IMAGES
of America

SALEM
OHIO

I0806419

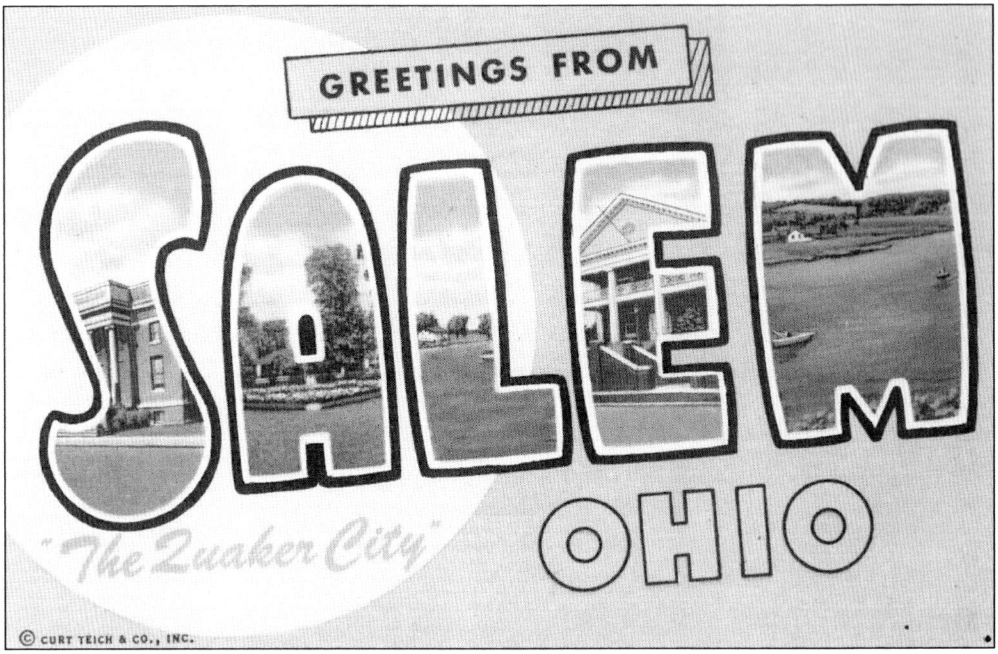

The name "Salem" comes from the word "Jerusalem," which means "City of Peace." A Quaker named Zadok Street Sr. came from Salem, New Jersey, in 1805. He, along with John Straughan from Pennsylvania, founded the new Ohio town in 1806.

IMAGES
of America

SALEM
OHIO

Dale E. Shaffer

ARCADIA
PUBLISHING

ISBN 978-0-7385-8738-7

Published by Arcadia Publishing
Charleston, South Carolina

Printed in the United States of America

Library of Congress Catalog Card Number: 98-85878

For all general information contact Arcadia Publishing at:
Telephone 843-853-2070
Fax 843-853-0044
E-mail sales@arcadiapublishing.com
For customer service and orders:
Toll-Free 1-888-313-2665

Visit us on the Internet at www.arcadiapublishing.com

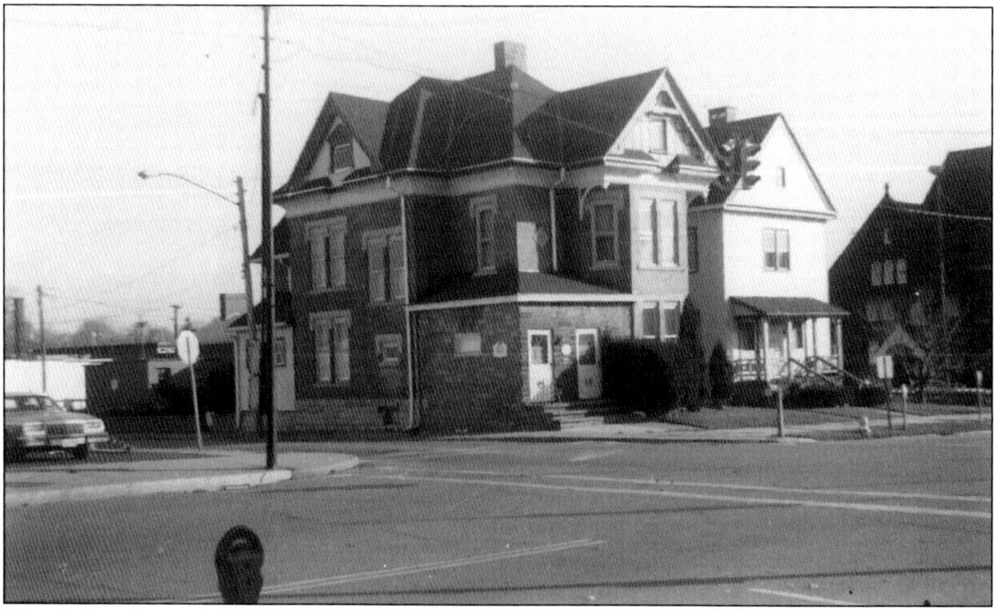

The Salem Historical Society was founded July 29, 1947. Its museum, located at 208 South Broadway Avenue, consists of four buildings, including Freedom Hall, which is dedicated to those who fought to abolish slavery. On display are hundreds of interesting artifacts—legacies of yesteryear—that give life to the past. The collection is a meaningful and tangible part of the Salem story.

Contents

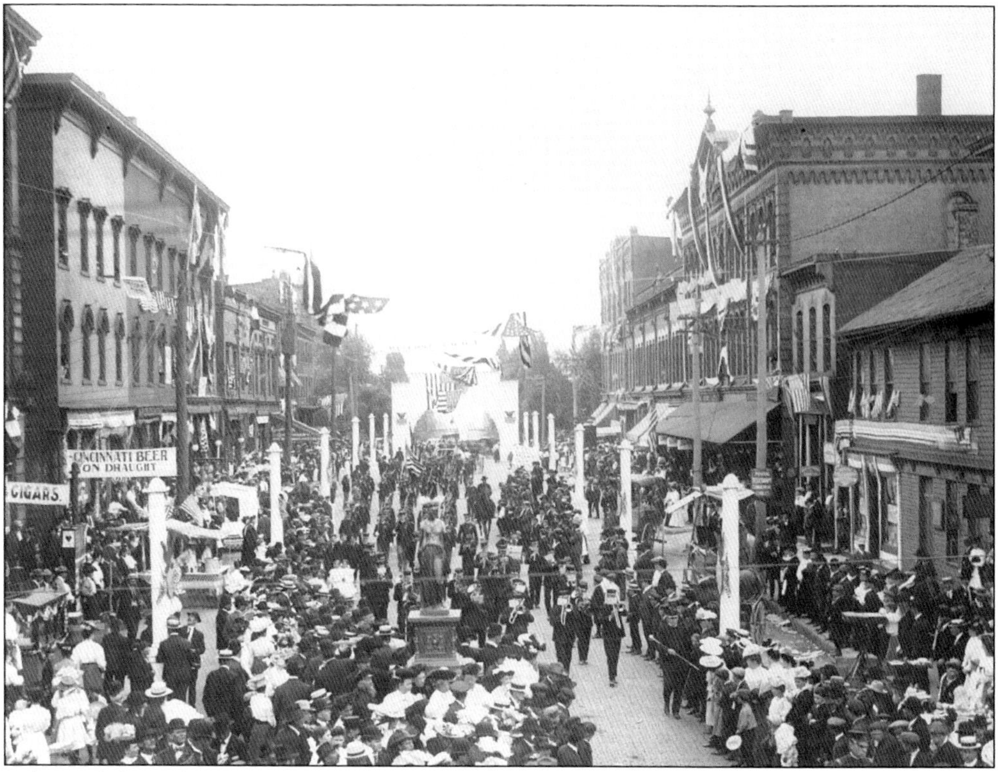

Salem celebrated its centennial June 20–23, 1906. This photo was taken on South Broadway Avenue. The four days of celebration were devoted to Old Settlers' Day, Anti-Slavery Day, G.A.R. Day, and Greater Salem Day. Millions of gummed stickers, envelopes, and postcards were printed to advertise the centennial. Gummed labels were stuck on envelopes sent out by businessmen, and on trunks and suitcases carried by men traveling throughout the United States.

Acknowledgments

Numerous people have contributed information to this book. Special thanks must go to Josephine Rupe, Director of the Salem Historical Museum, and Caroline Lehwald, her predecessor for 20 years. Most of the photographs used came from the Museum's collection. The efforts of these two ladies in organizing and preserving the many historical images and artifacts relating to Salem's past is greatly appreciated. Without access to these resources, I could not have composed this book.

To those Salemites who, through the years, have donated historical photographs to the Museum's collection, to the many volunteer staff members, and to all other persons who showed interest in the book, added valuable bits of information, and helped verify the accuracy of names, dates, and events, I express my gratitude.

Introduction

The 233 photographs presented in this book are intended to give a brief, but broad, pictorial view of what the past was like in a little Quaker town called Salem, Ohio. They cover a time period of over 100 years—from 1850 to 1956—showing the downtown of yesteryear, old buildings, businesses, trolley cars, homes, and the people as they looked, worked, and played in earlier times. Descriptive captions add historical meaning to each photographic scene.

This book is not intended to present a complete, detailed history of Salem from the town's founding in 1806 to the present. Rather, its scope is limited to selected scenes from the past. Every photo is a conversation piece with a unique story to tell, which represents a small part of the city's history.

Pictures taken in 1906 show how Salem celebrated its centennial, how the people dressed, the forms of transportation used, and what the buildings looked like. Some of these structures are gone now, but many are still standing, having been restored to their original architectural appearance. This book is timely as Salem's upcoming 200th birthday will be in 2006.

Historic scenes are important because they show the changes that have taken place in a city's landscape, including streets and layout. Collectively, this information forms a historical portrait that depicts the town's uniqueness.

Photographs of the old town hall (1847–1952) are historic, not just because the old building no longer exists, but because of the famous orators and reformers who spoke there on important issues like slavery and women's rights—people like Frederic Douglass, William Lloyd Garrison, Wendell Phillips, Sojourner Truth, James Garfield, Susan B. Anthony, Elizabeth Cady Stanton, Lucretia Mott, Dr. Anna Shaw, and Ralph Waldo Emerson.

Recorded history is unique in that it is lasting and retains its value for future generations. Our past is not something that we leave behind, but rather something we incorporate into our daily lives. Each of us needs a "mental standing ground" outside our own time frame in order to be more perceptive observers within it. No person can fully understand his or her own community and society without comprehending its evolution. A city that does not know its past does not know itself.

History presented in book form has many advantages. It is more permanent than speech, which means that its contents can be shared, studied, and reflected upon by more people over a longer period of time. Also, the photographs in a book can do much that speech cannot. The spoken word rushes by and is gone, but the written word and visual images endure.

When the Northwest Territory was opened in 1800, and it was declared that no slavery could legally exist there, members of the Society of Friends (Quakers) migrated north in great numbers. Over 800 families moved into the Ohio Territory. Courageous, strong in their convictions, and firm in their faith, these God-fearing people had a deep desire to rear their families in surroundings free from the evil effects of slavery.

The first, hardy group of pioneers coming to the Salem area in 1801 came from New Jersey, Pennsylvania, Maryland, and Virginia. Members of the Society of Friends came because they were bitterly opposed to slavery. They found a vast wilderness, inhabited by Native Americans and plenty of wild animals. Peace was immediately made between the Redmen and the Friends.

In 1806 the settlement of Salem was plotted by Zadok Street and John Straughan. By 1807 the town had a post office and store, operated by John Street, son of the co-founder. Mail was delivered once a week by horse and carrier (originally by foot) from New Lisbon, the county seat. The early stage route through the area was established around 1824.

Salem was not incorporated until January 8, 1830. There was a town council consisting of a president, recorder, and five trustees. John Campbell was the first president. In 1852 the form of government was changed to a village, and a mayor was elected.

The town's first foundry was started in the 1830s, and that is where Thomas Sharp, in 1842, built the first steam engine. In 1844 a factory was established to card wool. Farmers Bank, Salem's first bank, was founded in 1846, and the First National Bank in 1863. On November 27, 1851, the first passenger train arrived in Salem.

Salem has always had the general image of being a quiet, conservative, and peaceful city—primarily because it was founded by Quakers and because its name literally means "City of Peace," which comes from the word "Jerusalem." Still with us today, after almost two centuries of time, are the influences which predominated over the early settlers.

The beauty and peacefulness of this small town exemplify the civic pride of its citizens. Among the town's most outstanding features are its crime-free atmosphere, school system, diversified industry, hospital facilities, museums, parks, churches, and proud heritage. Internationally known artist Charles Burchfield lived and painted in the Quaker city.

Some of the historical highlights in the city's past include its being the site of Ohio's first Women's Suffrage Convention (the second in the nation) in 1850; being part of the Underground Railroad with many abolitionist supporters; being the headquarters of the Western Anti-Slavery Society and the city where the *Anti-Slavery Bugle* newspaper was published; being the early seat of the label industry where the first gummed labels in the United States were made; and, in 1929, being the first city in Ohio to have a high school night football game performed under lights.

Salem has long been the industrial manufacturing center of the area, providing jobs for thousands of workers from miles around. Product names like Mullins, Deming, Silver, Eljer, American Standard, and Bliss have long been an important part of the Salem and world economies.

Hopefully, this book of images will help introduce readers to historic Salem, and serve future generations as a convenient reference source of factual information.

One

Downtown Scenes

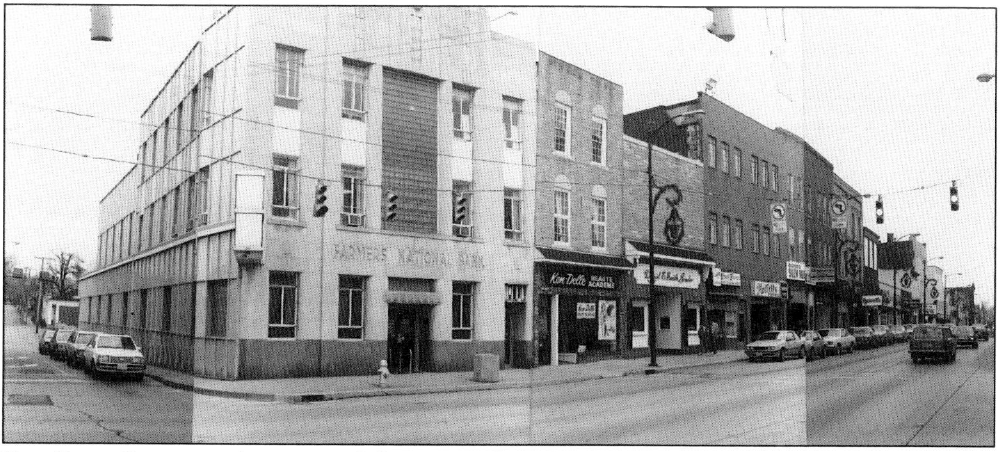

East State Street in downtown Salem, near Broadway Avenue, as it looked in 1980. The downtown has since been renovated and the buildings restored.

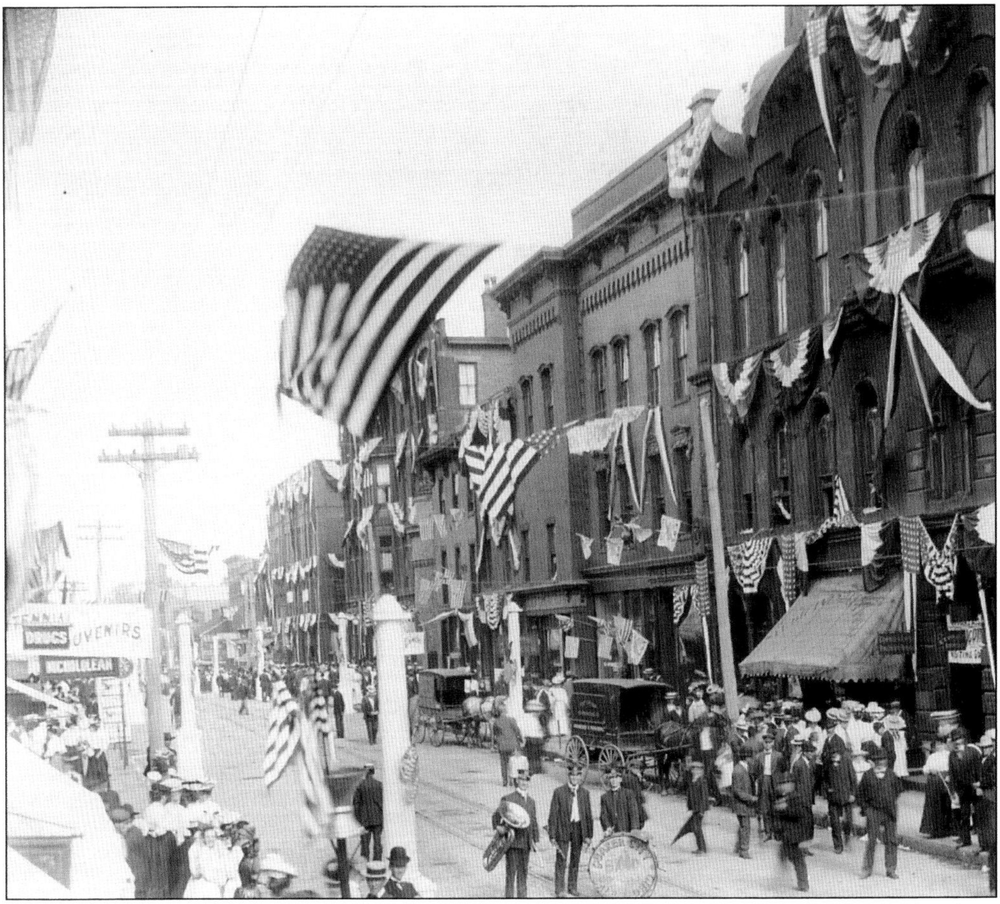

A centennial photograph taken on State Street in the middle of downtown Salem. President Theodore Roosevelt extended birthday greetings, and Judge Webster Street, great-grandson of the city's co-founder Zadok Street Sr., attended the event. On its final day a surprise announcement was made presenting the city with a 25-acre public park, named Centennial Park.

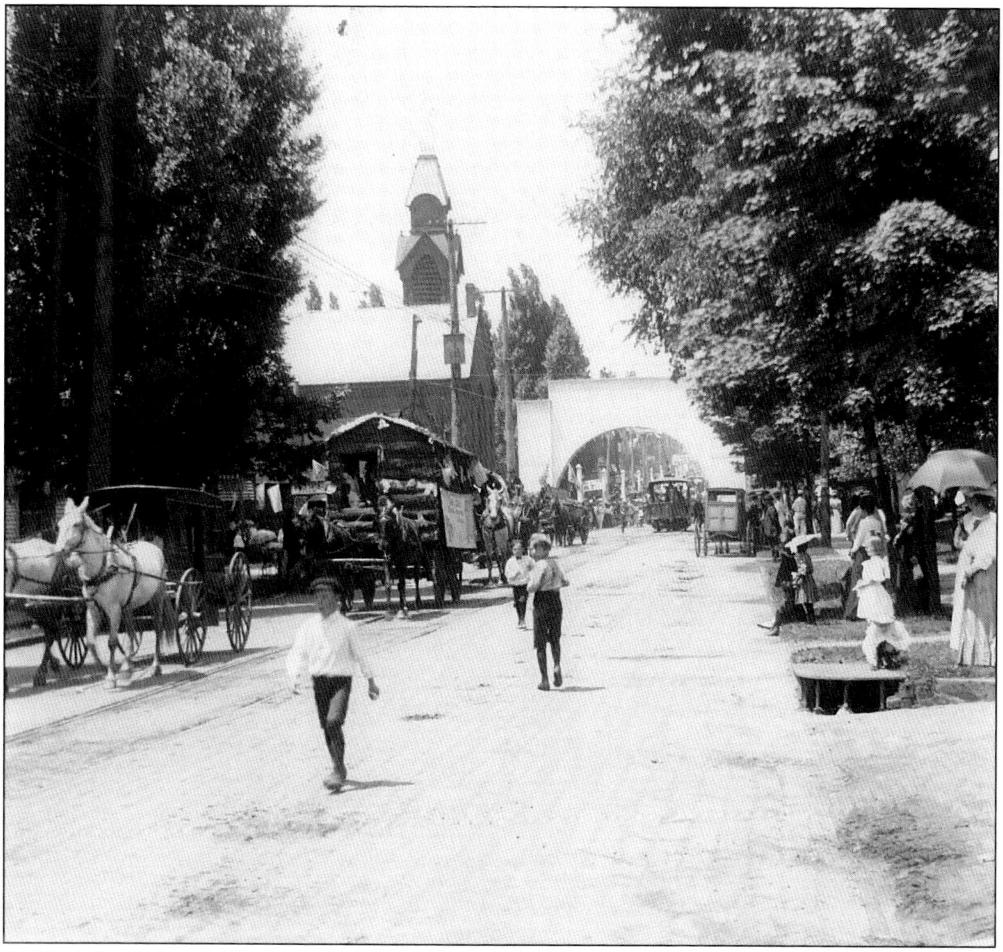

A 1906 Centennial photograph, looking west on East State Street from Vine Avenue. Harry W. Lewis of Atlantic City was contracted to decorate the city and arrange a court of honor. Decorations included the construction of three lighted arches. Parades were the main feature. One was a slavery parade with the oldest inhabitant of Salem, Mrs. Mary Kelly, age 104, born and raised in slavery, riding in the main carriage.

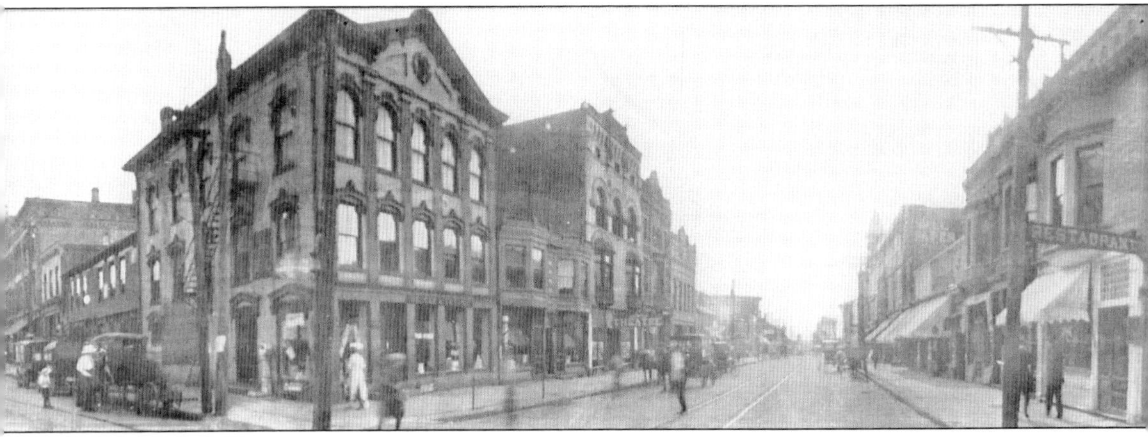

A 1906 panoramic view of downtown Salem, looking east and west on State Street (left image), and south on Broadway Avenue (right image). The drinking fountain was removed in 1911, the

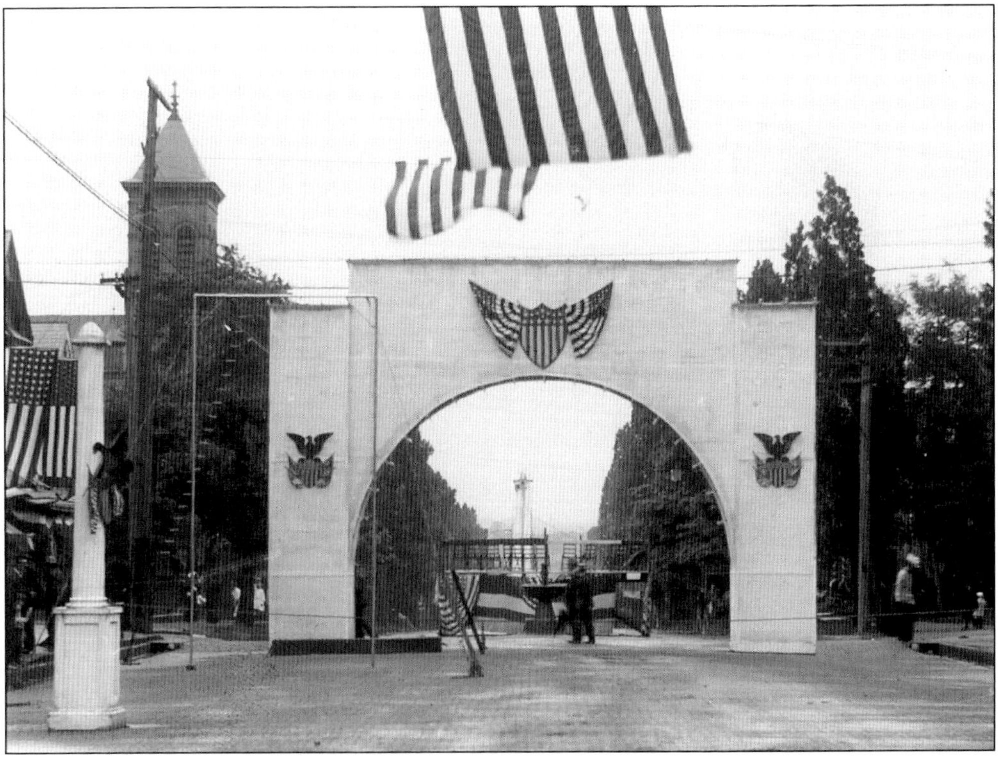

A 1906 centennial photograph showing one of the arches being constructed on South Broadway Avenue, near Pershing Street. At the left is the old Methodist Church building. Booker T. Washington spoke on the afternoon of June 22 under a large tent on the Columbia Street School lawn. His speech was the climax of a program arranged for Anti-Slavery Day. Dr. Washington's address was titled "The Regeneration of a Race."

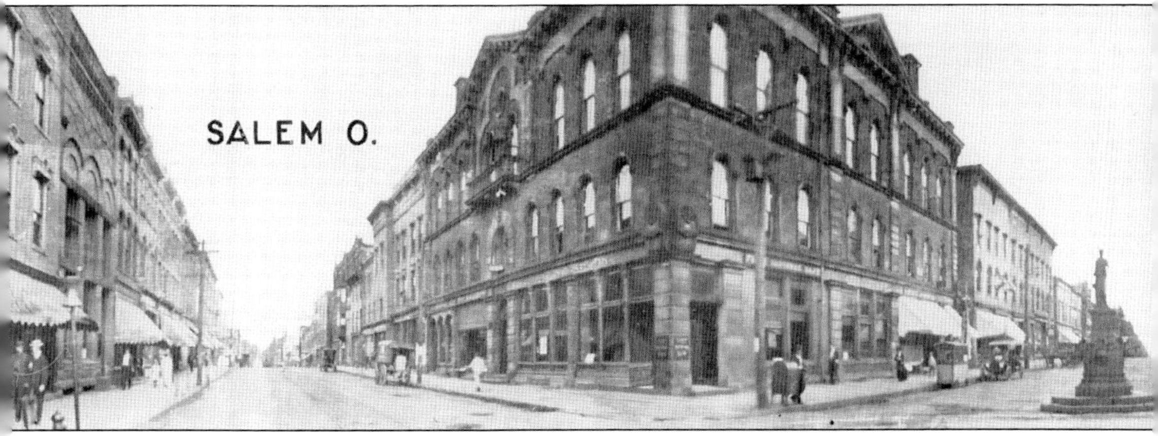

same year Salem's trolley system ceased operations. To the left of the statue is Popcorn Jim's cart. Most of the old buildings are still standing.

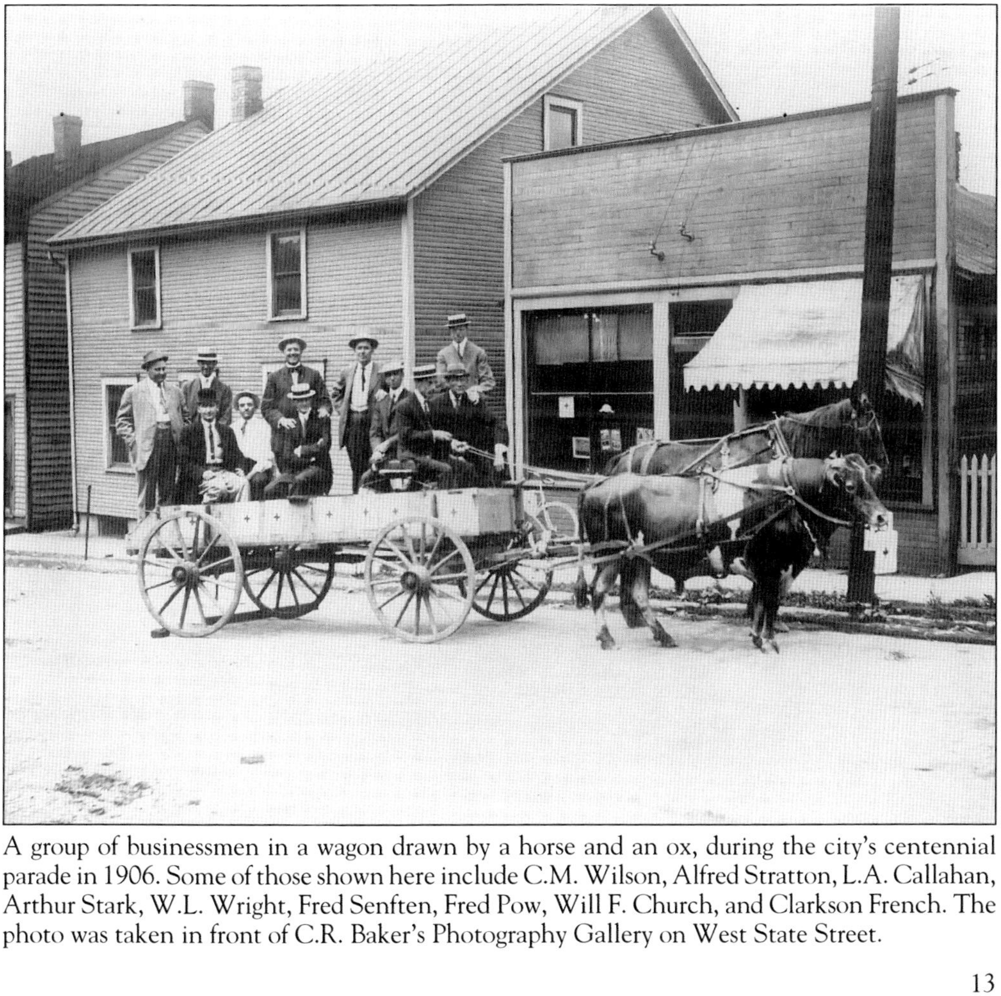

A group of businessmen in a wagon drawn by a horse and an ox, during the city's centennial parade in 1906. Some of those shown here include C.M. Wilson, Alfred Stratton, L.A. Callahan, Arthur Stark, W.L. Wright, Fred Senften, Fred Pow, Will F. Church, and Clarkson French. The photo was taken in front of C.R. Baker's Photography Gallery on West State Street.

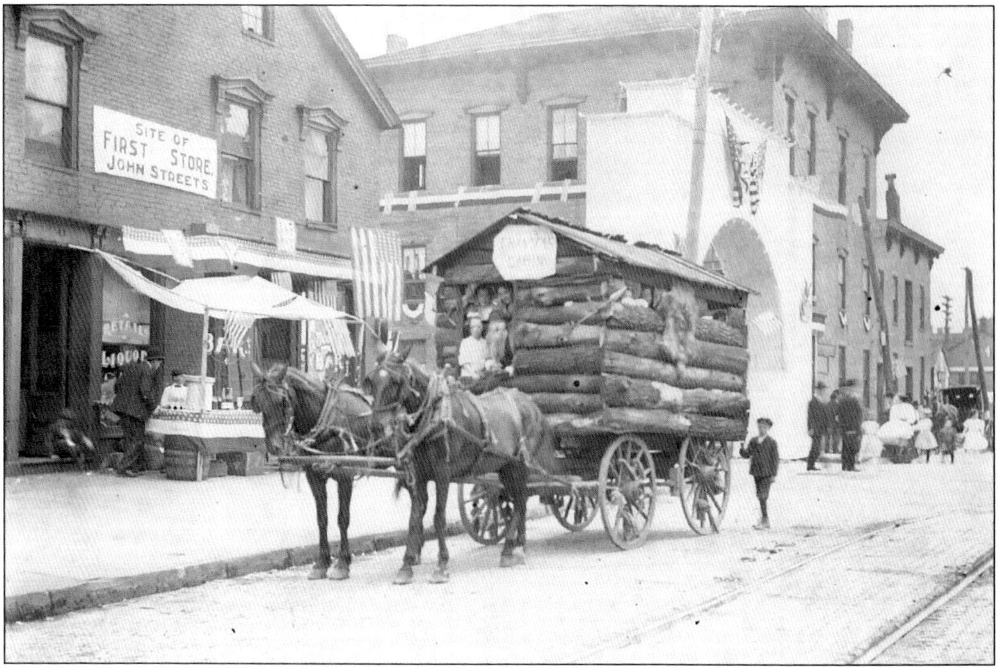

A photograph taken in 1906 during Salem's centennial celebration. The building at the left, on the southwest corner of State Street and South Ellsworth Avenue, was the site of Salem's first store and post office, operated by John Street, son of Zadok Street Sr. (co-founder of Salem). At right is the Anderson Block. Note the Salem Electric Railway tracks.

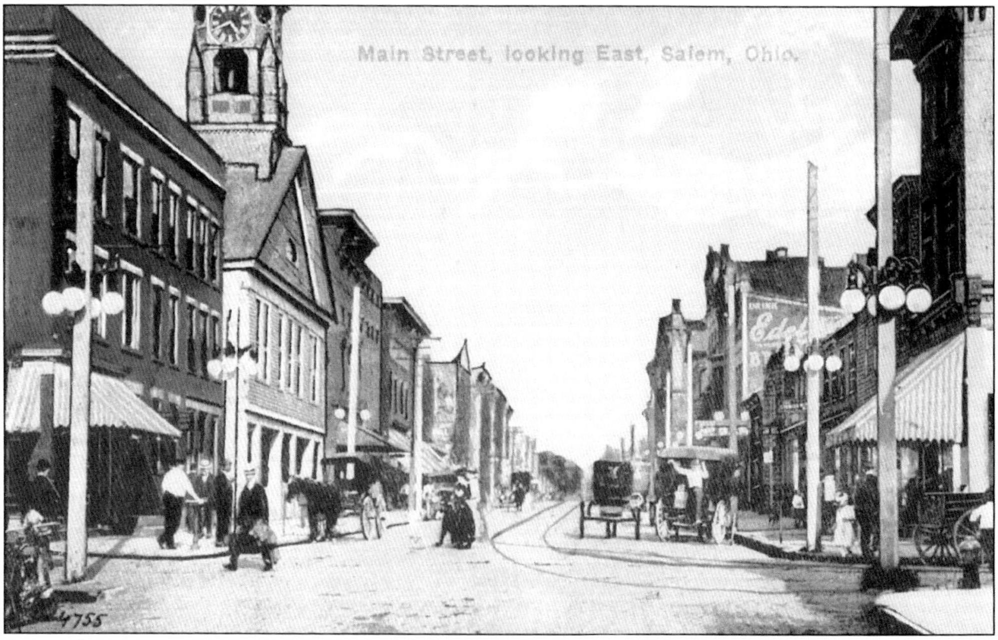

An early 1900s scene of Main (State) Street, looking east from Ellsworth Avenue. The time of day was 4:42 p.m. Most vehicles were drawn by horses. One car and one motorcycle can be seen. The tracks are for the Salem Electric Railway (1890–1911). The corner building at right still stands.

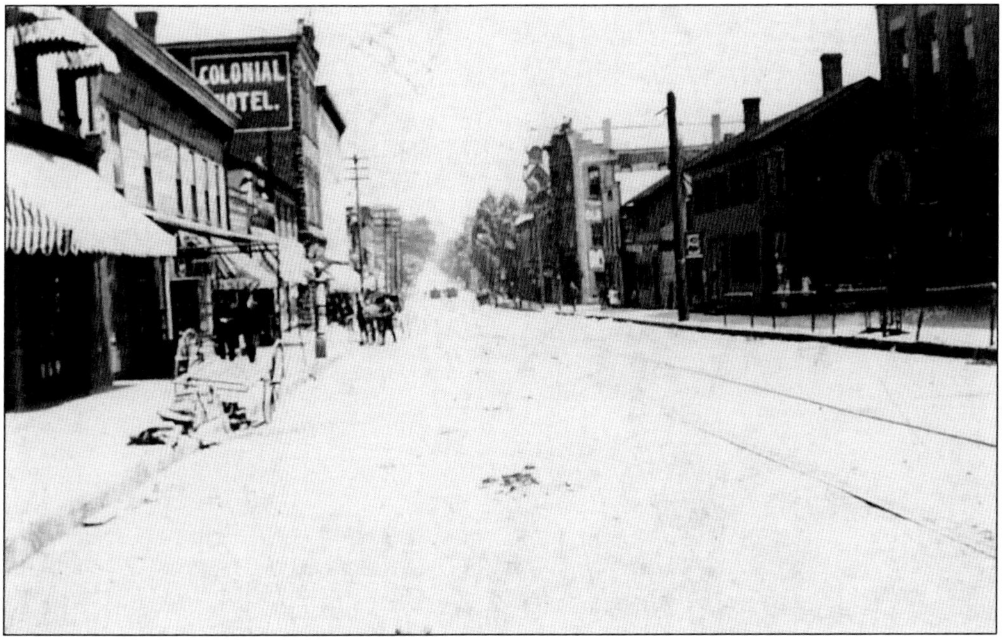

A photograph of East State Street, looking east from Lundy Avenue, taken in the late 1890s. The building at the left with "Colonial Hotel" advertisement is the Grand Opera House. The tracks in the street are for the Salem Electric Railway (1890–1911).

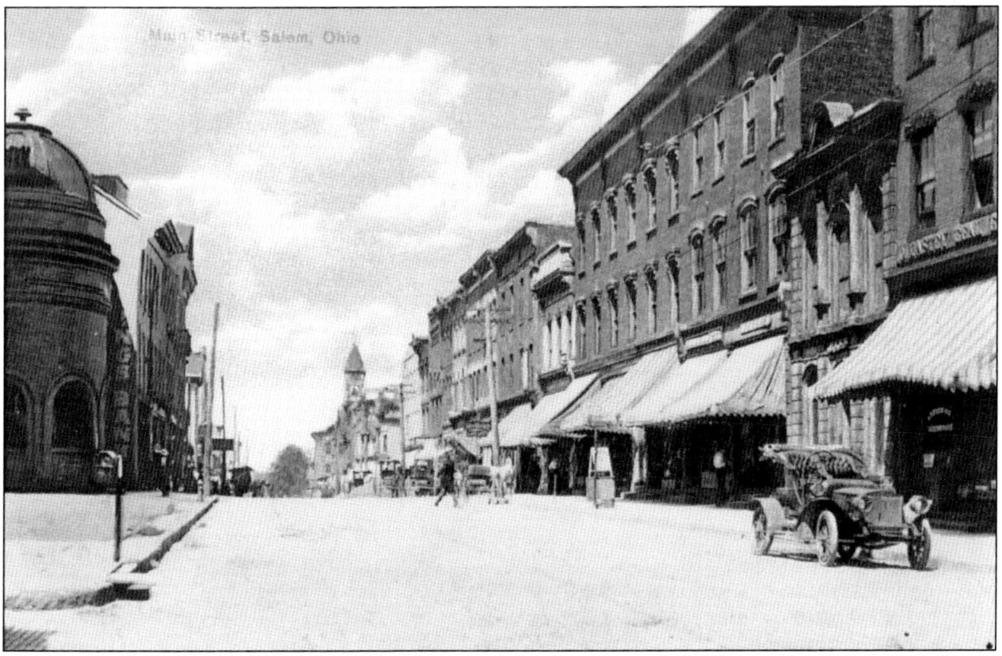

Salem's Main (State) Street in the early 1900s, looking west from Lundy Avenue. Citizens Savings Bank (1903–31) is at the left, and Astry's Real Estate office is on the right. Centered in the background is the old town hall (1847–1952).

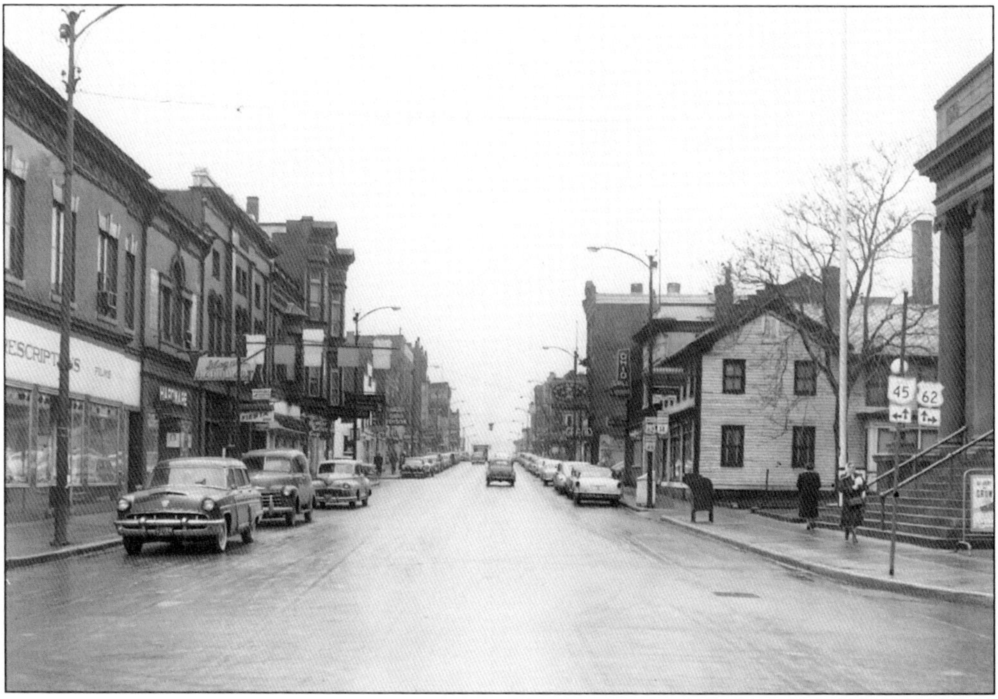

Downtown Salem as it looked in the 1950s. The view is west from Lincoln Avenue. On the right is the old post office, which was torn down in 1962. The buildings on the left are still standing.

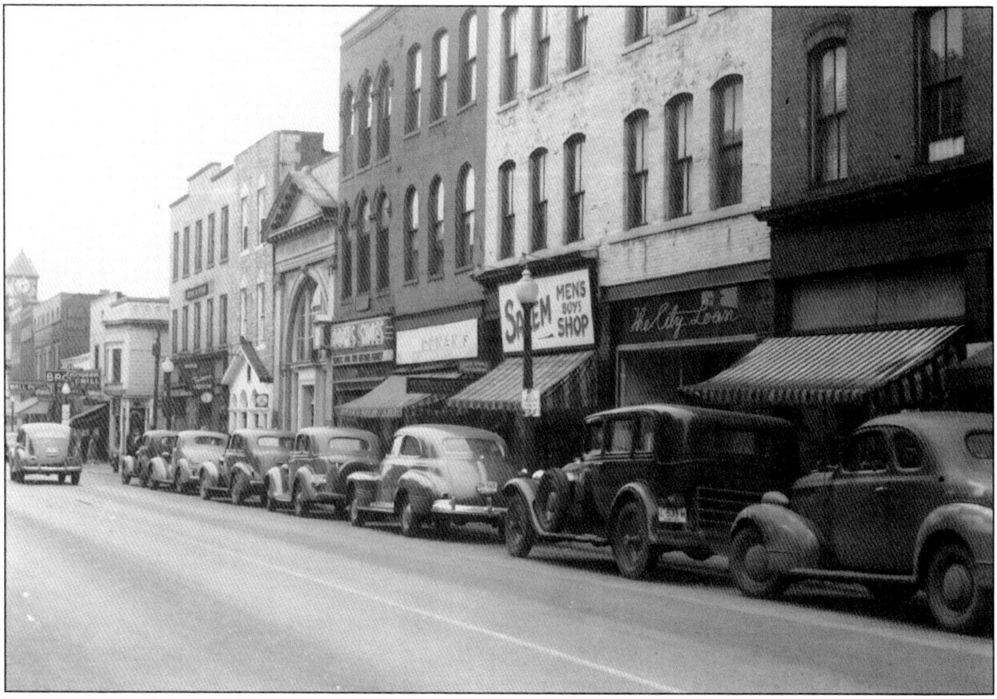

Downtown Salem in the 1940s. At left is the old town hall, which was razed in 1952. Most of these buildings have since been restored to their original appearance.

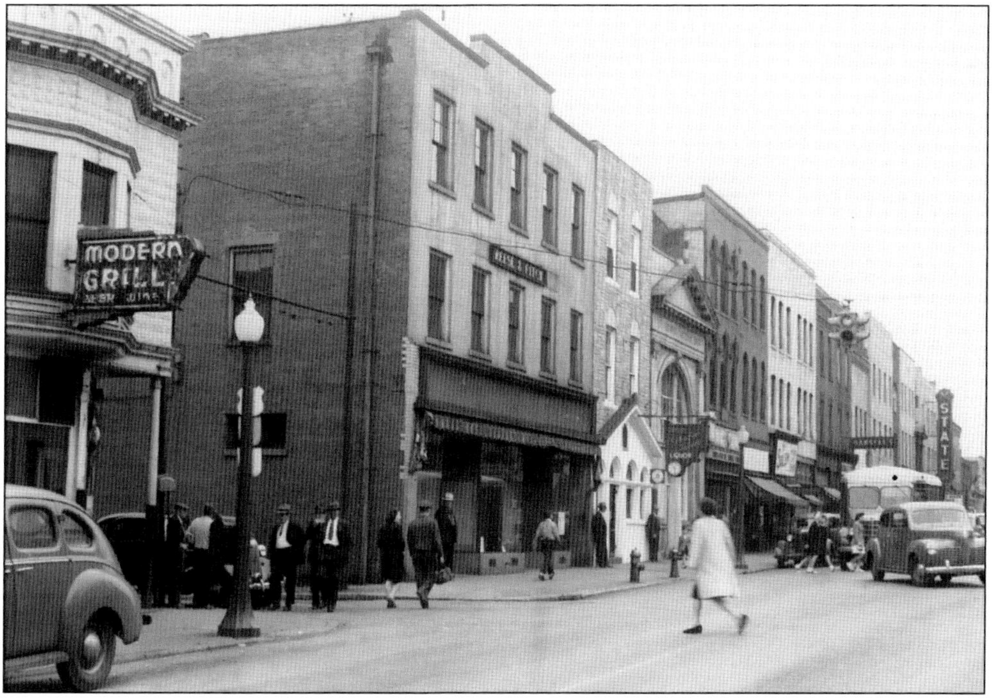

Downtown Salem in the 1940s. The vacant building once housed Woolworth's Five-and-Ten. Next to it was Jesse Schafer's Tavern and the Farmers Bank. These buildings still stand today. The State Theater is now the Salem Community Theater.

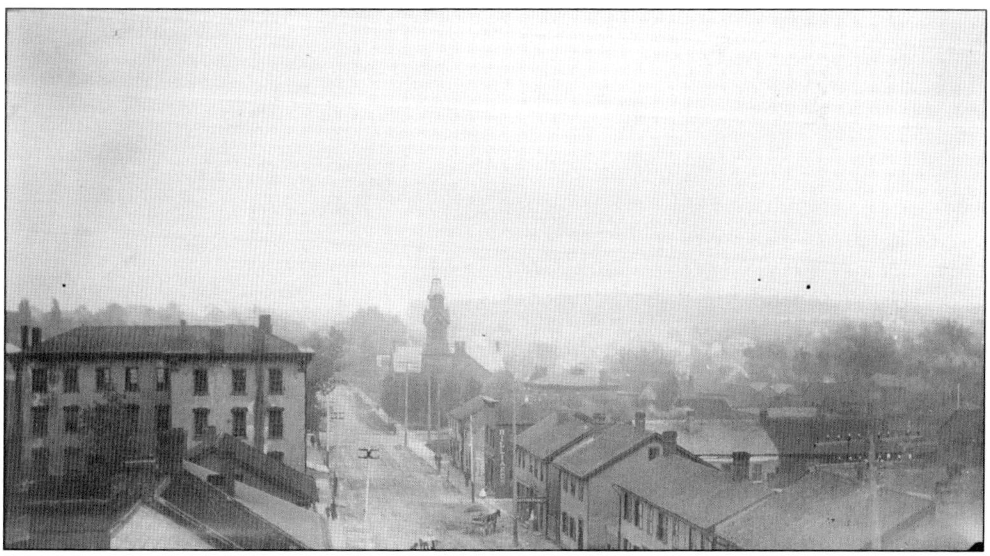

An 1880s view looking east from atop a downtown building on State Street. The building at the left was the old American Hotel, the city's tallest structure. Shown in the center is the old Baptist church, which burned down in 1947.

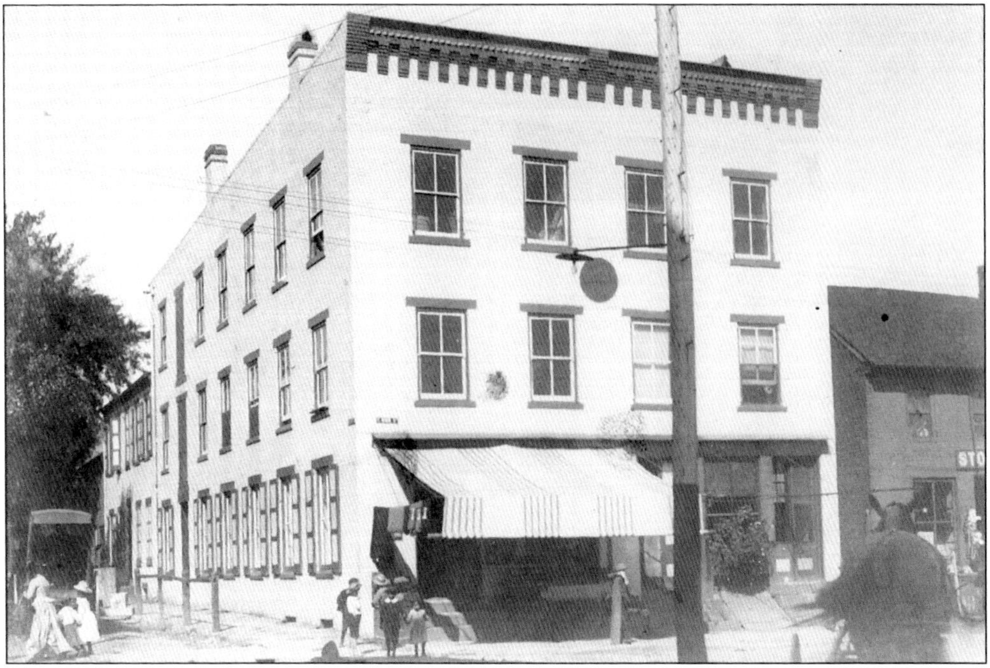

A *c*. 1888 photograph of the northeast corner of East State Street and North Lundy Avenue. Salem's first incandescent lights had just been installed when this photograph was taken. Note the woman on the left dressed with a bustle, and the small boys wearing Quaker wide-brimmed hats.

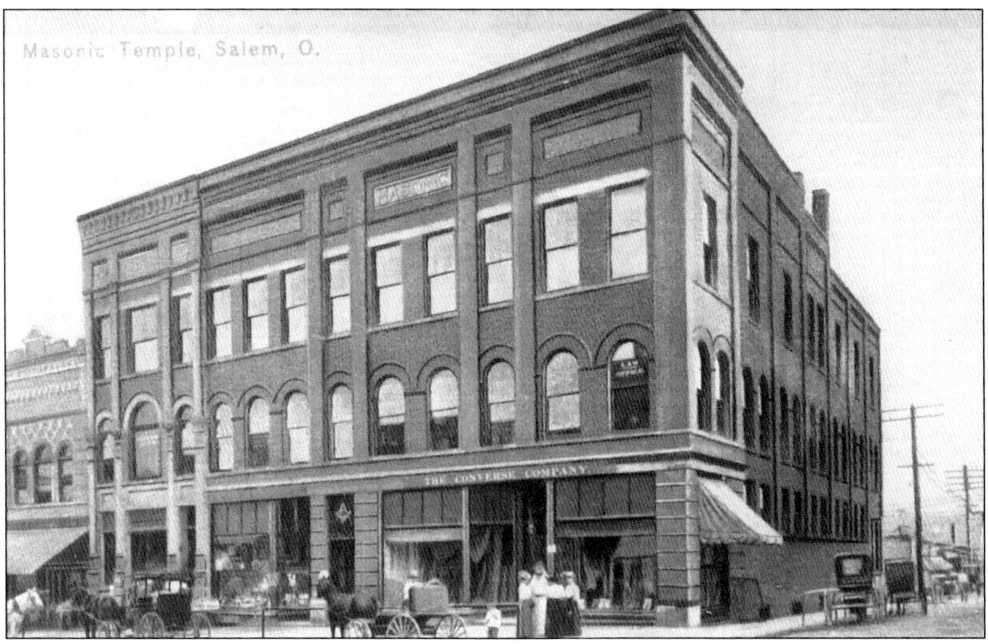

The Masonic Block on the southeast corner of East State Street and South Lundy Avenue, erected in the early 1890s. Lodge rooms were on the third floor, and the Converse Company was on the ground floor. In the 1920s the Masons moved into their new temple at 788 East State Street, dedicating it on June 27, 1923.

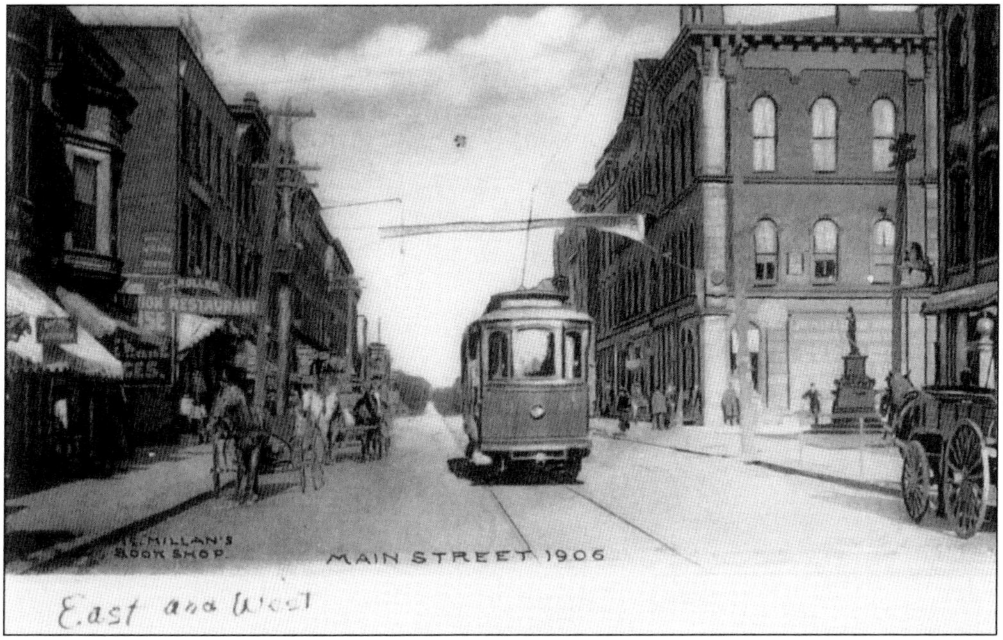

A 1906 image showing one of the Salem Electric Railway cars heading west downtown on East State Street, passing Broadway Avenue. The Salem Electric Railway, organized by Dr. J.M. Hole and others, operated from 1890 to 1911. It was taken over by the Milton Davis family in 1892. Salem was one of the first towns in the United States to have electric trolleys. Most other cities pulled their trolley cars with horses and cables.

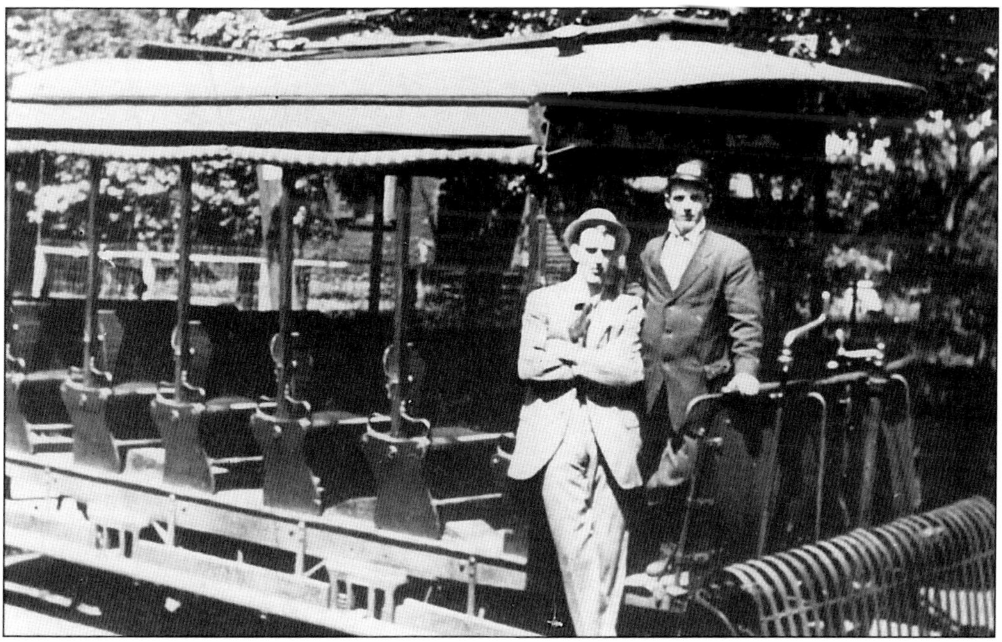

A Salem Electric Railway summer car, used for transporting passengers to the Salem Fair Grounds east of the city. Often they were loaded, with people hanging all over them. Sometimes they towed second cars like trailers. The cars had no front or back ends. They traveled in both directions without the motorman having to turn them around.

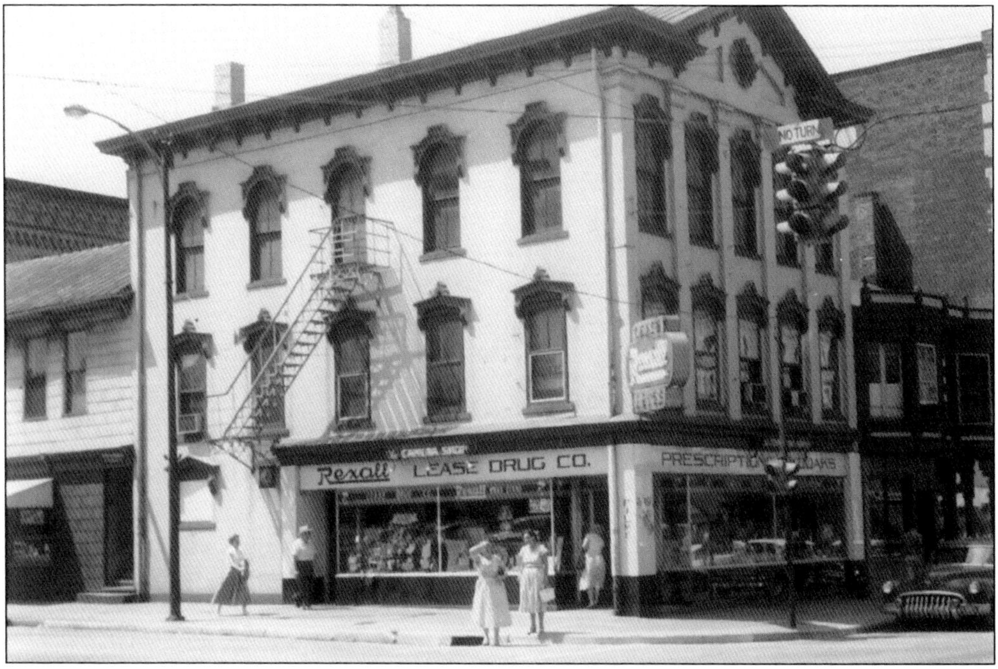

An early 1950s photograph of the Lease Drug Company in the Whinnery Block on the southwest corner of East State Street and South Broadway Avenue. The building was erected before the Civil War. Dr. John C. Whinnery, a dentist, once owned the building and had his offices there. The Whinnerys were active in the anti-slavery movement.

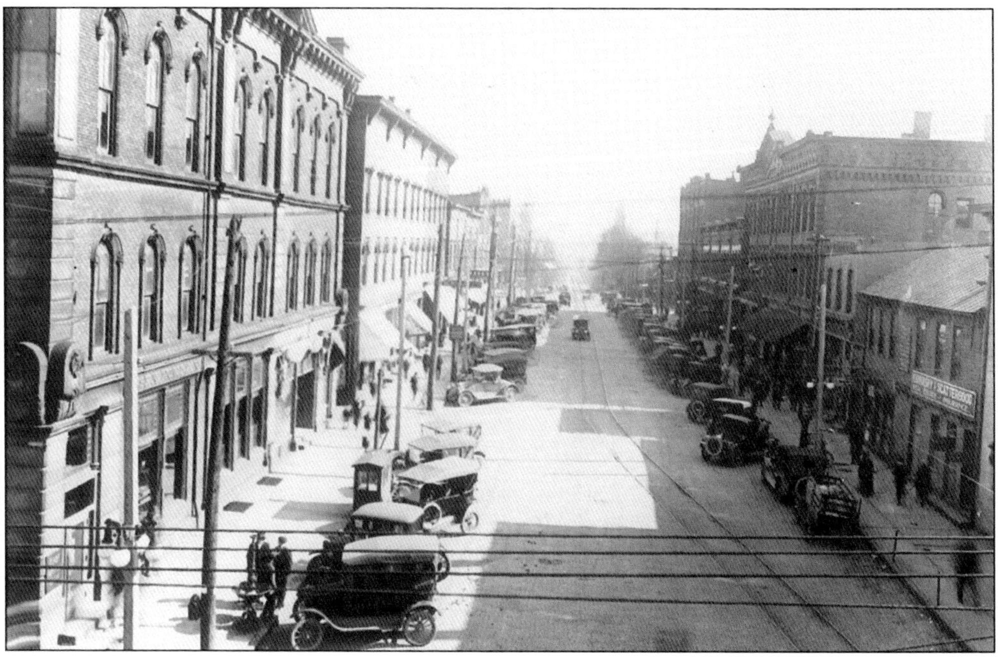

A photograph taken around 1915 of South Broadway Avenue looking south. At left, in front of Concert Hall, is Jim Ramsey's popcorn and taffy stand. The tracks are for the Y&O Electric Railroad, which operated between Salem and East Liverpool from 1905 to 1931.

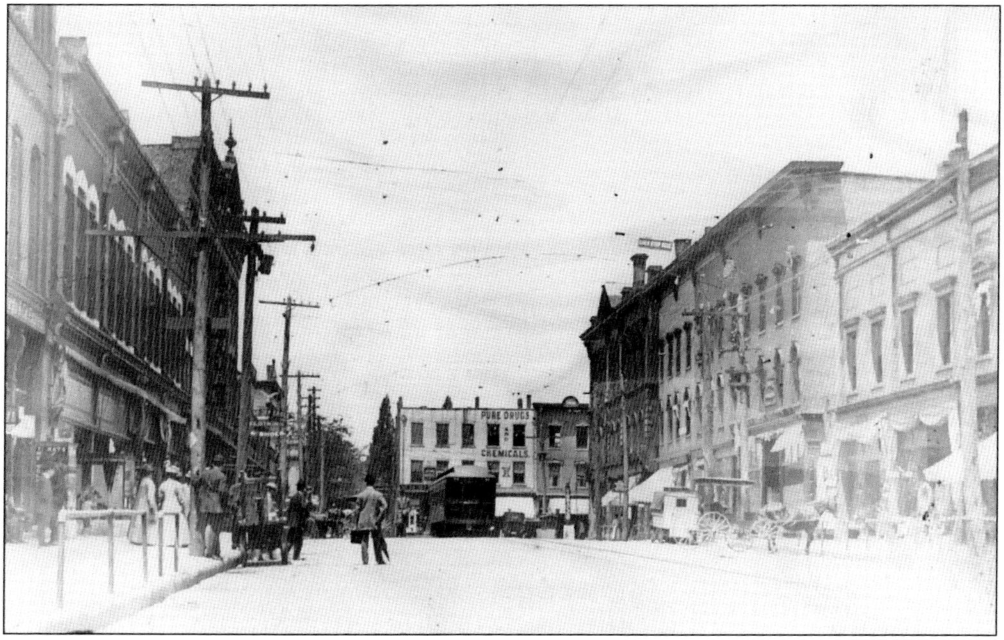

An early 1900s scene looking north on South Broadway Avenue. Note the Y&O Electric Railroad car in the center heading for East Liverpool. Passengers at the left are waiting to board. Hitching posts were still in use.

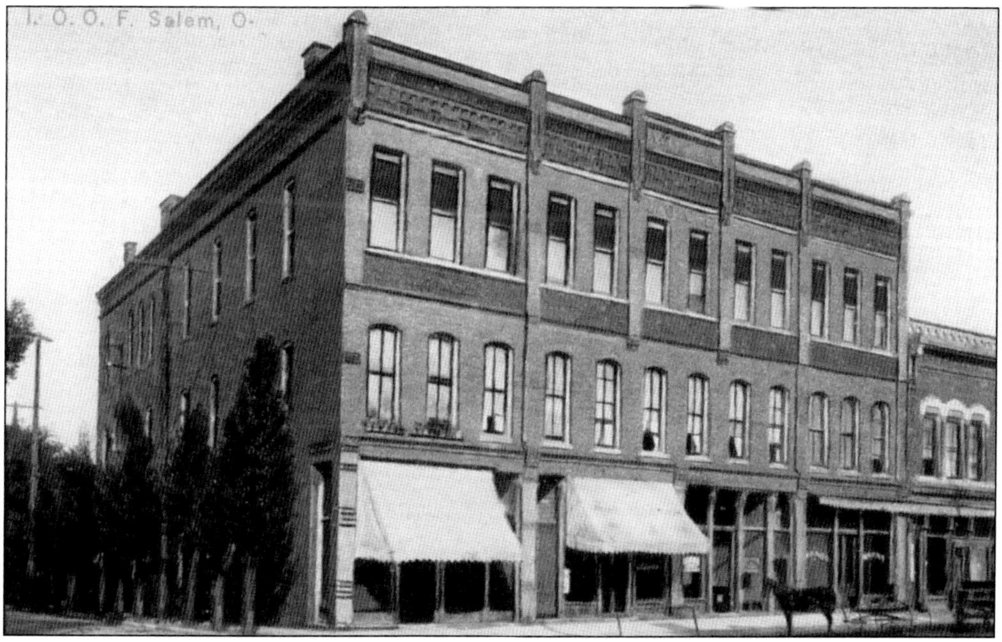

The Wilbur Block stands on the northeast corner of East Pershing Street and South Broadway Avenue. Its name came from John Wilbur, leader of a branch of the Society of Friends. In 1854 the Friends divided into two sects—the Wilbur Friends and the Gurney Friends. The Gurney Block is a few doors to the north. J. Twing Brooks erected the two buildings in the early 1870s.

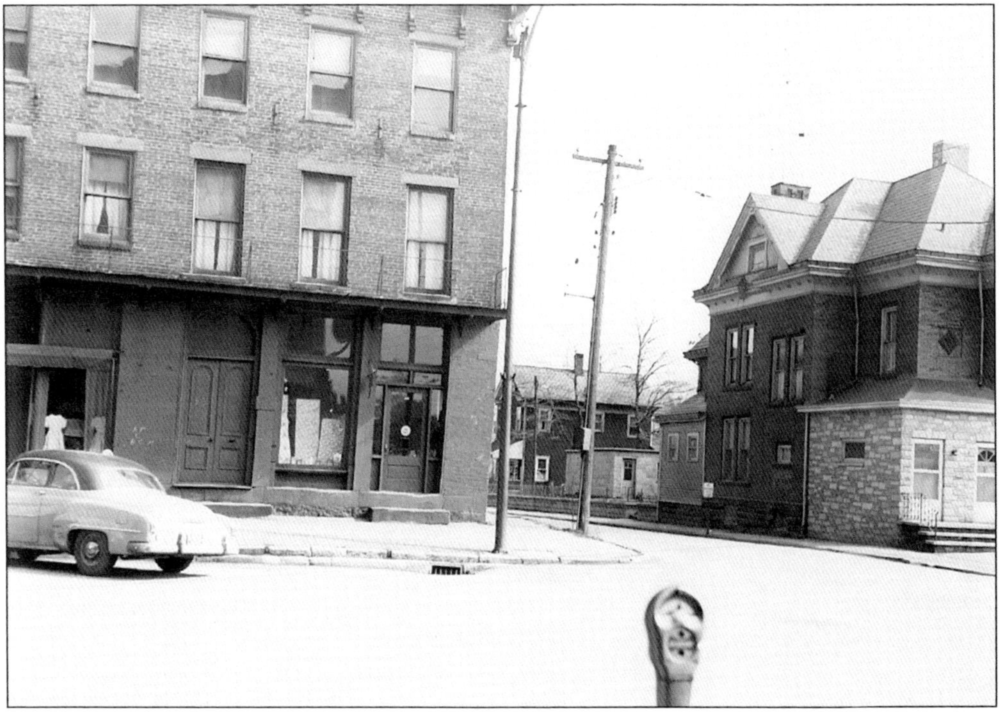

A 1960s photograph of South Broadway Avenue and East Pershing Street showing the Redinger Building on the left, and Schell's Tavern on the right. The Redinger structure was built in 1860 by a Mr. Folger, who called it the Broadway Building. He operated a hotel there, known as the Broadway House. It was later converted into apartments. Fred Redinger bought it in 1910 and used the building for a wallpaper store. It was razed in 1970.

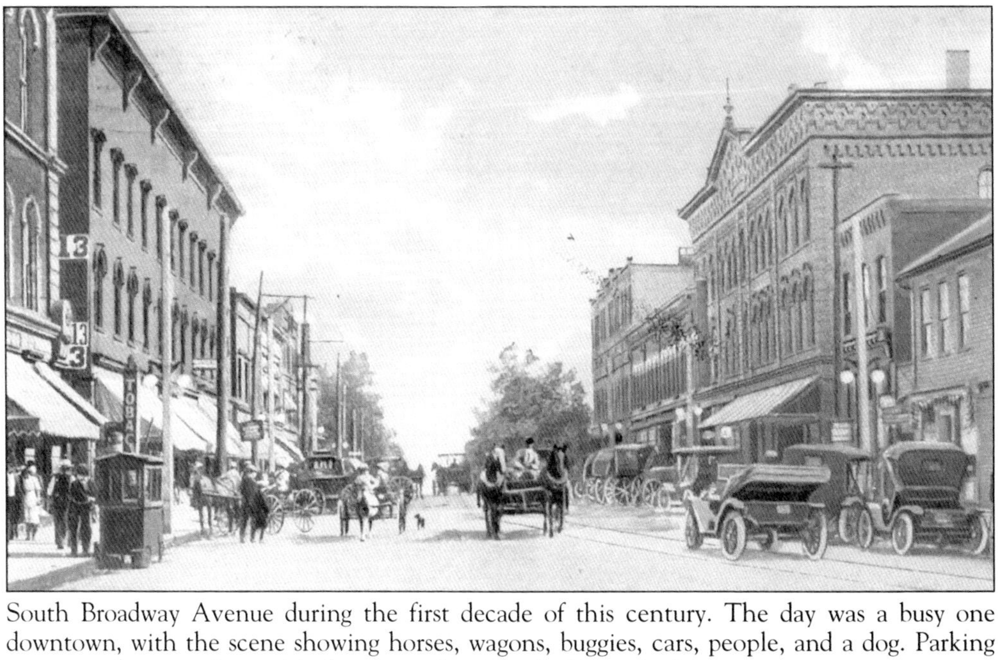

South Broadway Avenue during the first decade of this century. The day was a busy one downtown, with the scene showing horses, wagons, buggies, cars, people, and a dog. Parking appears to be at random, with the car on the right double-parked.

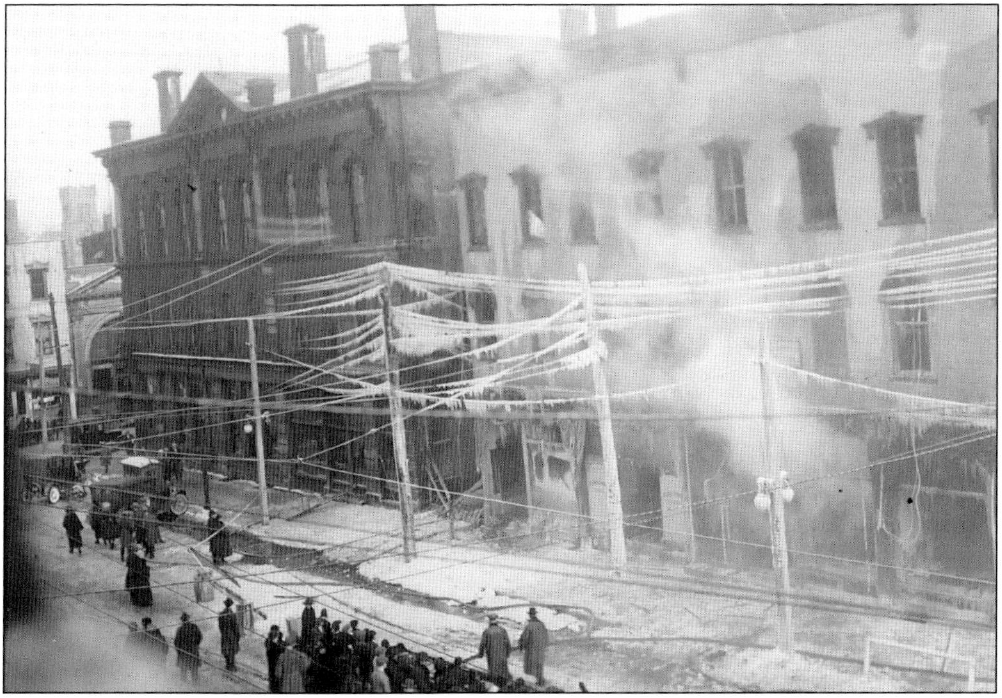

One of the worst fires in downtown Salem, February 23, 1924. The blaze began around 9:30 p.m. on a cold night. Two three-story brick buildings on South Broadway Avenue were completely destroyed. It lasted for ten hours. Hundreds of volunteers from all walks of life nobly rose to the emergency. The next morning Y&O Railroad workmen had to chop ice from the tracks so the car on that line could leave the city.

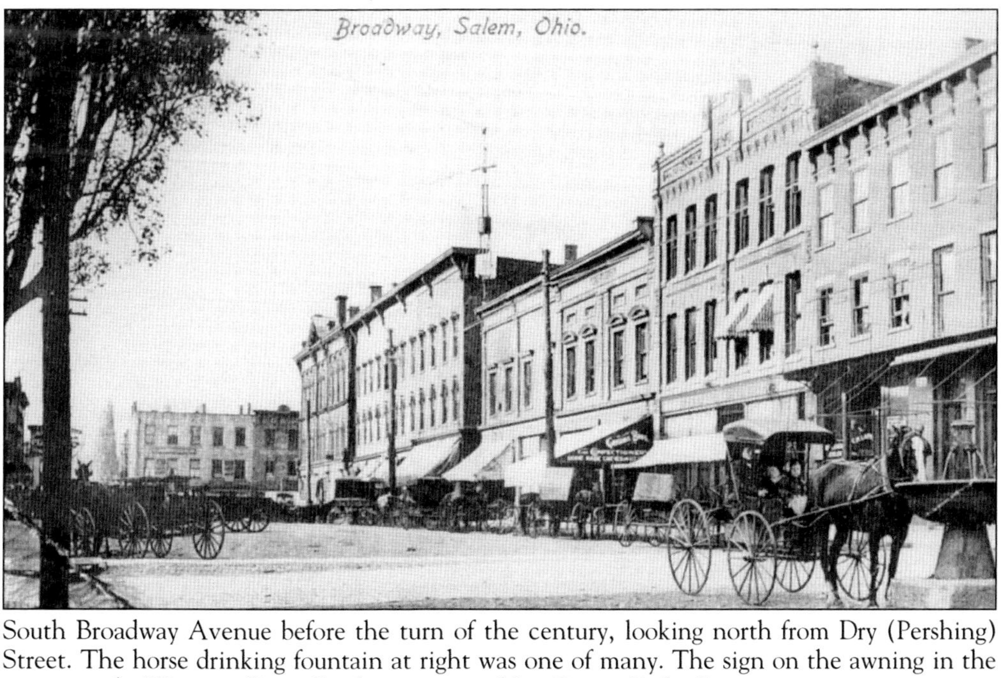

South Broadway Avenue before the turn of the century, looking north from Dry (Pershing) Street. The horse drinking fountain at right was one of many. The sign on the awning in the center reads: "Gregoris Bros. Confectionery and Ice Cream Parlor."

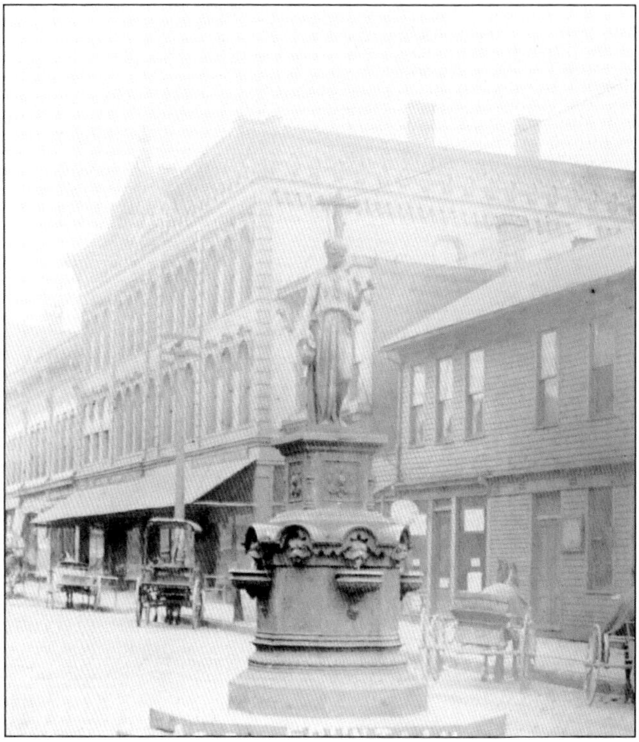

"Hebe," the large statue and drinking fountain that once stood in the middle of South Broadway Avenue near State Street. Hebe, in Greek mythology, was the goddess of youth. Tradition invested her with the power to make old people young again, and it is said that she rejuvenated Hercules. She was removed from the scene in 1911.

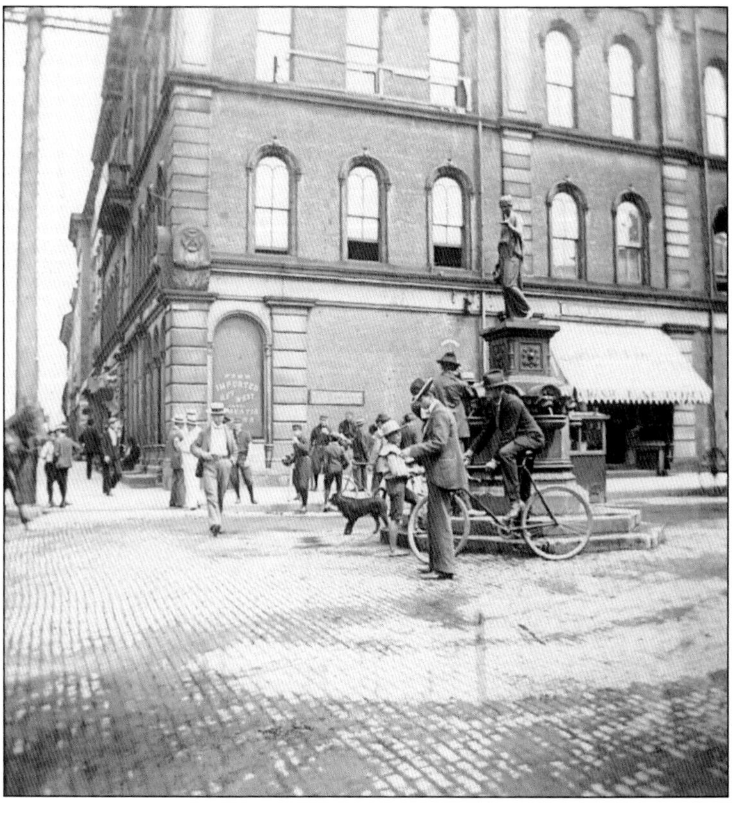

A c. 1899 photograph showing the drinking fountain and "Hebe" statue on South Broadway Avenue. The corner building is the Pow Block (1860–1929), with Concert Hall above. The awning at right is for the Sorg and Juergens Cigar Factory. Note "Popcorn" Jim Ramsey's cart in front of the cigar store. The Y&O Railroad tracks do not appear because the first Y&O car did not arrive in Salem until 1908.

This parade took place one Saturday afternoon in downtown Salem in celebration of the 1956 Sesquicentennial. None of the stores shown remain in business today, but the buildings still look about the same.

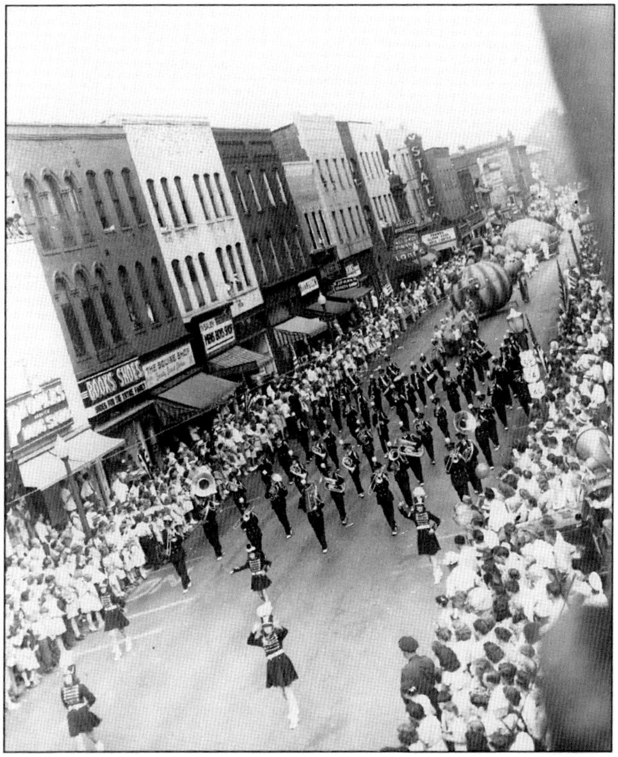

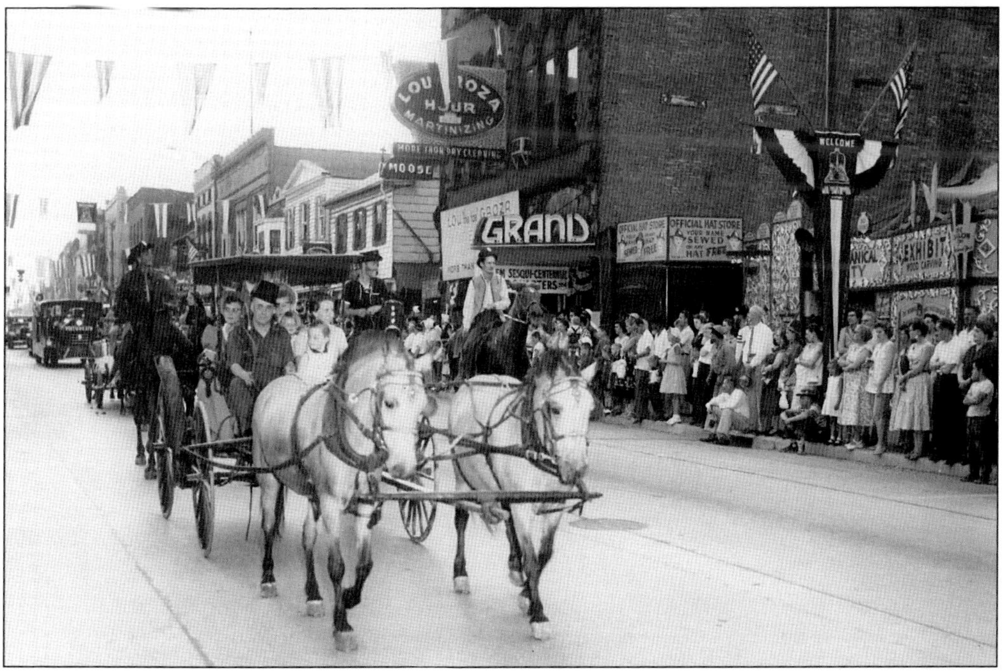

Salem's downtown was well decorated for the sesquicentennial parade in 1956. The last movie shown at the Grand Theater was on April 10, 1955, and titled *Son of Paleface*, starring Bob Hope. Built in 1889, the structure was originally called the Grand Opera House. John Philip Sousa's band played there in the late 1890s.

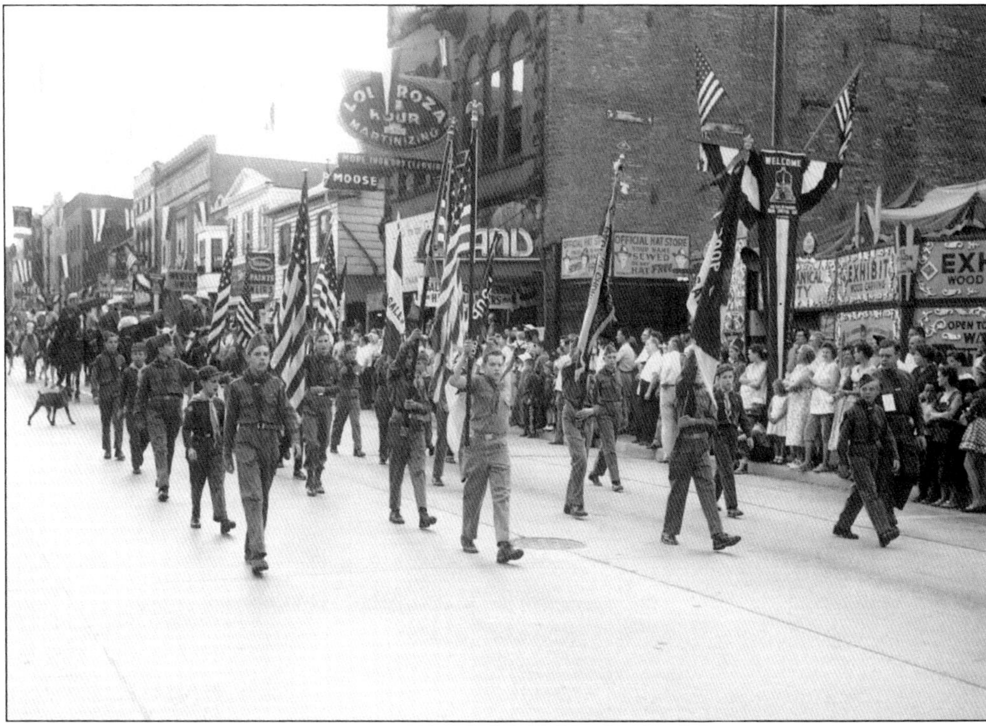

One of Salem's many Boy Scout troops in the 1956 Sesquicentennial Parade. The town's 200th birthday will be held in 2006.

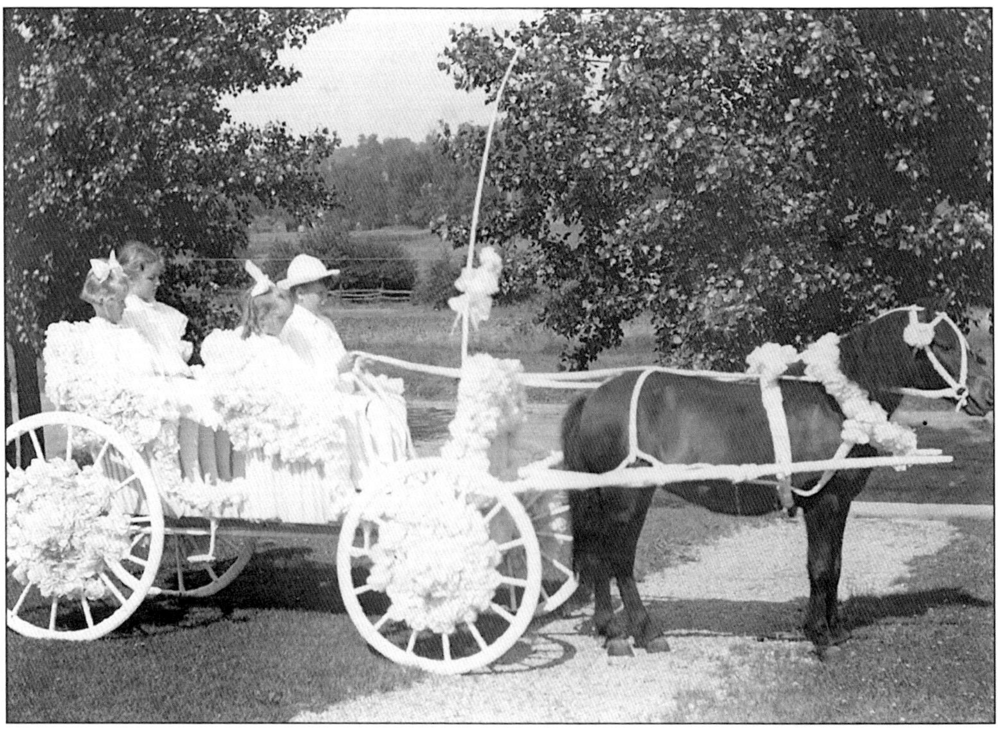

Four youngsters in a pony-drawn buggy, beautifully decorated for a parade in the early 1900s.

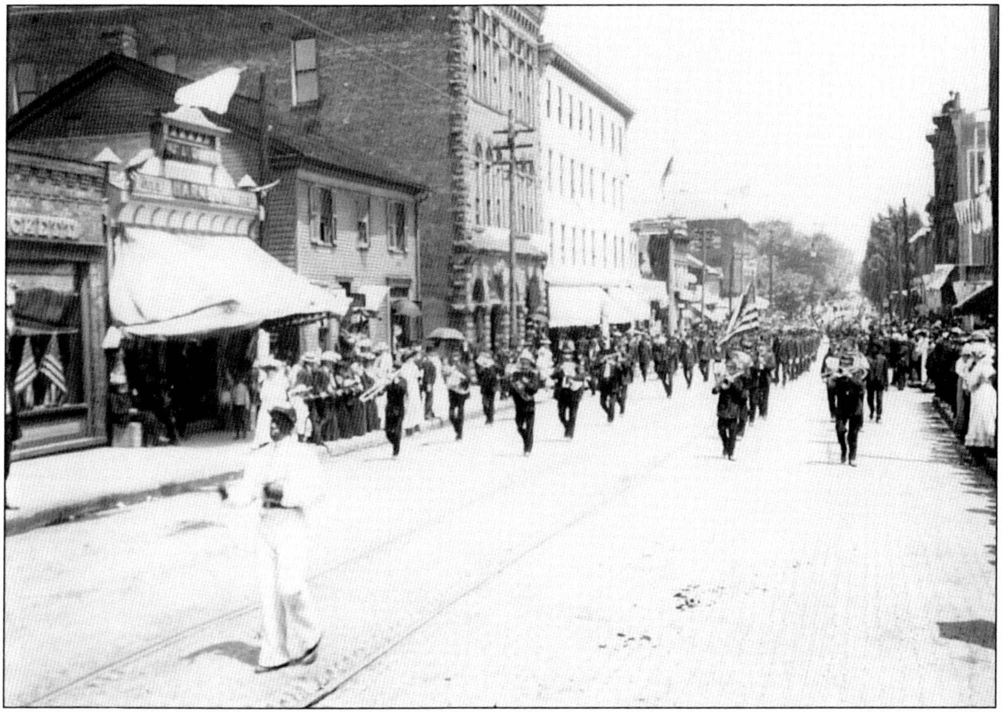

An early 1900s parade in front of the old Grand Opera House and Colonial Hotel on State Street. Some of the buildings are no longer standing.

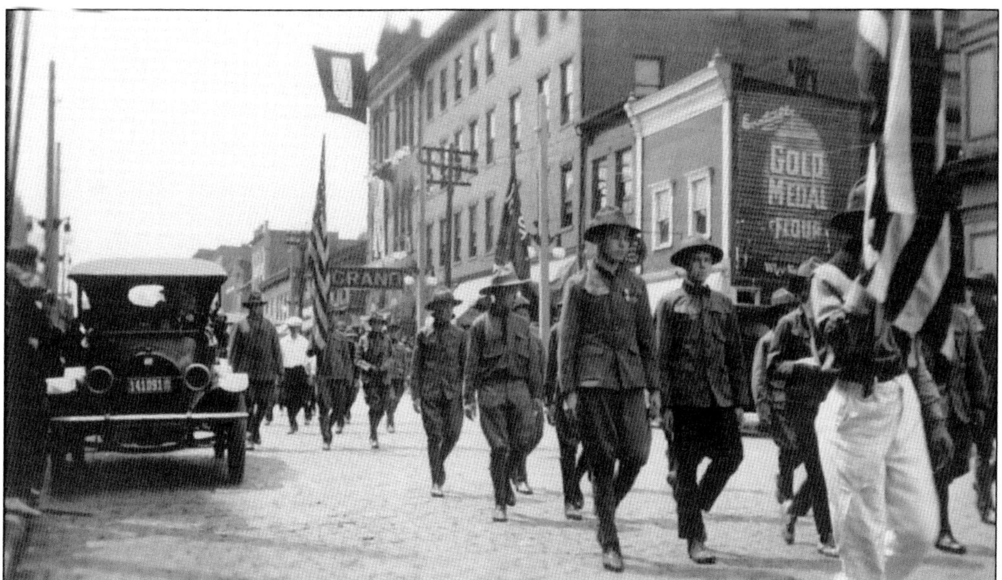

World War I Company D doughboys marching east on State Street in 1917. Most of the buildings shown here are no longer standing.

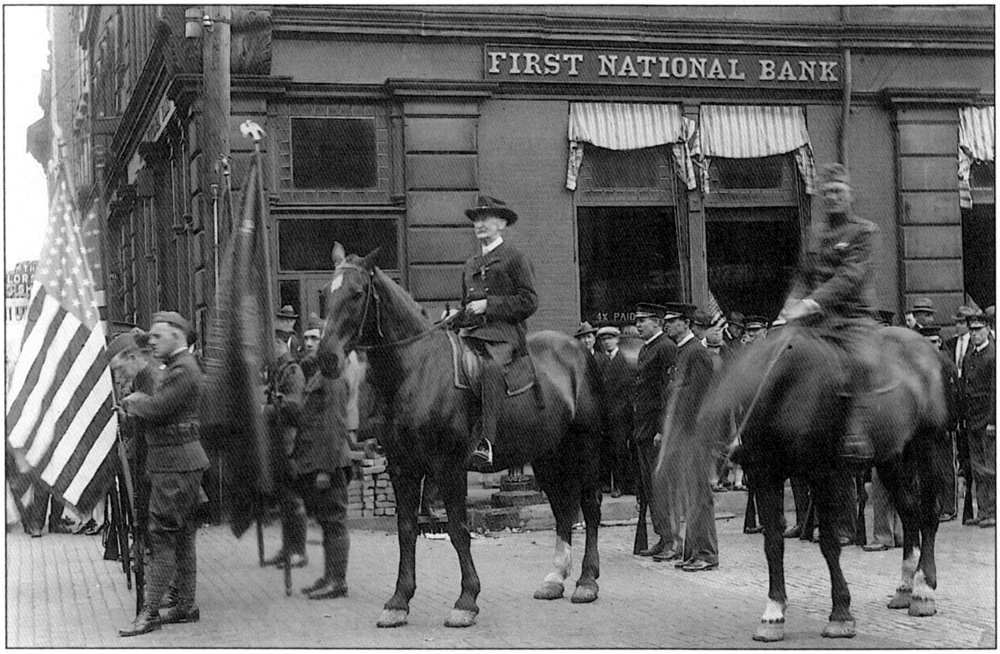

Charles Bonsall (center), Salem's last Civil War veteran, a prominent figure in Memorial Day parades. He is shown here in full dress uniform in the 1920s. He died at age 97 on February 25, 1937. The bank building on the southeast corner of State Street and South Broadway Avenue was replaced in 1929. Concert Hall was on the third floor, where many famous entertainers such as Tom Thumb and Mark Twain performed.

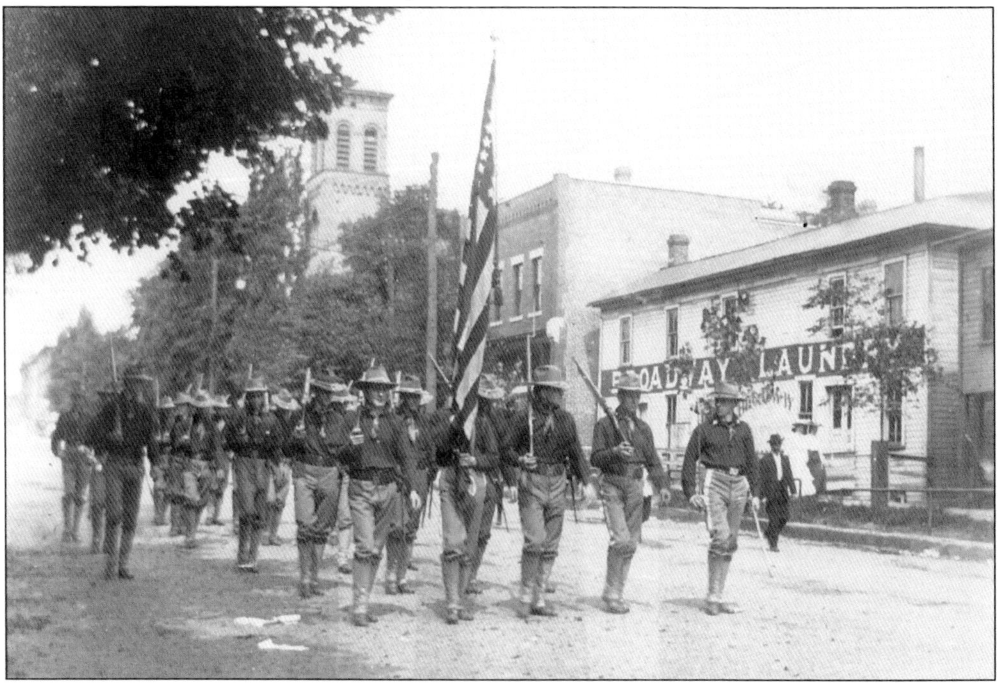

Spanish-American War veterans on South Broadway Avenue in the early 1900s. The Methodist church was replaced in 1911, and Broadway Laundry now operates as American Laundry.

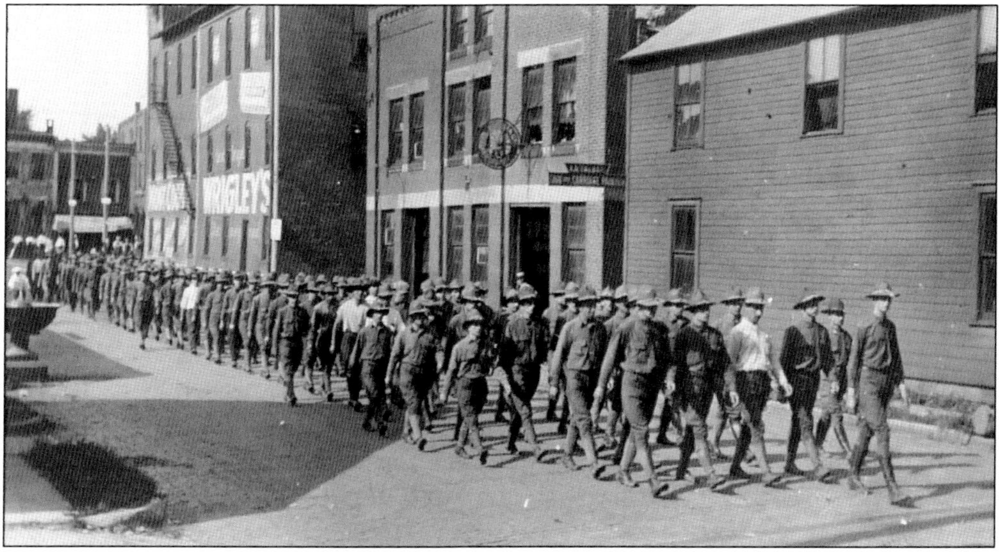

World War I recruits in June of 1917. They are marching south on Penn Avenue. Captain Percy Tetlow was commander of the newly formed Company D of the Ohio 10th Infantry. The unit of volunteers trained in Salem for three months before being sent to Camp Sheridan, Alabama, and Camp Lee, Virginia.

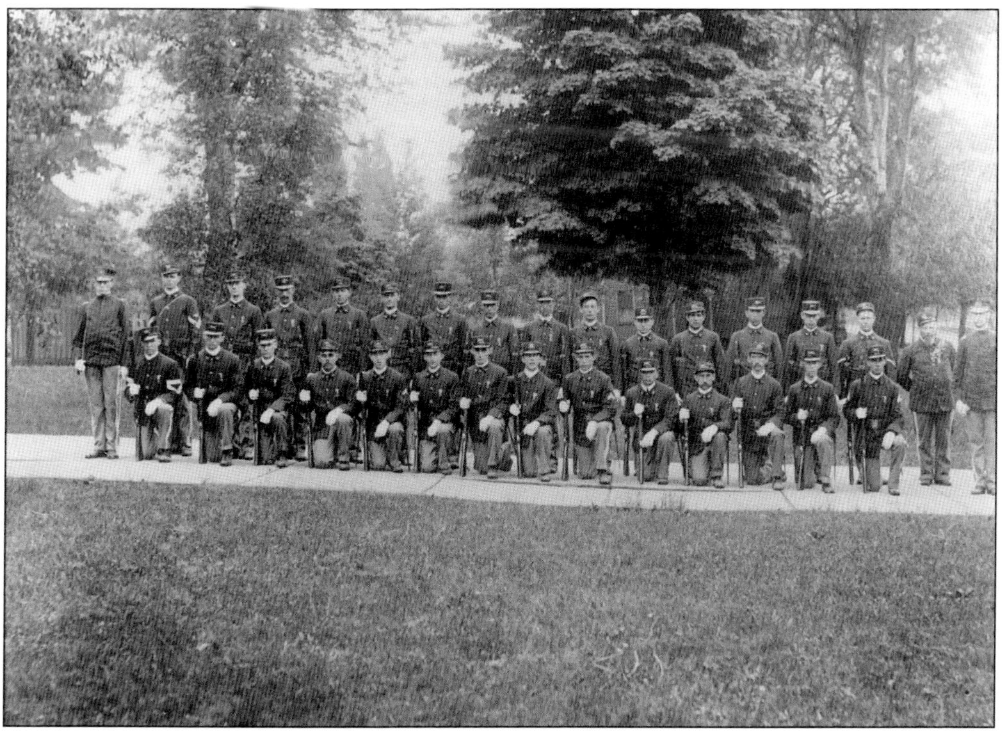

Members of Phillip Triem Camp 43 (Civil War), Company C, 1st Infantry, Ohio S.V. Reserves. This photograph was taken on May 30, 1904, in Salem.

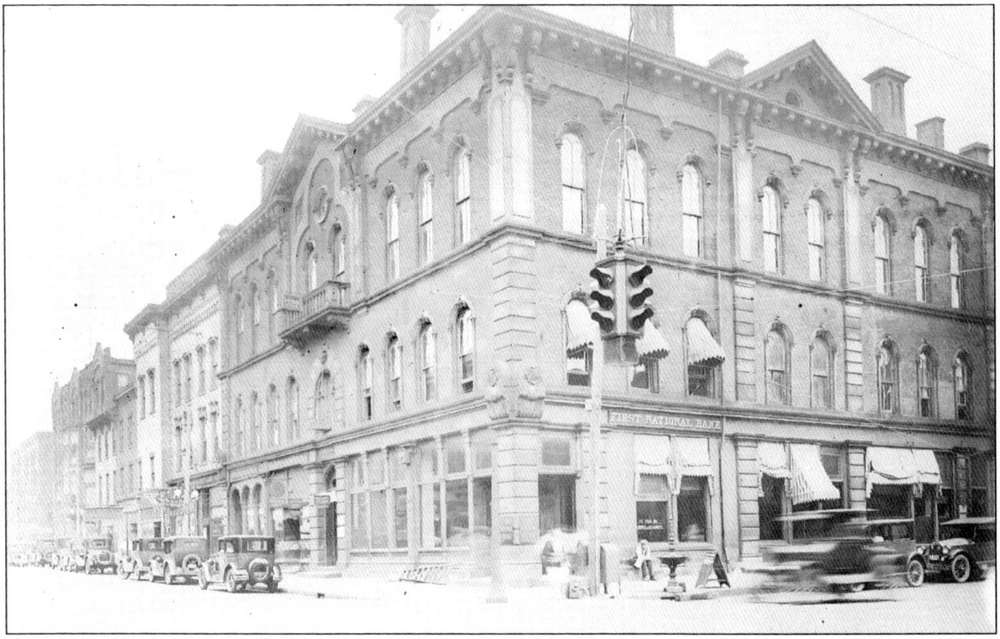

Salem's Pow Block, on the southeast corner of East State Street and South Broadway Avenue, built in 1861–62 by Alexander Pow. Concert Hall, once the center for entertainment and political gatherings, occupied the third floor. The First National Bank was on the ground floor, and Mr. Pow was its first president. The building was replaced in 1929 by the present limestone structure.

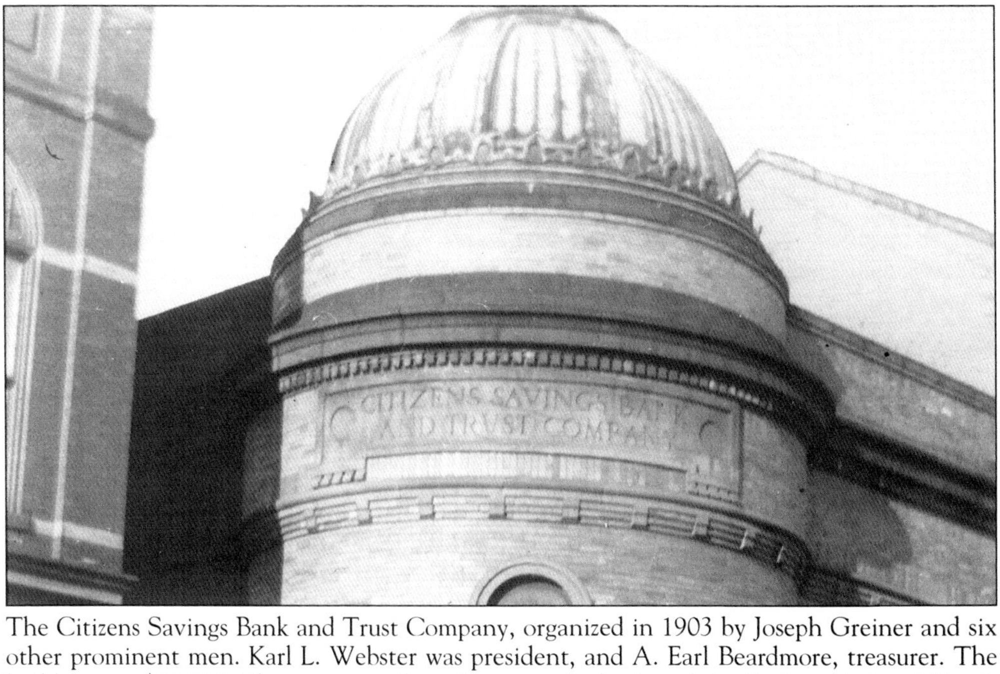

The Citizens Savings Bank and Trust Company, organized in 1903 by Joseph Greiner and six other prominent men. Karl L. Webster was president, and A. Earl Beardmore, treasurer. The building cost $28,000. There was a walkway between the bank and the Greiner-Brainard Hotel, which led to a parking lot. Frank Ehrhart had his aromatic popcorn stand in that walkway to serve shoppers on Saturday nights.

Two

Downtown Businesses

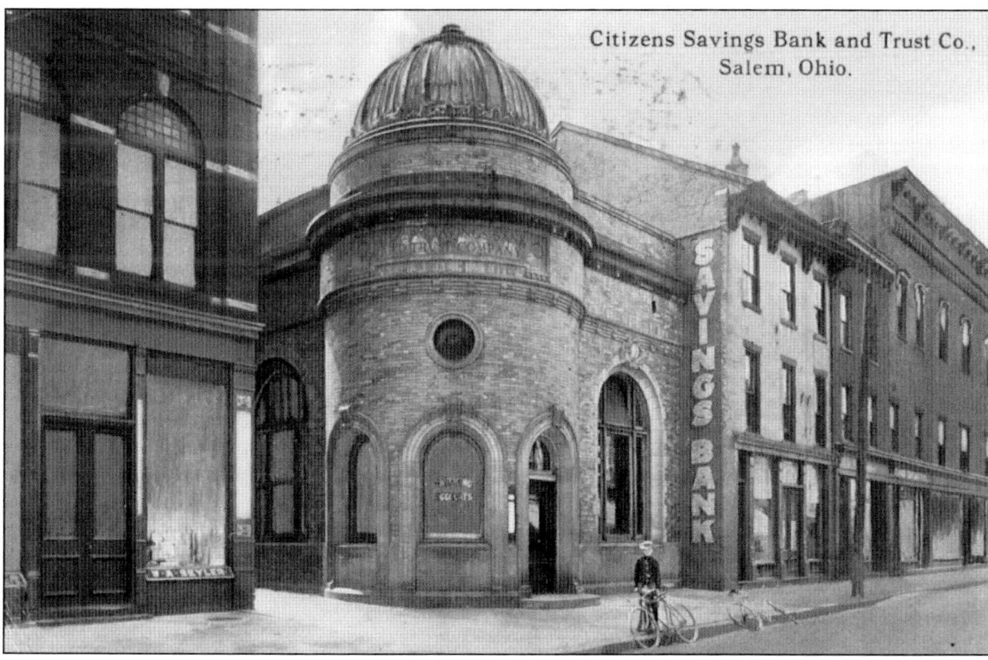

The castle-like building once located at 427 East State Street. This building, which housed the Citizens Savings Bank, was one of the most artistic structures in town. Founded in 1903, the bank closed during the Depression in 1931. Ira Brainard was one of the incorporators and stockholders. The structure was torn down in the 1930s to make room for the Nyktus building. On the left is the Greiner-Brainard Hotel.

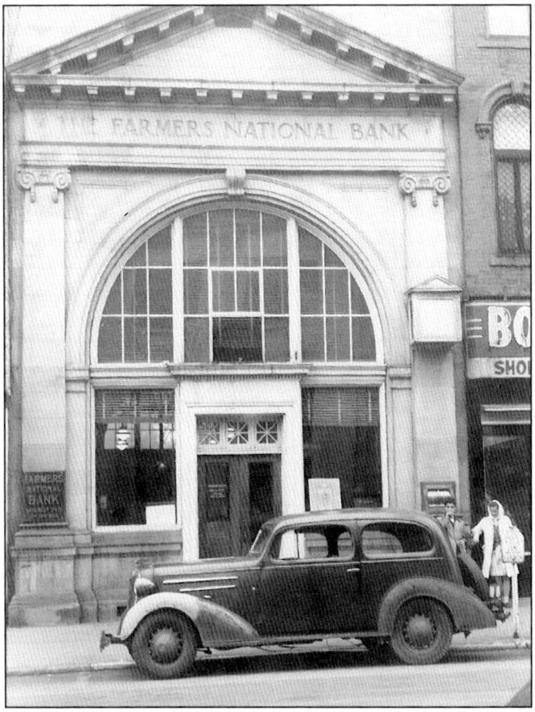

The Farmers Bank, once located at 340 East State Street. The bank was chartered in 1846 as a branch of the State Bank of Ohio. While Zadok Street II (grandson of Salem's co-founder) was the prime mover in founding the bank, Simeon Jennings was chosen as the bank's first president. The bank remained at this location for 89 years, although the building was renovated in 1925. The photo was taken around 1940.

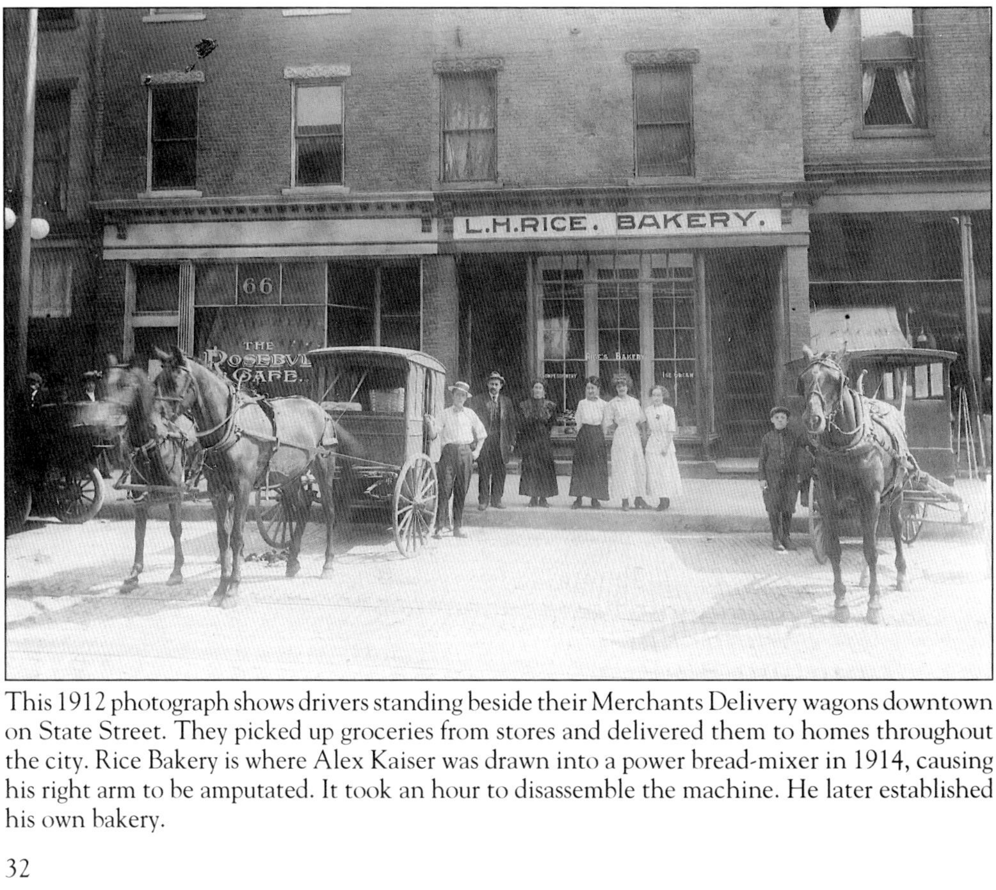

This 1912 photograph shows drivers standing beside their Merchants Delivery wagons downtown on State Street. They picked up groceries from stores and delivered them to homes throughout the city. Rice Bakery is where Alex Kaiser was drawn into a power bread-mixer in 1914, causing his right arm to be amputated. It took an hour to disassemble the machine. He later established his own bakery.

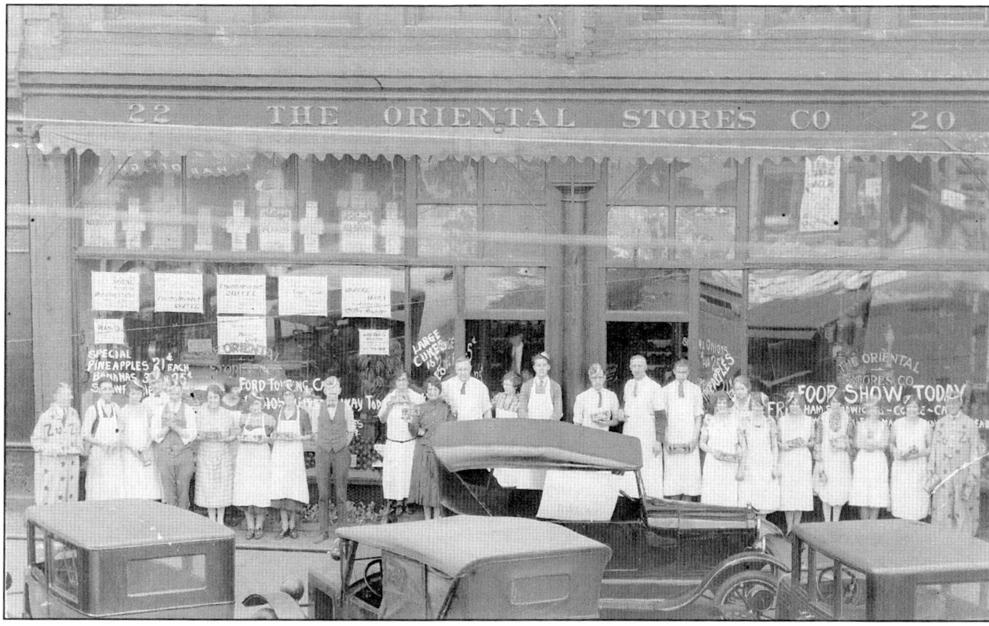

The Oriental Market on South Broadway Avenue, owned by Harvey E. Eakin. This was the first self-serve store in Salem, and the largest general store in Columbiana County. It sold high-quality goods in the store and by mail. Cut glass from Czechoslovakia, fine china from France and Germany, and dinnerware from England were displayed throughout the store. Mr. Eakin was an inventor, and one of his biggest sellers was a fruit jar sealer.

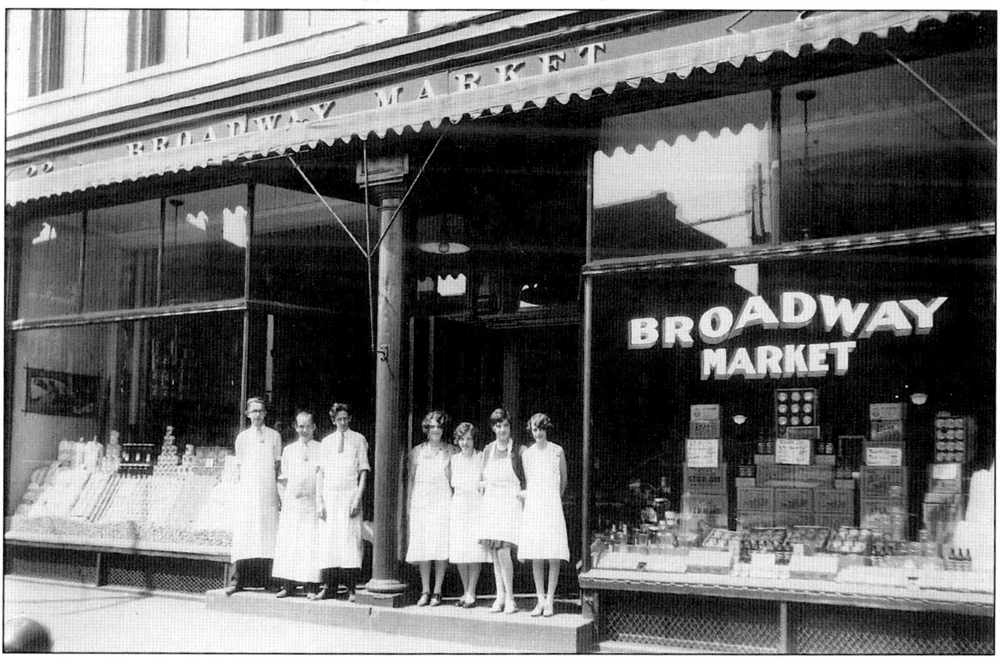

Broadway Market. Roy S. Hostetler bought the Oriental Company store in 1930 and changed the name to the Broadway Market. Kroger's took over the space in 1944, with a grand opening ceremony featuring "Flagpole Kelly" sitting on a pole high atop the building. The Gurney Building still stands today.

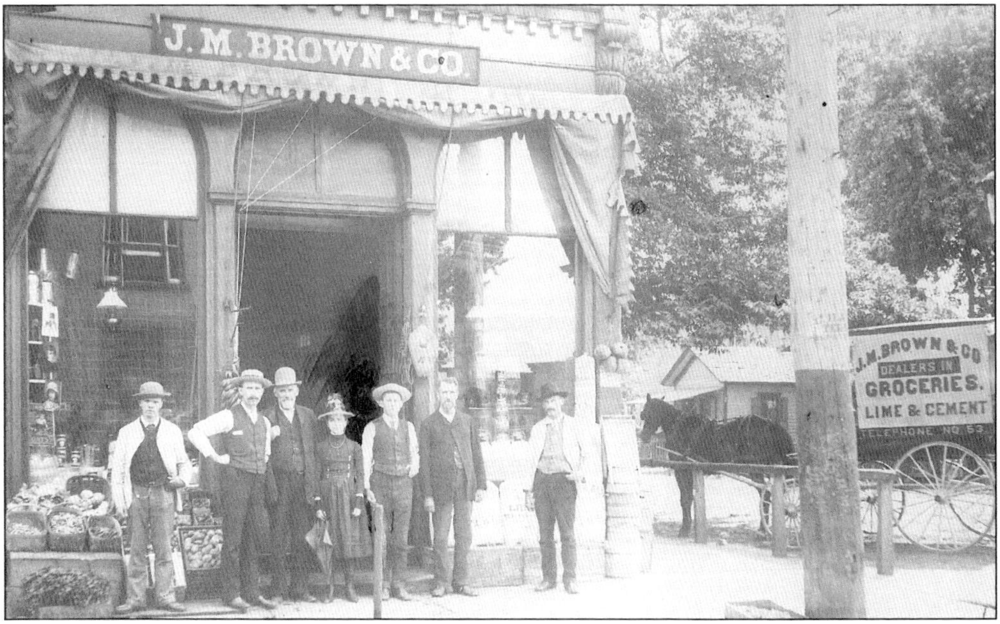

James M. Brown's grocery store (the building still stands), located on Brown's Corner, the southeast corner of State Street and South Ellsworth Avenue. In 1905 it was probably the oldest firm in Salem, having been established in 1857. It sold the first roasted coffee in town. About 1910 the store became the Smith Company.

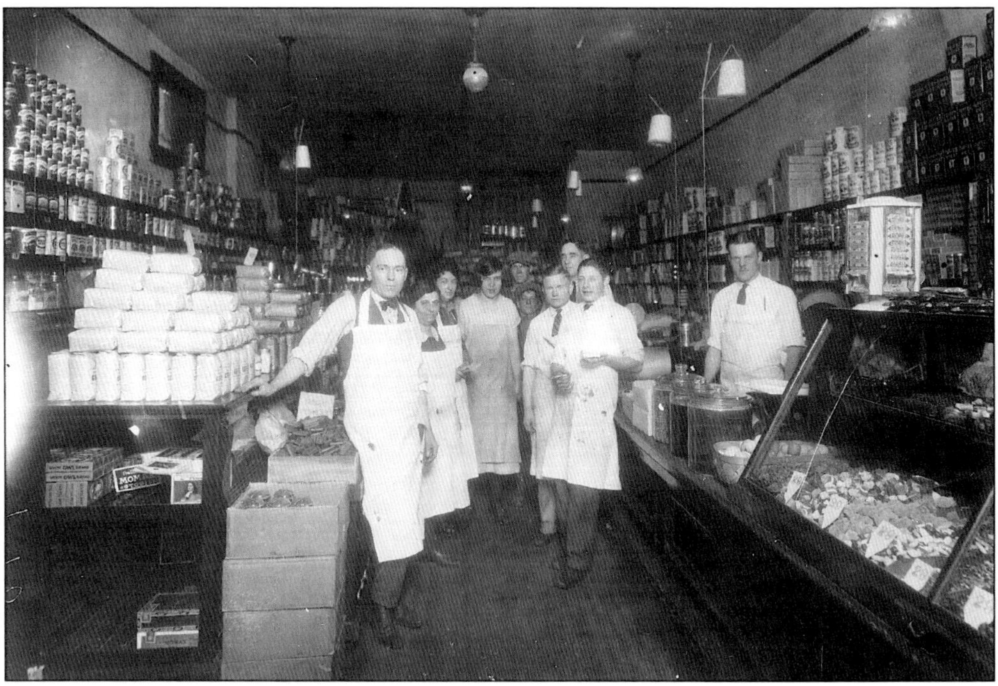

Harroff's Grocery, located on South Broadway Avenue during the first half of this century. At left is Harry Harroff, with his wife behind. Leo Wacksmith, the butcher, is at the far right.

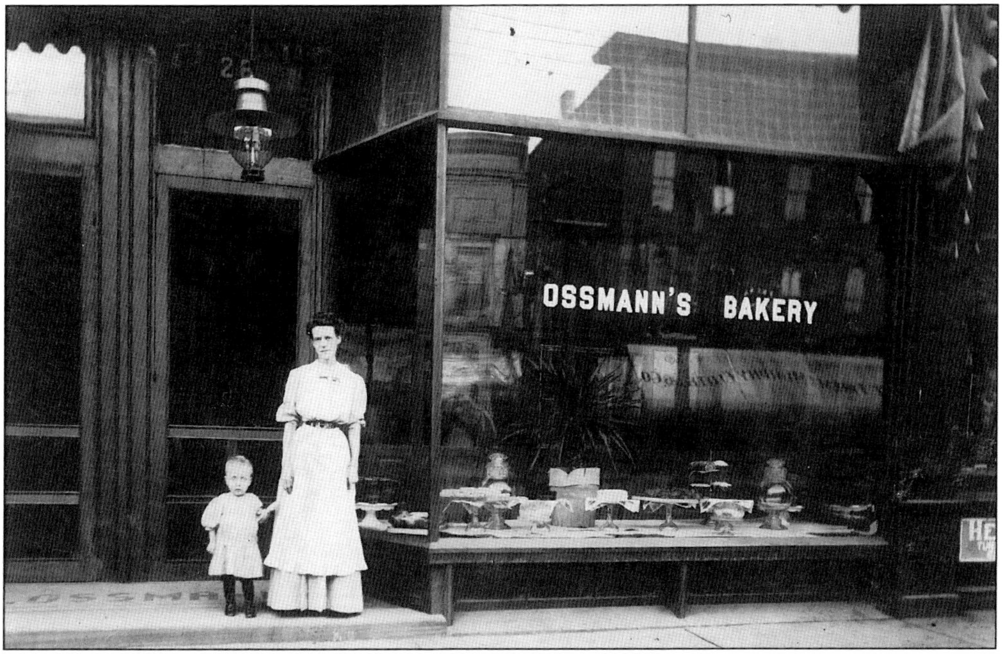

Conrad Ossmann's bakery, located at 167 South Broadway Avenue in 1902–1903. His wife and son appear in front. Later it became the J.L. Davis Bakery. The building still stands today.

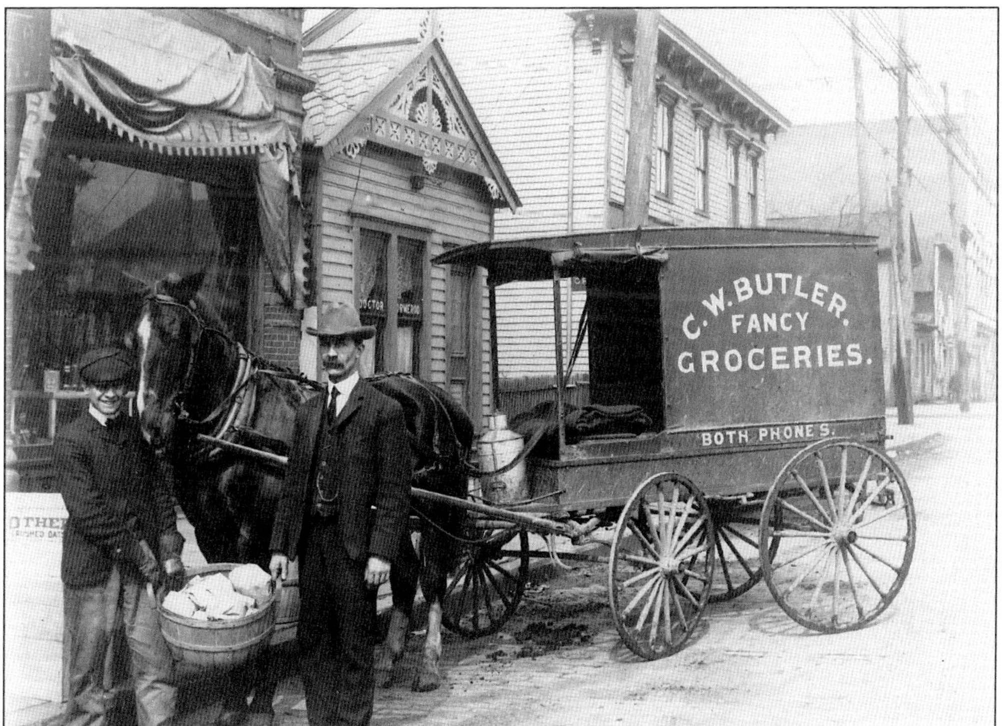

C.W. Butler loading his wagon. At the turn of the century, many of the small mom-and-pop grocery stores in town delivered to homes. Note the lettering indicating that there were two phone systems in town at the time.

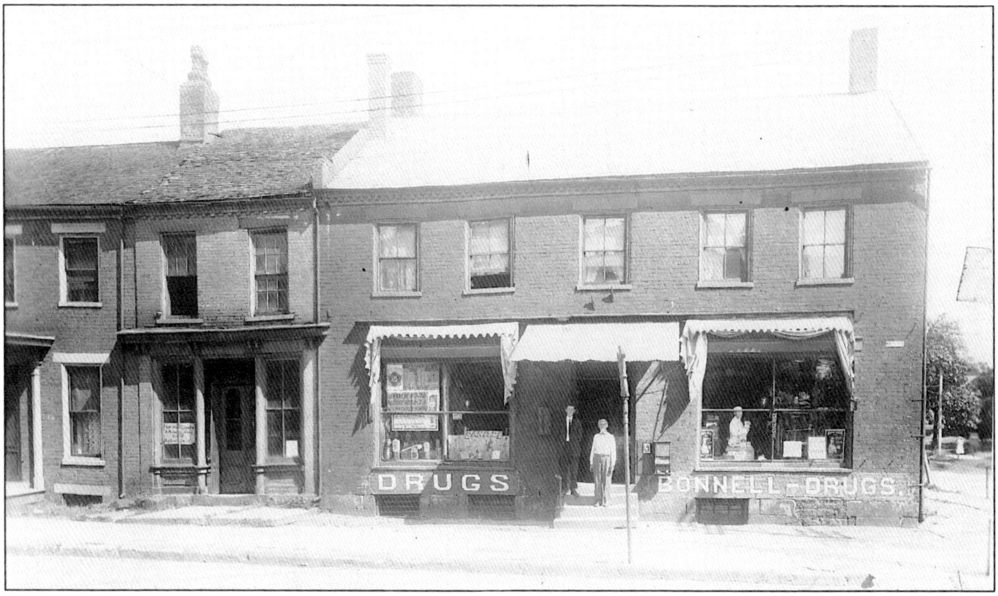

Bonnell's Drug Store, located on the northwest corner of East State Street and North Lincoln (Garfield) Avenue in the early 1900s. This photograph was taken about 1910 when the Salem Electric Railway trolley was still operating. Neither of these buildings stand today.

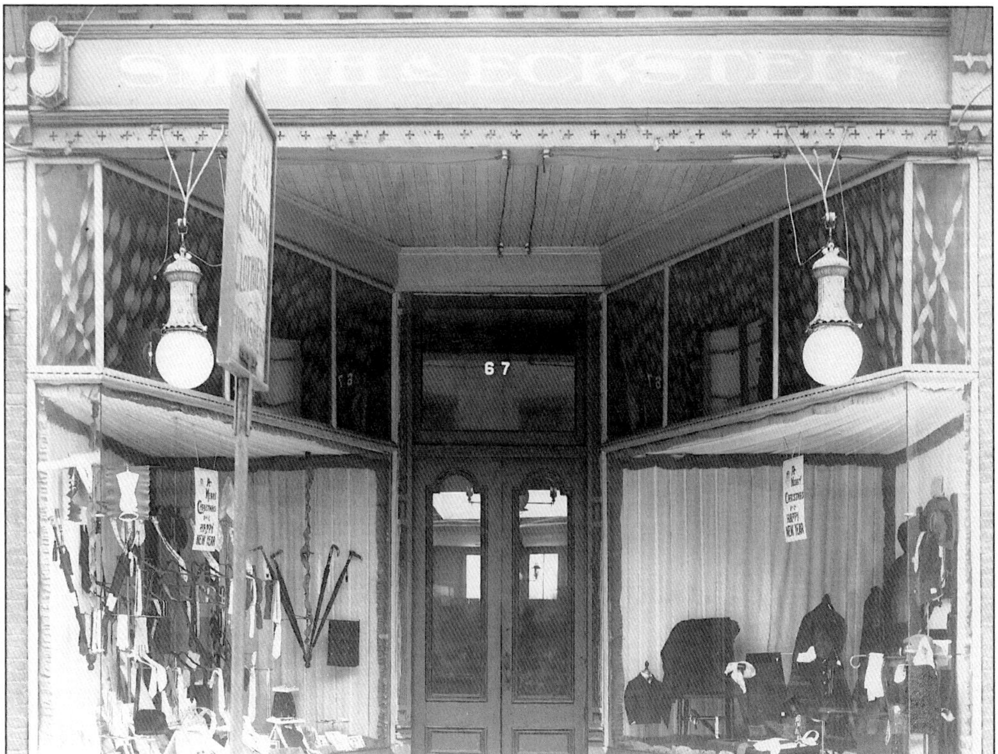

Smith and Eckstein, purveyors of fine clothing. The store windows are decorated for a Christmas season in the early 1900s. Note the special electric lighting. The building still stands today at 420 East State Street.

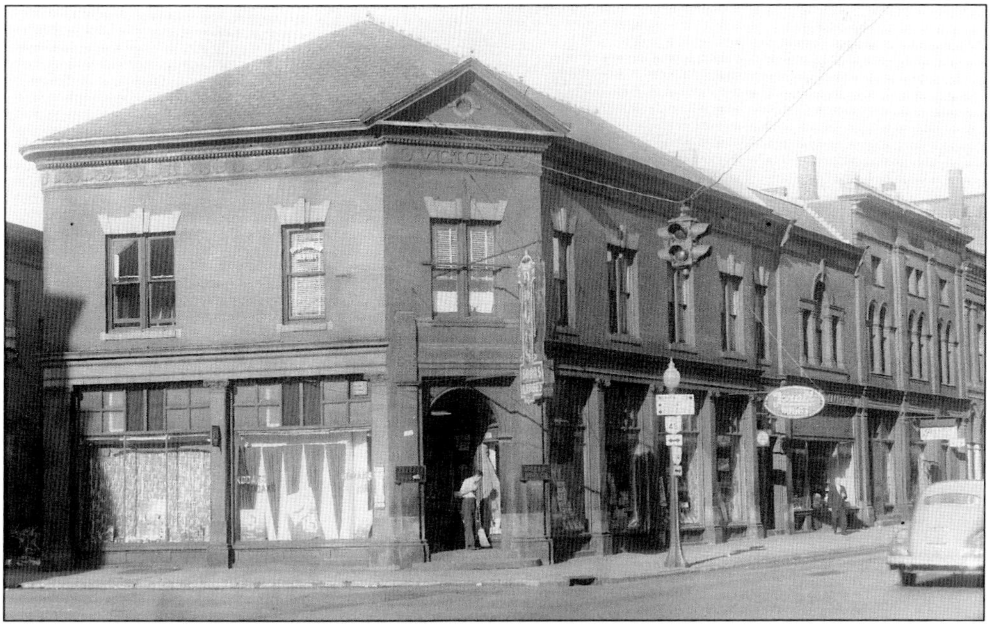

The Victoria Building, located on the southwest corner of East State Street and South Lincoln Avenue. This building housed Lease's Drug Store in the 1940s, when this photograph was taken. Dr. Joseph J. Hurray, a dentist, had his office on the second floor. Connected to this structure are the Exchange and Manila Buildings, all erected by J. Twing Brooks in the 1890s. Initially, the ground floors were used as a stable.

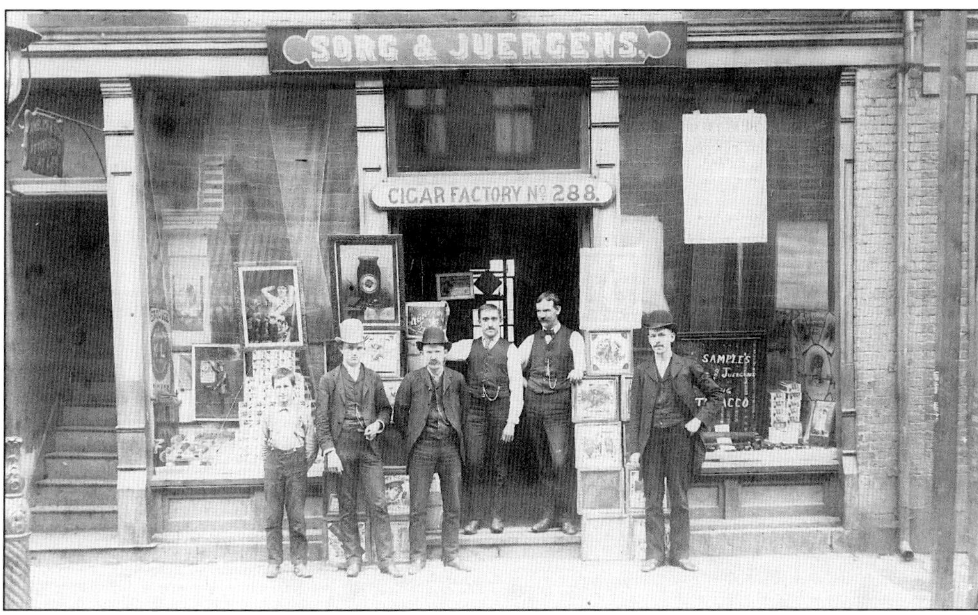

Cigar Factory No. 288, owned and operated by J.G. Sorg and Otto C. Juergens in the late 1880s. They are shown standing in the doorway of their store. The partnership was dissolved in 1890, and Juergens continued the business on South Broadway Avenue.

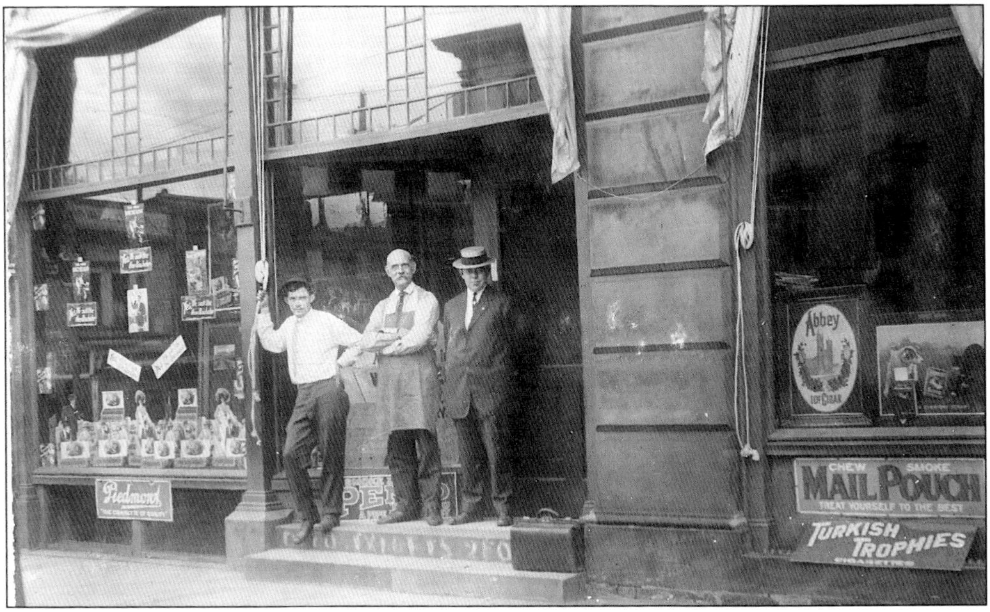

Bill Juergens and his father, Otto Juergens, with a friend in front of Juergens Cigar Store, located on South Broadway Avenue in 1915. This was a favorite meeting spot for Democrat politicians.

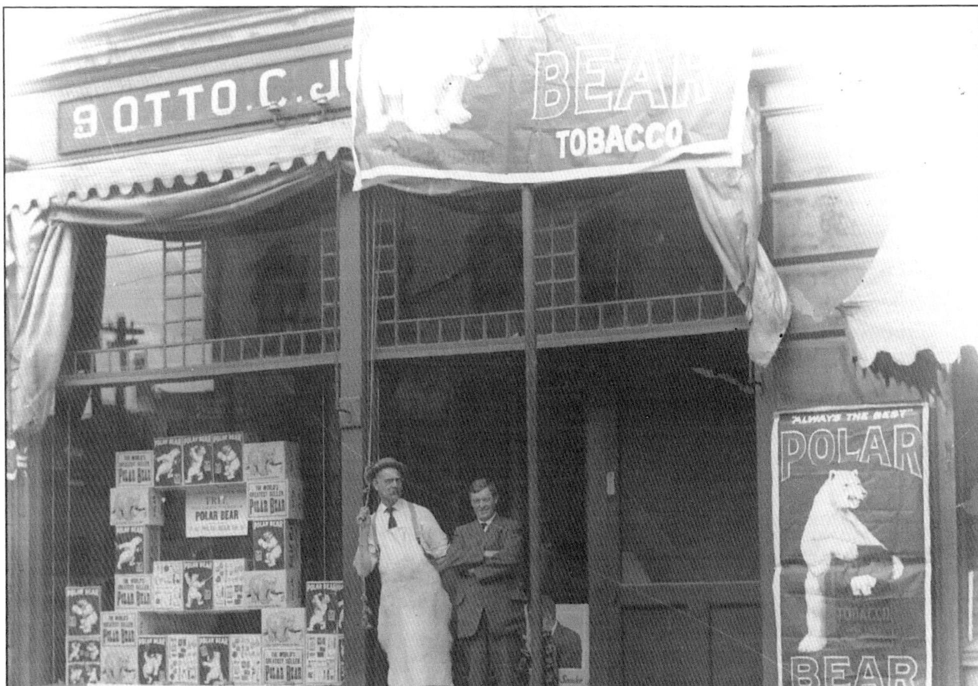

Otto C. Juergens (at left), a cigar-maker by trade, in 1911 standing with a friend in front of his store. Located in the First National Bank building on South Broadway Avenue, this store was a popular gathering place for men, and was frequently referred to as "Tammany Hall" (a once-popular name for the Democratic Party in New York City).

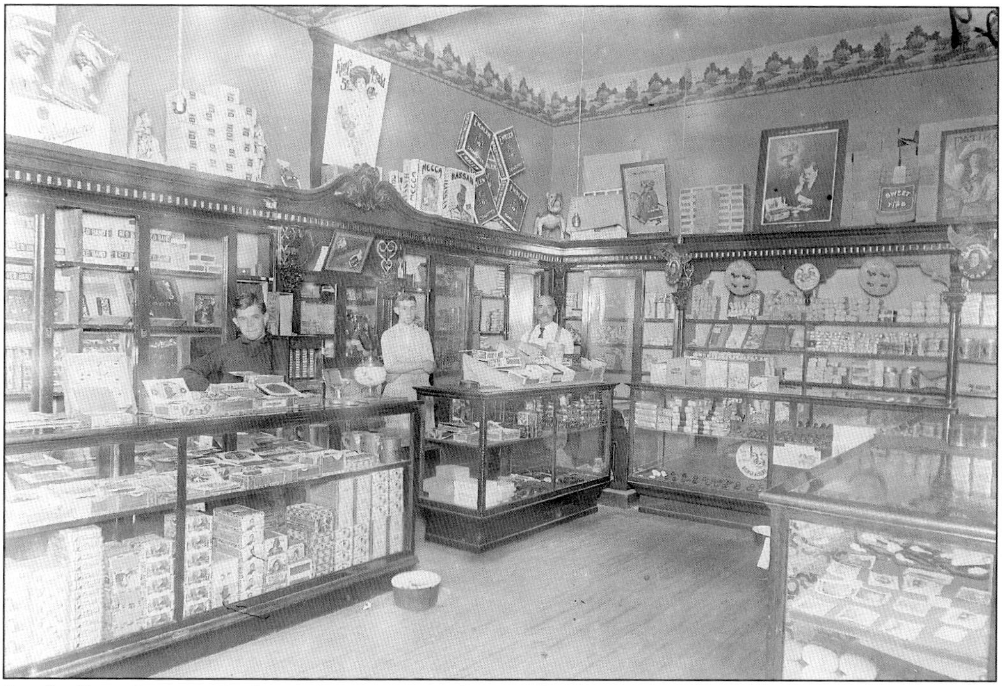

Inside Otto Juergens's Cigar Store on South Broadway Avenue in 1907. The people are Carl Juergens, Sam Fleisher, and Otto Juergens. Note the spittoon. At the turn of the century Salemites were consuming approximately 1,000 pounds of snuff per year. Scotch, or yellow snuff, was most in demand. It was rubbed on the gums. Copenhagen, or black snuff, was used in the nose.

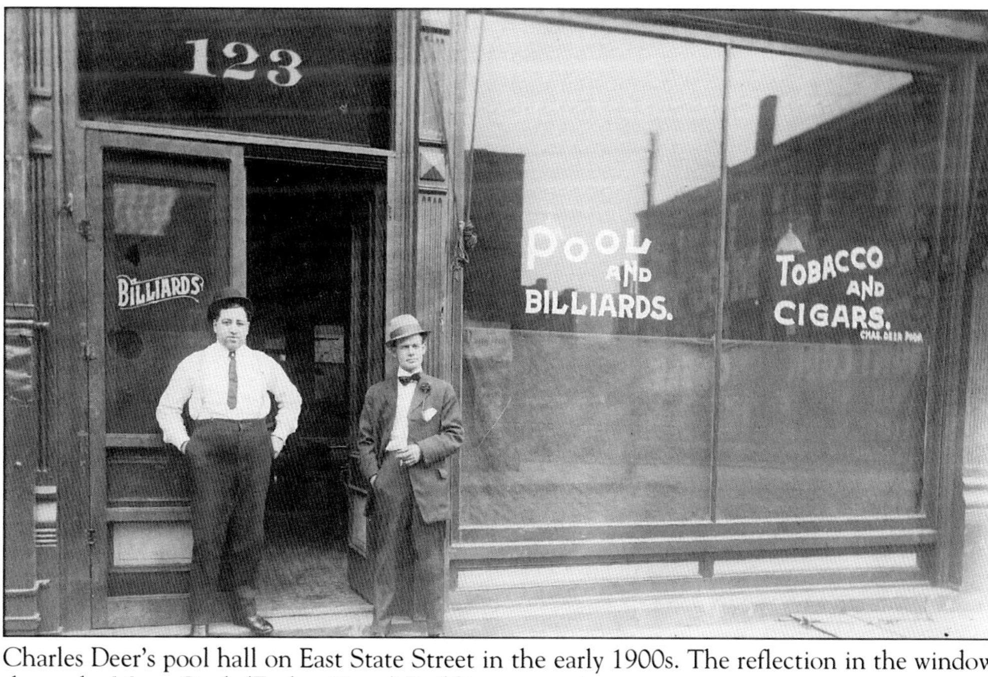

Charles Deer's pool hall on East State Street in the early 1900s. The reflection in the window shows the Mont Cook (Endres Gross) Building across the street.

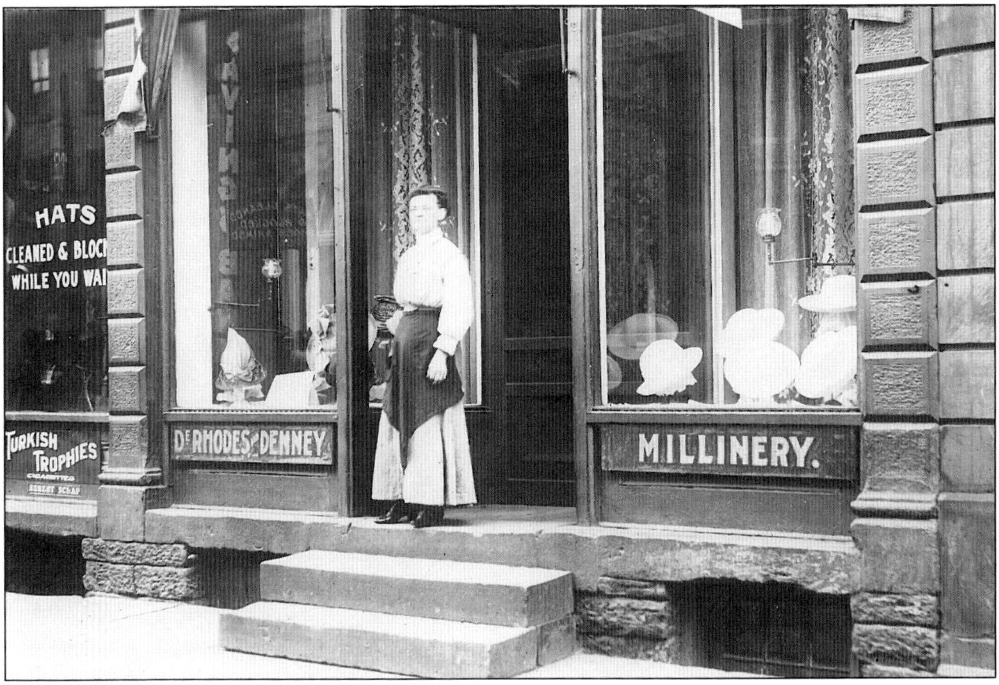

Mrs. Frank DeRhodes in front of the DeRhodes and Denney Millinery on East State Street. Mrs. DeRhodes's daughter was Mabel Doutt, who was the last owner of the store in the 1950s. The store dealt with all types of hats, bonnets, and headdresses for women.

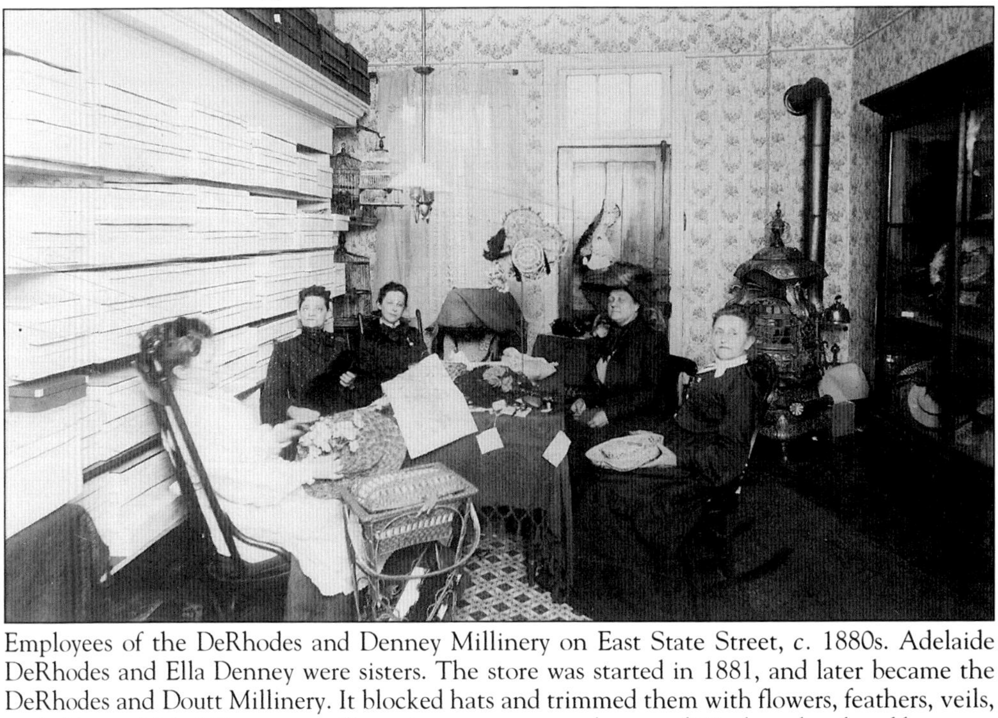

Employees of the DeRhodes and Denney Millinery on East State Street, *c.* 1880s. Adelaide DeRhodes and Ella Denney were sisters. The store was started in 1881, and later became the DeRhodes and Doutt Millinery. It blocked hats and trimmed them with flowers, feathers, veils, and ribbons. Mabel Doutt was still serving customers at the age of 90 when she closed her store in the 1950s.

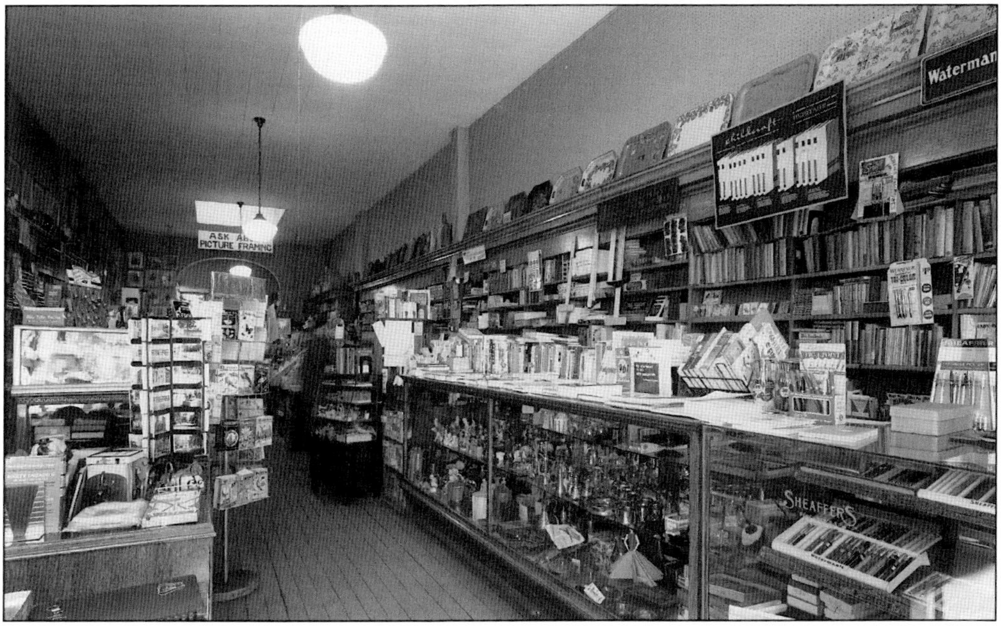

MacMillan's Bookstore. Established in 1859 by Joel MacMillan, this was once Salem's oldest store. The sign over the door read: "Things Out of the Ordinary." There was an enticing smell in this store coming from a vast combination of things—ink, library paste, notebooks, rubber erasers, crayons, paint sets, chalk, fountain pens, poster board, craft paper, and books. The building still stands today.

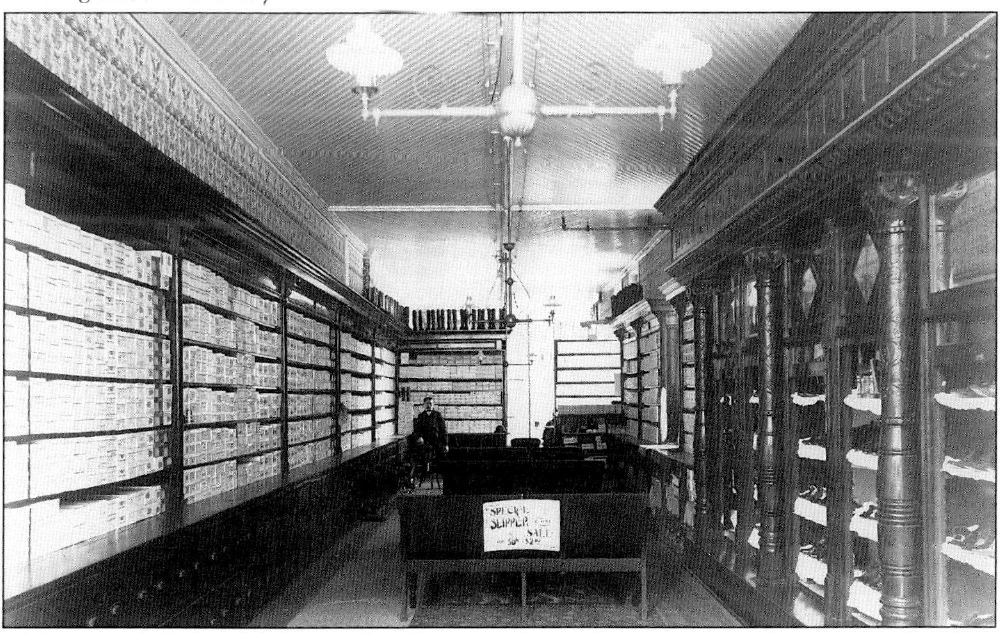

Frank R. Speidel's shoe store, located on South Broadway Avenue. Electricity had not yet become available in Salem when this photograph was taken—note the gas lights. The store was consumed by fire in 1924. Two three-story brick buildings were completely destroyed in the spectacular blaze. There are no shoe stores in downtown Salem today. The Speidel residence, incidentally, is the present Arbaugh-Pearce-Greenison Funeral Home.

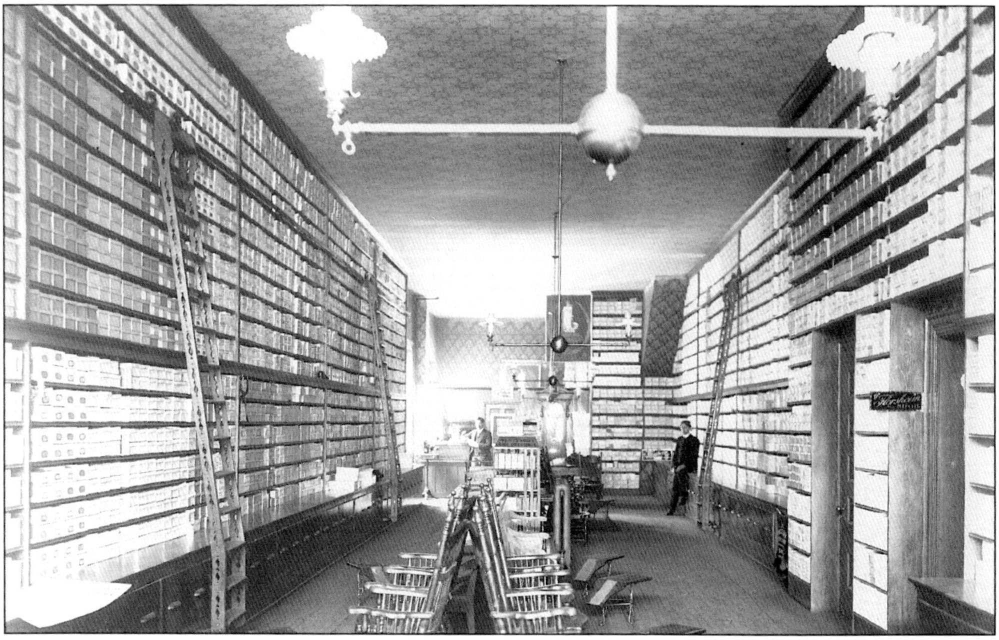

Charles Chalfant's shoe store, located in the Greiner-Brainard (Metzger) Hotel in 1890. Note the gas lights and ladders that slid on rails. This building is no longer standing.

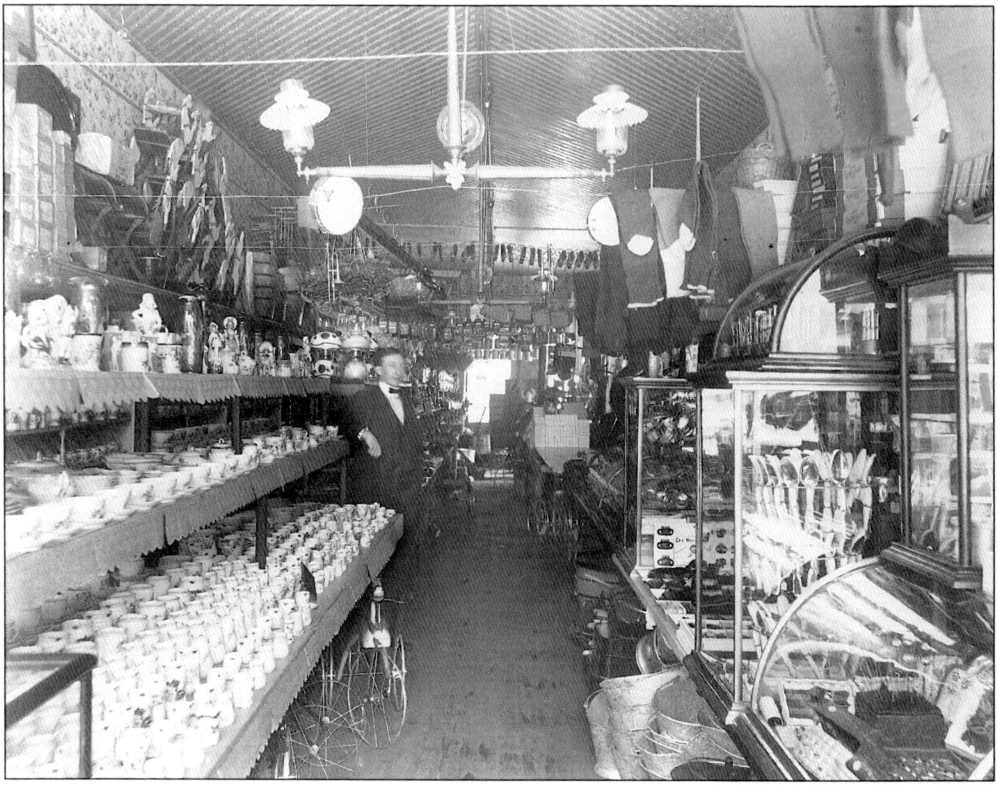

Farmer and Getz, owners of a store filled with a wide variety of notions, knickknacks, and useful articles. Note the gas lights, tricycles, and coal buckets.

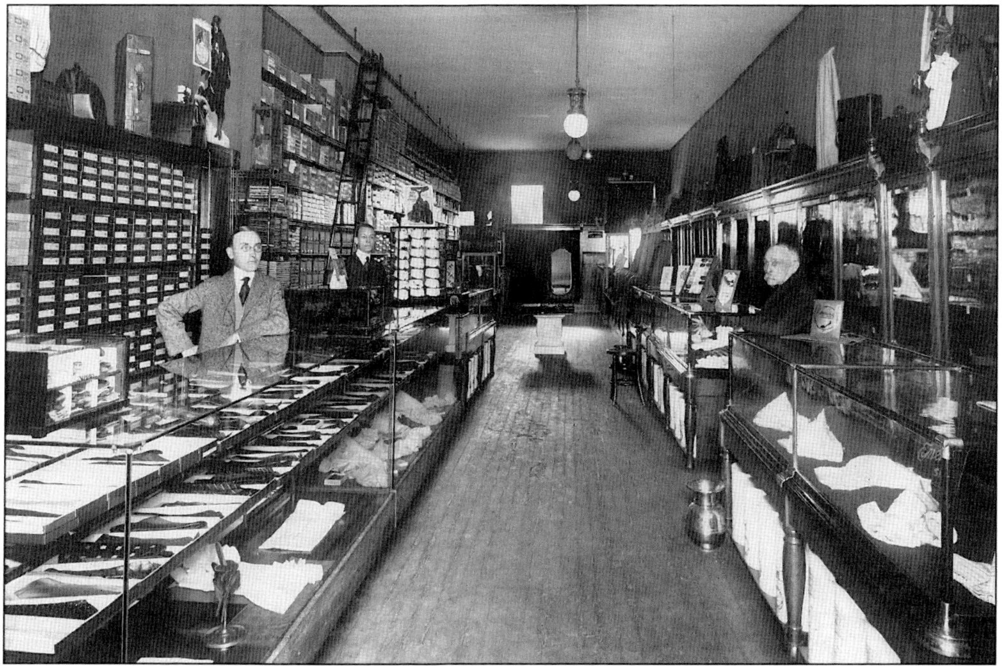

The J. Atchison and Son men's clothing store, located at 420 East State Street in 1914. W. Sherman Atchison and his father operated the store. The building still stands today. This store later became the Fitzpatrick-Strain Company. Sherman opened another store called the Salem Wall Paper and Paint Company. In 1909 he was Salem's postmaster, and for five years he and Frank Y. Allen managed the Grand Opera House.

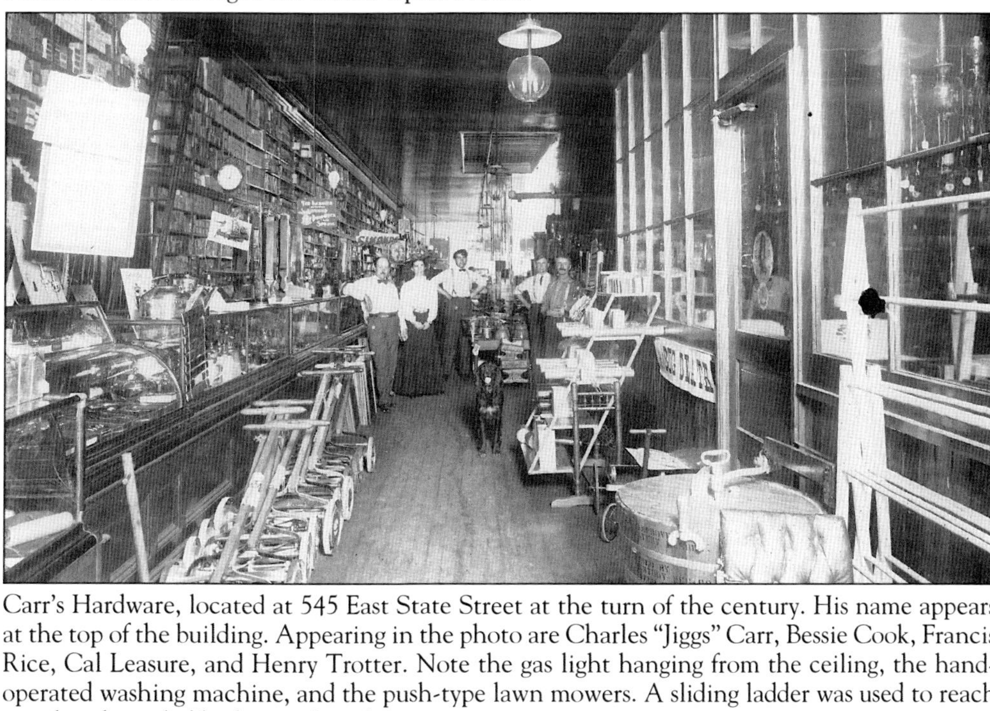

Carr's Hardware, located at 545 East State Street at the turn of the century. His name appears at the top of the building. Appearing in the photo are Charles "Jiggs" Carr, Bessie Cook, Francis Rice, Cal Leasure, and Henry Trotter. Note the gas light hanging from the ceiling, the hand-operated washing machine, and the push-type lawn mowers. A sliding ladder was used to reach merchandise piled high out of reach.

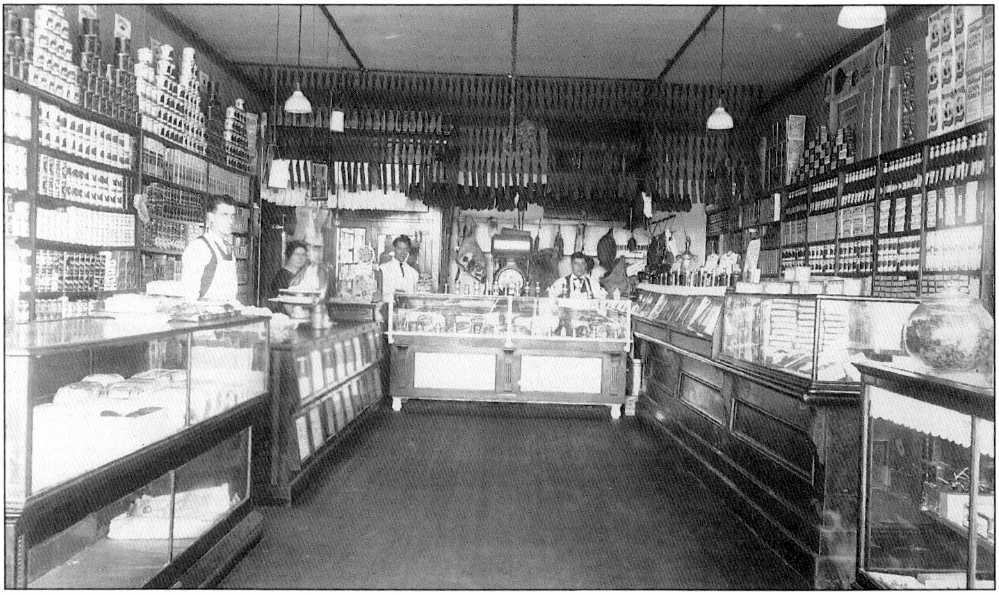

Hoperich's Grocery, a mom-and-pop store, located on the southwest corner of South Lundy Avenue and Aetna Street (later moved to Perry Street). This photo was taken in 1926 and shows Phil Wack, Pearl Hoperich, Frank Hoperich, and Fritz Hoperich. Dr. Harold Hoperich, grandson of Frank, practiced medicine in Salem for many years.

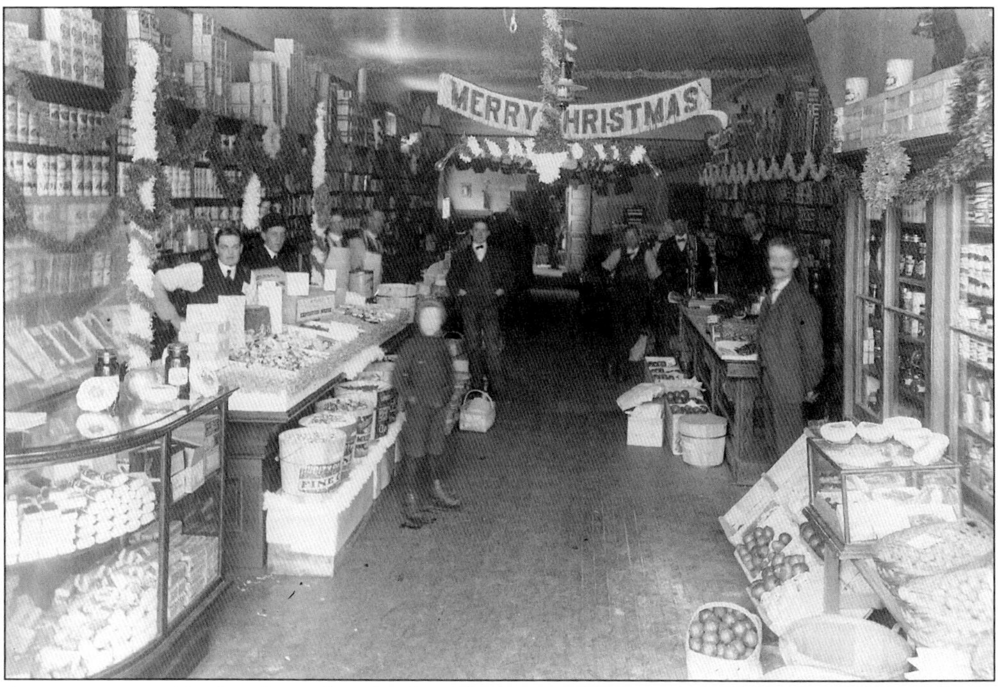

A grocery store filled with goodies for the Christmas season. Entering this store is like walking into the 1890s. A lot of foodstuffs were displayed in bulk in baskets and unfinished kegs. Scoops were essential. Long tongs were used to reach high items stacked against the wall. Remember the hanging scales, and the cast-iron, wire string-holder shaped like a cone hanging from the ceiling?

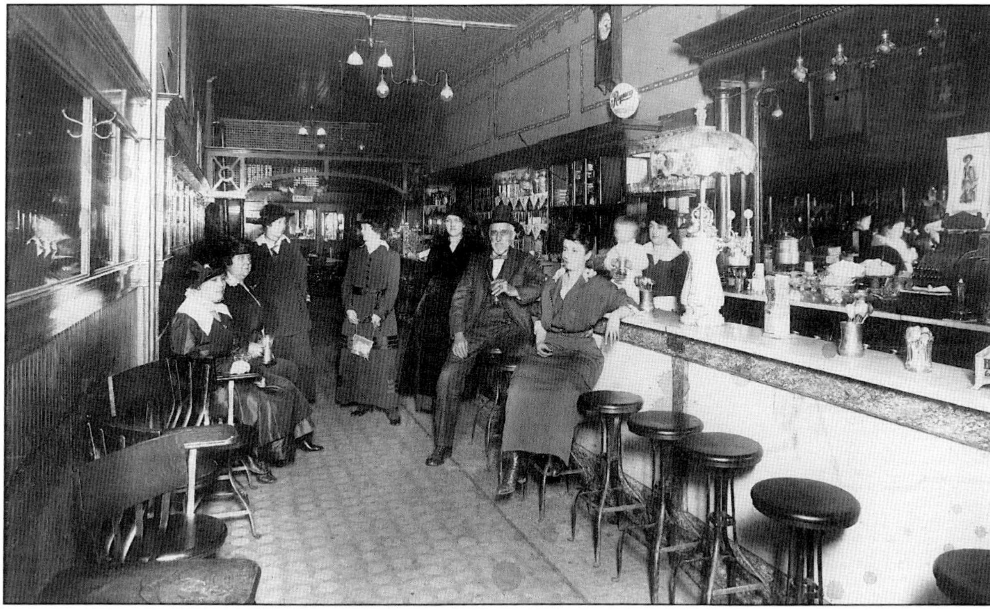

Wolf's Confectionery on East State Street, a popular spot in the late 1800s. For over a hundred years, soda fountains were an American institution—as American as apple pie, baseball, and hot dogs. Most drugstores had them because they appealed to the national taste. The confectionery is where people could enjoy a refreshing soda, sundae, milkshake, or coke. It had an open atmosphere and was a fun place to socialize.

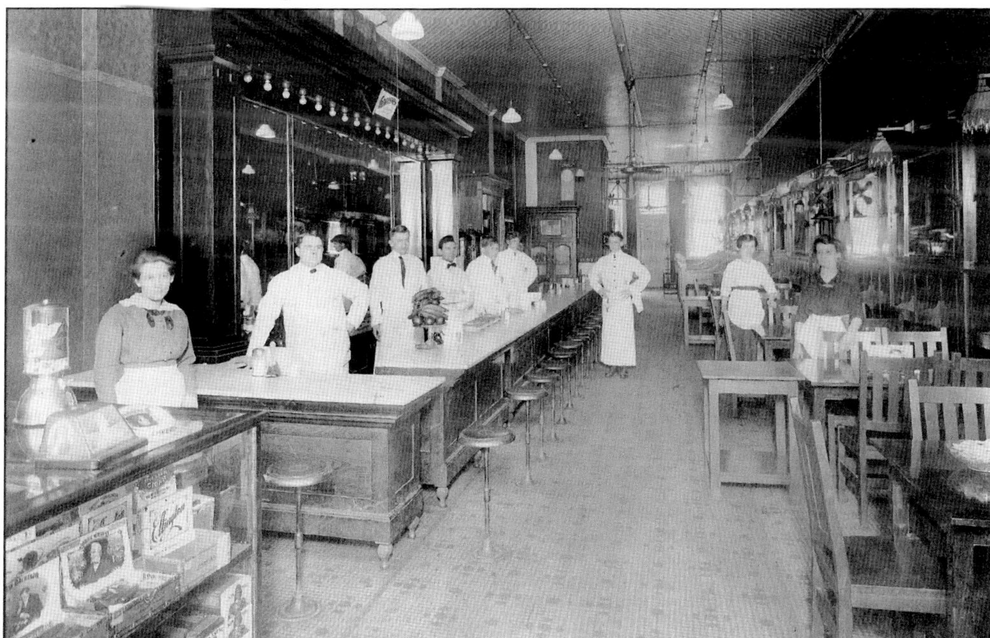

Trotter's Restaurant, one of Salem's popular eating spots in 1917. It was located in the Greiner-Brainard (Metzger) Hotel building on East State Street. Charles E. Trotter is at the left and Virgil Rakestraw is in the center. A specialty of this restaurant was fried oysters. The Salem Electric Railway trolley would pick them up and deliver them to customers along the line.

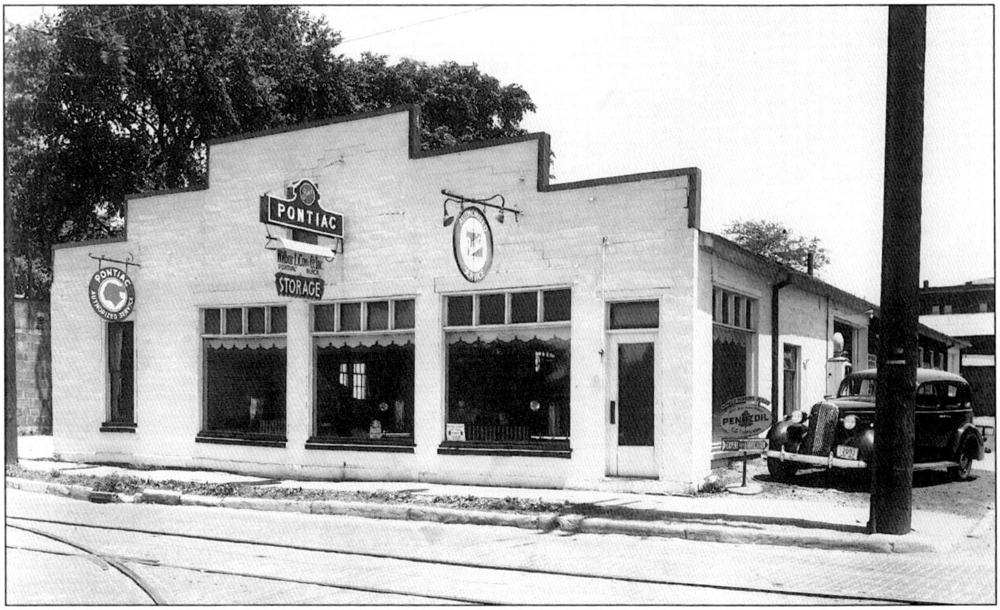

The building erected by Dallas Keller on North Ellsworth Avenue in the 1920s to house his automobile dealership. He sold the first Pontiac in Salem in 1926. Wilbur Coy took it over in the early 1930s and sold Buicks and Pontiacs. The track in the street was used by the Y&O Railroad and the Stark Electric Railroad.

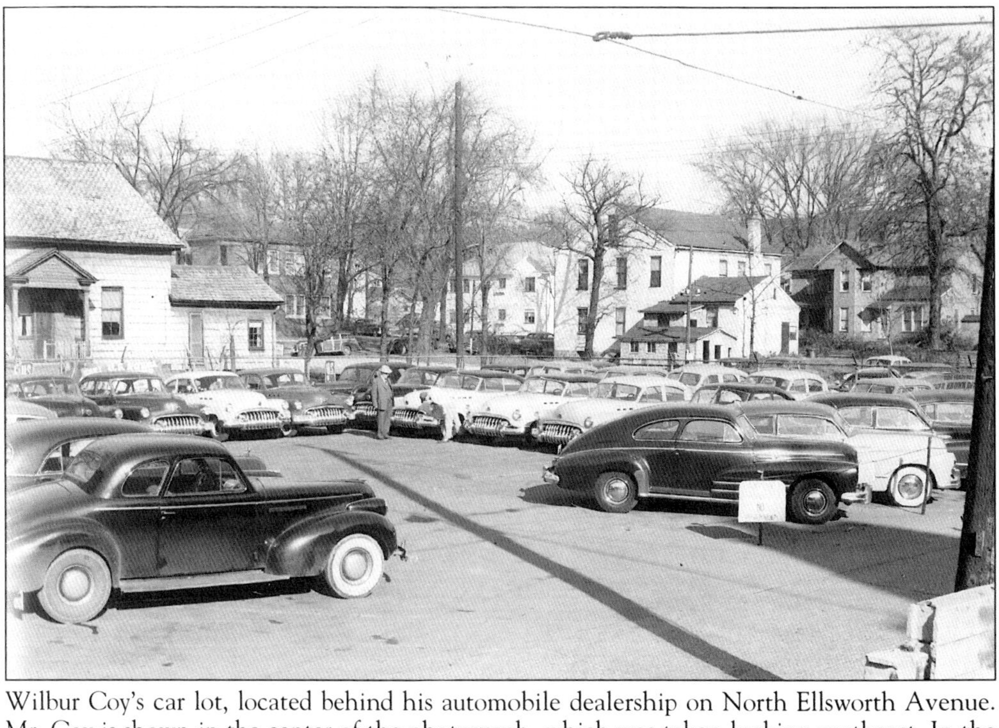

Wilbur Coy's car lot, located behind his automobile dealership on North Ellsworth Avenue. Mr. Coy is shown in the center of the photograph, which was taken looking northeast. In the background is the Clinic hospital and at left is an apartment building on East Second Street—part of the old Hicksite Meeting House.

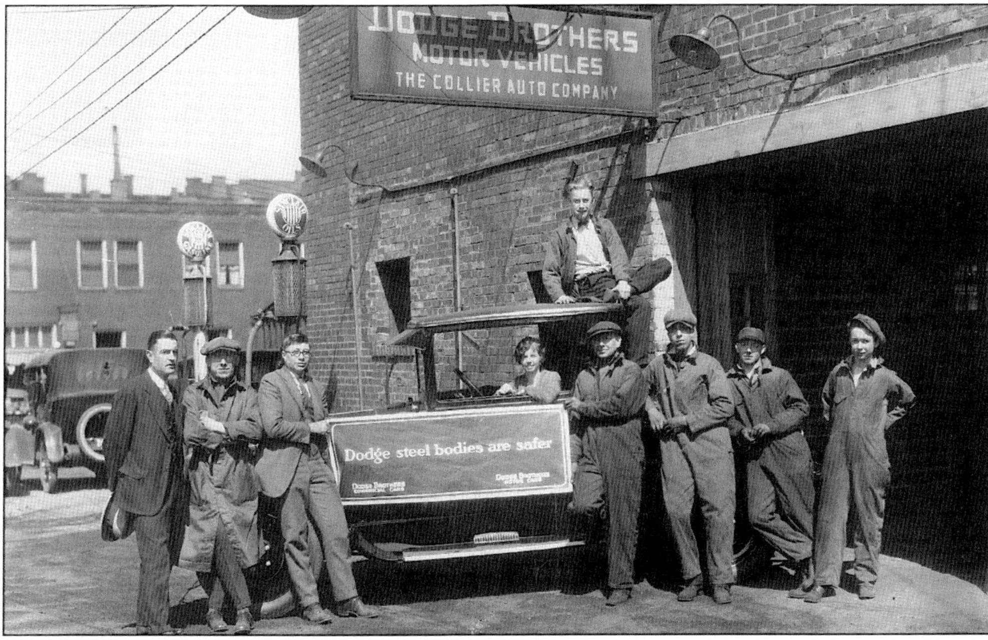

The Collier Auto Company Dodge dealership, located at 655 East State Street in the late 1920s. P.J. Collier was president and treasurer, and A.P. Morris was vice-president and secretary. This photo was taken at the back of their shop in the alley between South Lincoln Avenue and Penn Avenue. At left, on Penn Avenue, is the Sinclair gas station, now the site of MiMi's Coffee Shop.

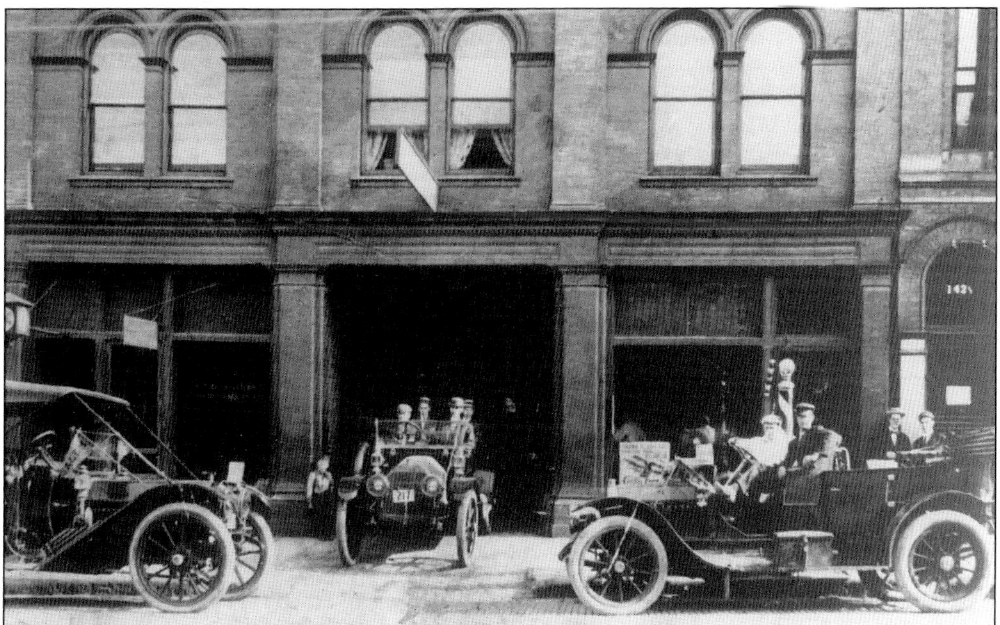

A June 1911 scene outside an automobile agency at 645 East State Street. On the left is a 1910 Oldsmobile Limited, owned by Samuel Grove Sr., owner of the Grove Chewing Gum Company. Riding in the car on the right are Fred and James Brinton Gibbons. Note the steering wheel is on the right-hand side of the car in the center. The building still stands today.

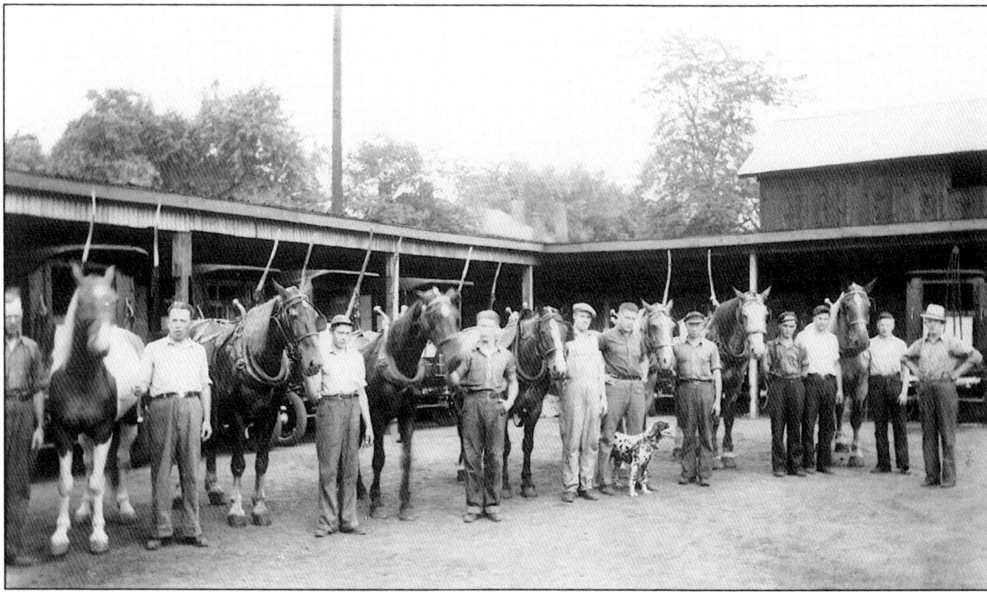

Employees of Les Cobb's Merchants Delivery with their horses at the stables on Sugartree Alley, behind the old town hall. During the early decades of this century, Les Cobb's Merchants Delivery picked up groceries and products from Salem businesses and delivered them to homes throughout the community. One resident recalls two kittens in a box being delivered to her home by this service. Three horses perished in a fire there in 1926.

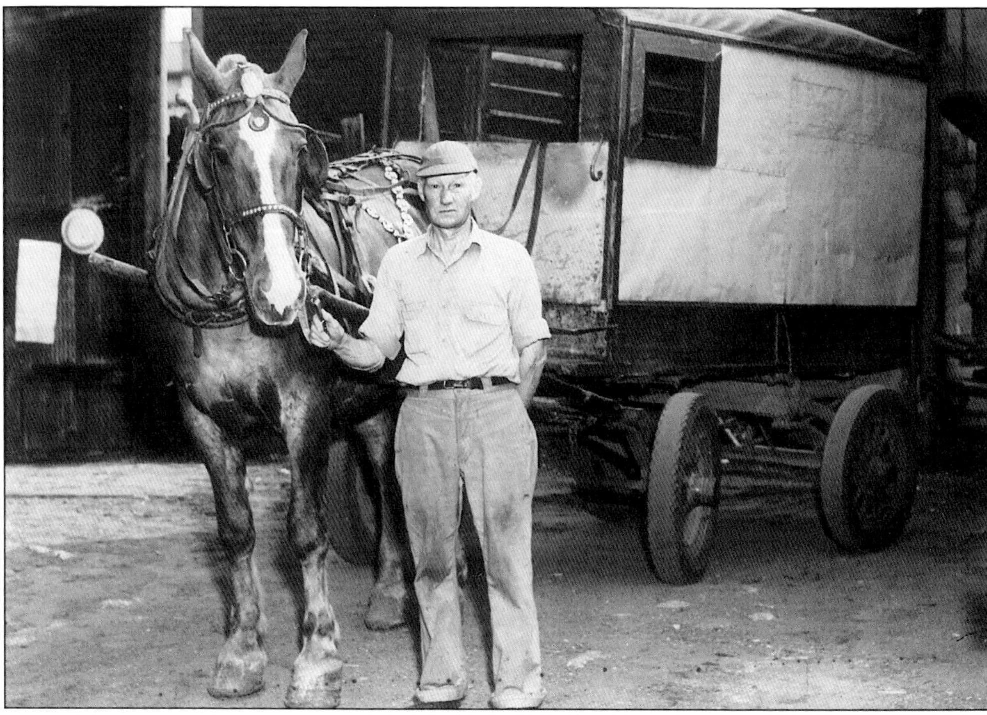

Merle "Red" White beside his Merchants Delivery wagon in 1951. These horse-drawn wagons were in use until the early 1950s. The horses were gentle, and children enjoyed petting them and feeding them apples.

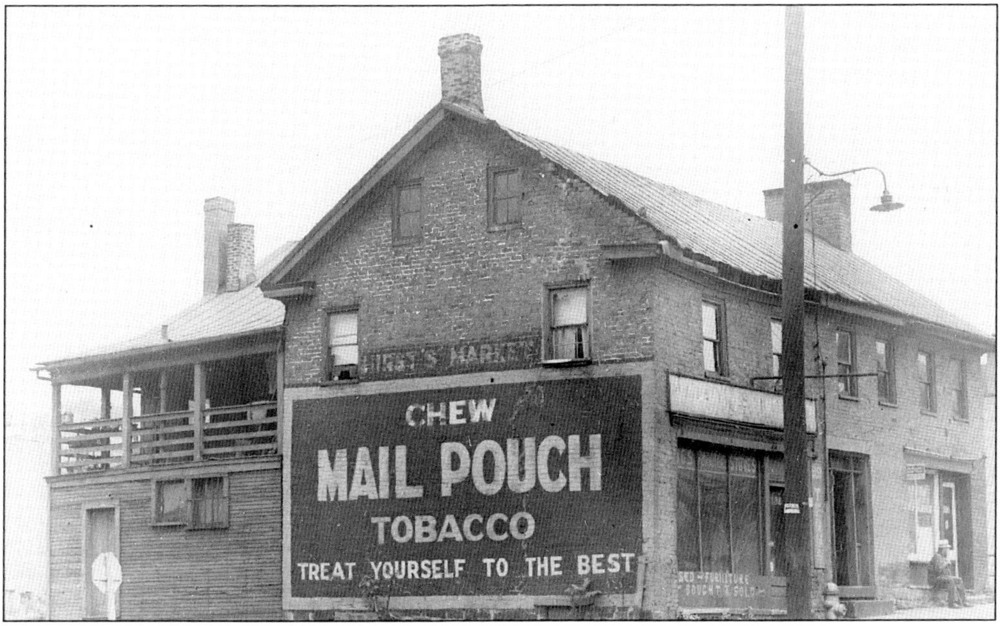

John Webb's Tavern, Salem's first brick hotel/tavern. Built in 1814, it was located on the northeast corner of West State Street and Howard Avenue. Later, the property was used by Simeon Jennings, Salem's first banker. This corner site was part of "Original Salem," and a very busy intersection in the early days. Catercornered from this site was William Heacock's log cabin tavern/hotel, built in 1809.

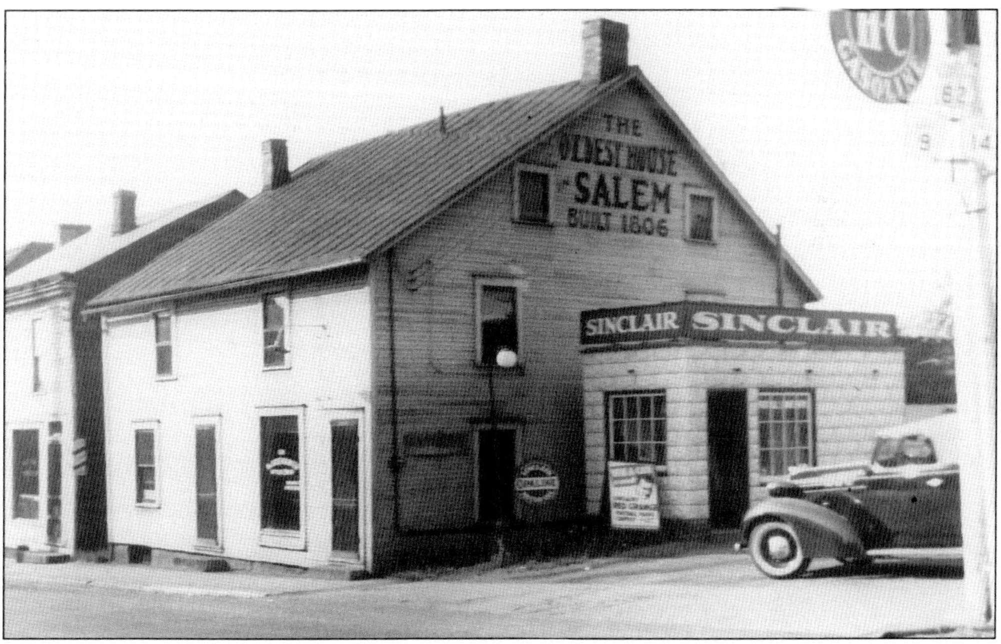

The structure on West State Street that housed the Morning Star Bottling Works in the 1930s. When it was razed in 1937, workers found the original 1806 two-story log house of Zadok Street Sr., co-founder of Salem. Efforts to preserve it failed, but some of the wood from its logs was saved and used to make a replica of the log house for the Salem Historical Museum.

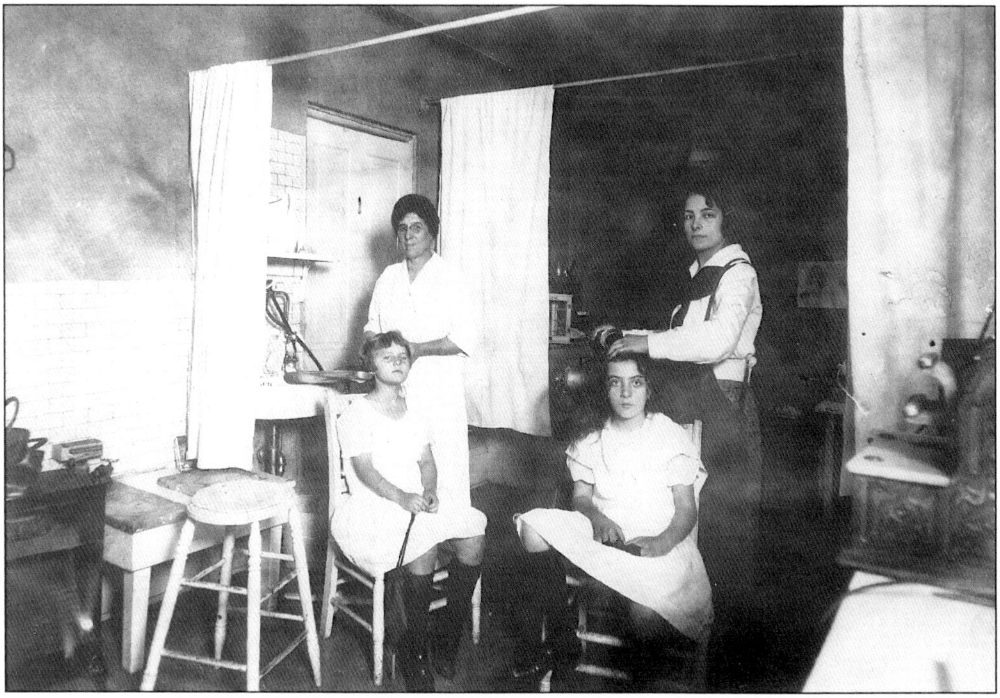

Clara Finney and Edith Ward working on the hair of Kathryn Litty and Margie Stewart. Clara Finney established Salem's first beauty shop in 1917. For years, on a part-time basis, she had gone to the homes of customers to give scalp treatments and use her electric curler. This was before permanents. In 1956 Miss Finney was 90 years old and still operating her beauty shop.

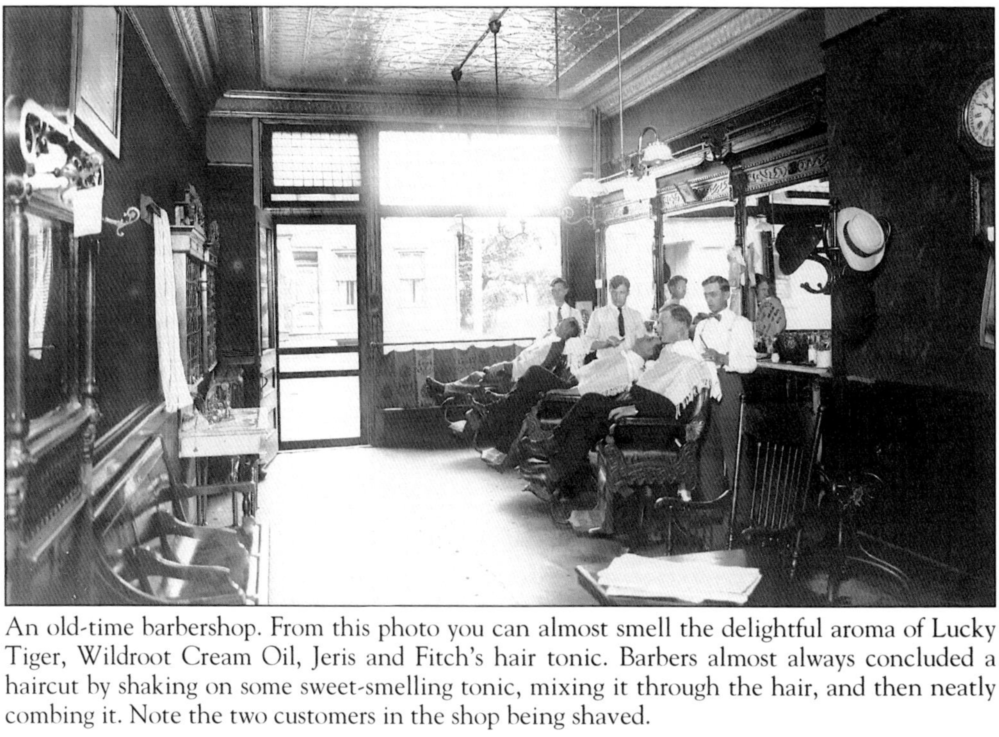

An old-time barbershop. From this photo you can almost smell the delightful aroma of Lucky Tiger, Wildroot Cream Oil, Jeris and Fitch's hair tonic. Barbers almost always concluded a haircut by shaking on some sweet-smelling tonic, mixing it through the hair, and then neatly combing it. Note the two customers in the shop being shaved.

Three

Special Buildings

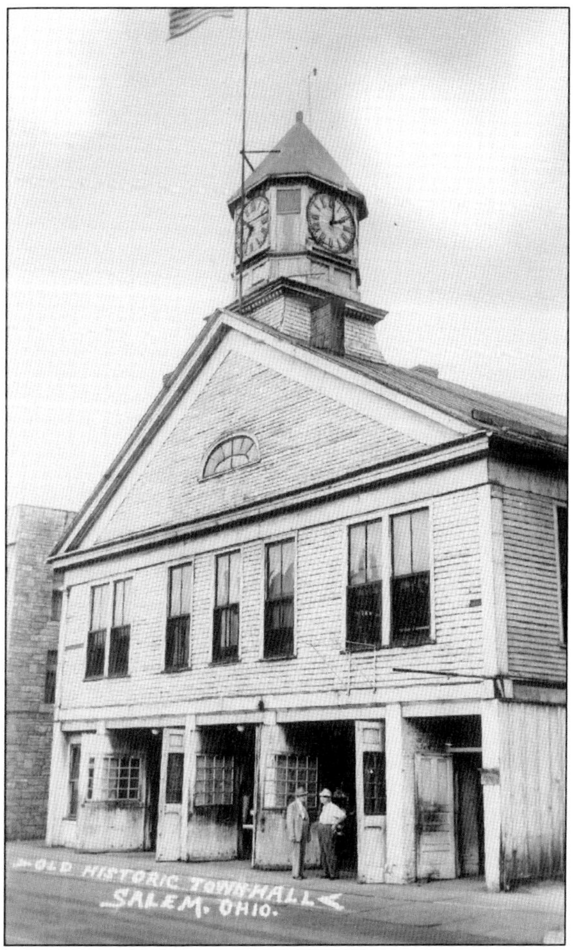

Salem's old town hall (1847–1952), once located on East State Street. This building is remembered historically for the spirited debates and reform speeches by famous 19th-century orators that took place here. It was referred to as the "Faneuil Hall of the West." Remodeling was done around 1910 to utilize the second floor for municipal offices and a dormitory for firemen. The stairs were originally in the center.

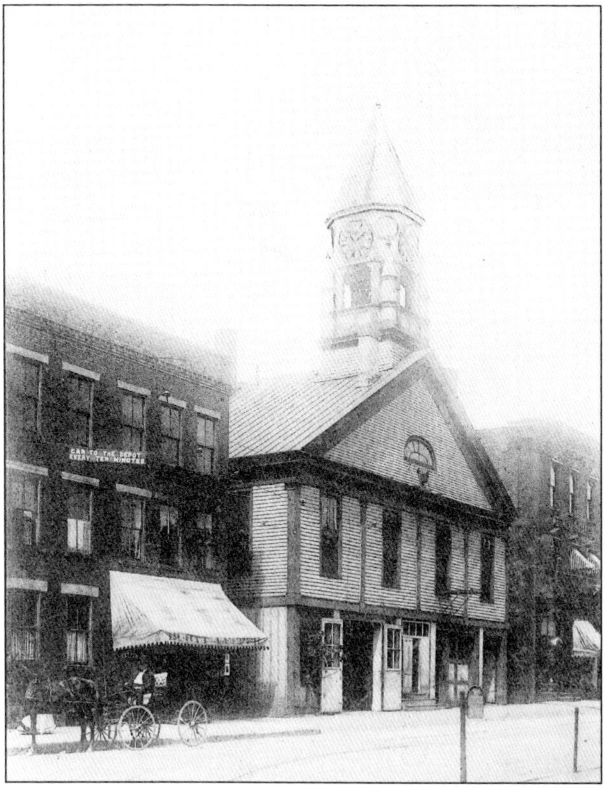

A turn-of-the-century photo of the town hall with a bell and clock in its tower. At left is the old American House building with a sign reading: "Car to the Depot Every Ten Minutes" (referring to the electric trolley). The bell was removed from the tower in 1933, and is now preserved at the entrance to Centennial Park.

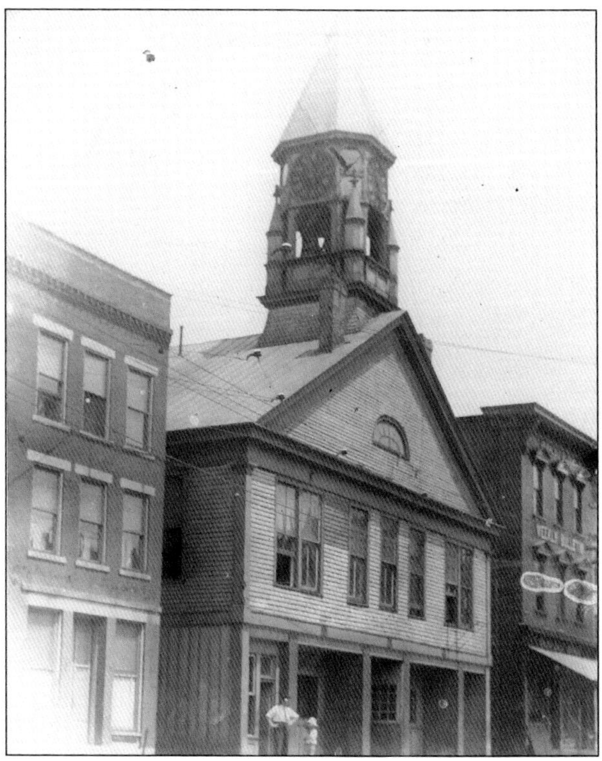

The town hall, originally called the Market House because a section of the ground floor was used for a market. A small room in one corner housed a little grocery store operated by Henry Davis. He also served as janitor, and rang the bell at 7 a.m., noon, and at 6 p.m., as well as when an old pioneer passed away, or a great calamity occurred.

Another view of the town hall. The site of the town hall was provided by the Salem Monthly Meeting of the Hicksite Friends. They deeded it to the city in 1844. Originally, the second floor was one big meeting room where speeches and discussions took place on major issues of the time. Bikers used the space to ride their high-wheelers, and audiences watched plays like *Uncle Tom's Cabin*.

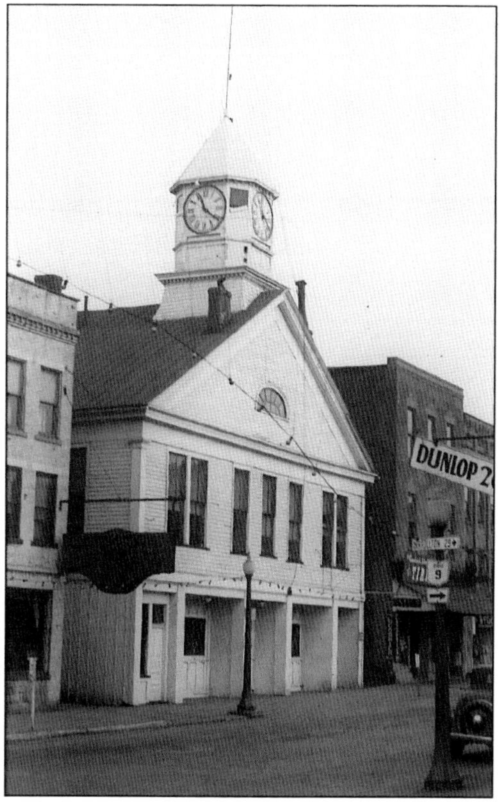

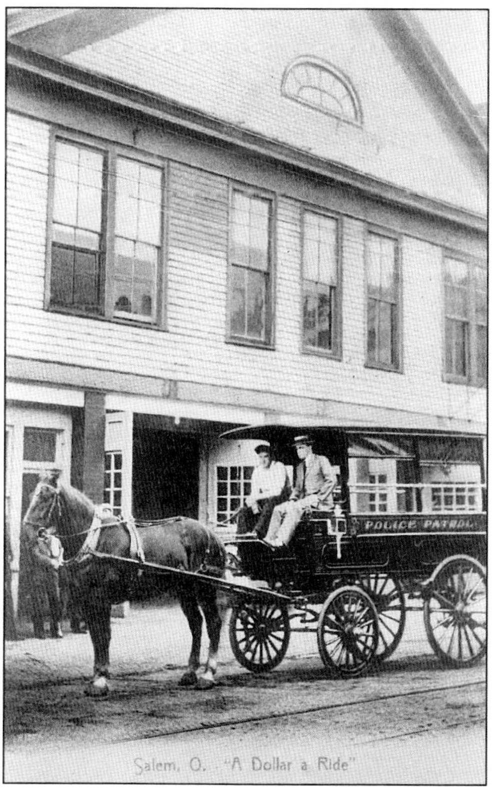

Salem's new police patrol wagon. On August 29, 1892, Salem's new police patrol wagon was delivered to city hall from Teegarden's carriage factory on Penn Avenue. The wagon was of regulation patrol style, with its body painted a deep blue trimmed in ebony. The words "Police Patrol" were lettered on each side of the wagon bed. Its wheels were decorated in red, with green and yellow trimmings.

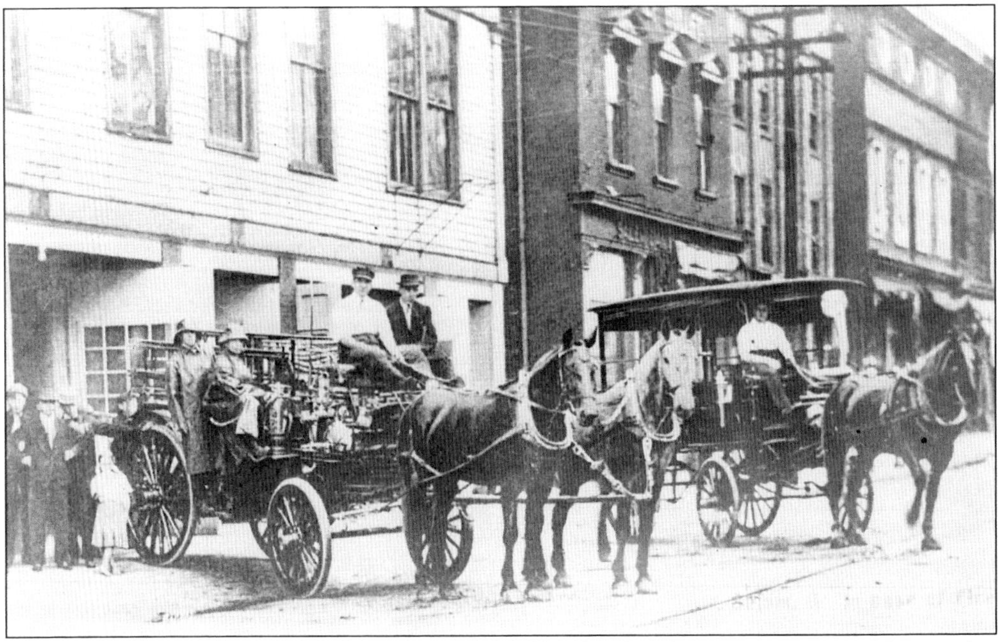

Salem's new hose and chemical wagon, purchased by the fire department in 1908. Its weight, with apparatus, was about 5,500 pounds. The wagon was an easy-running one that the team of horses had no trouble pulling. These horses were very spirited and were exercised every morning by the firemen. They were kept in stalls that opened immediately into the room where the fire apparatus was housed.

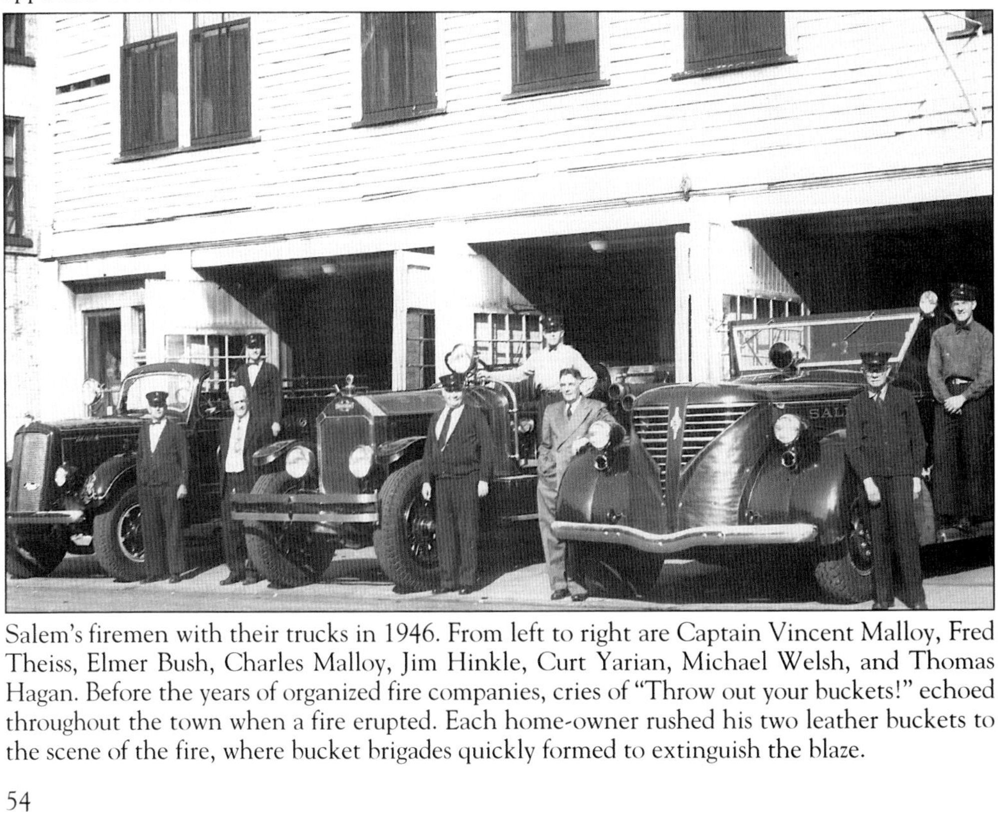

Salem's firemen with their trucks in 1946. From left to right are Captain Vincent Malloy, Fred Theiss, Elmer Bush, Charles Malloy, Jim Hinkle, Curt Yarian, Michael Welsh, and Thomas Hagan. Before the years of organized fire companies, cries of "Throw out your buckets!" echoed throughout the town when a fire erupted. Each home-owner rushed his two leather buckets to the scene of the fire, where bucket brigades quickly formed to extinguish the blaze.

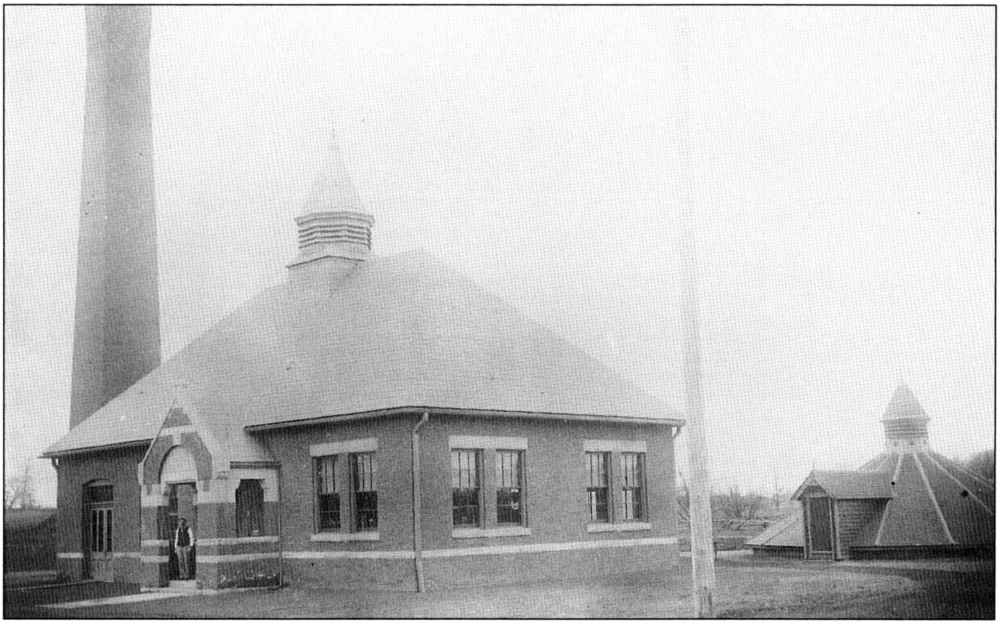

Salem's Water Works Pumping Station, still new when this photo was taken in 1887. Buckeye engines were originally used to pump water throughout the city. These were later replaced with electric pumps. A fire siren sat atop the roof, and a United States Geologic Survey benchmark was embedded in the south wall. The building was torn down in 1982. On the right is an underground water storage tank that served as a reservoir.

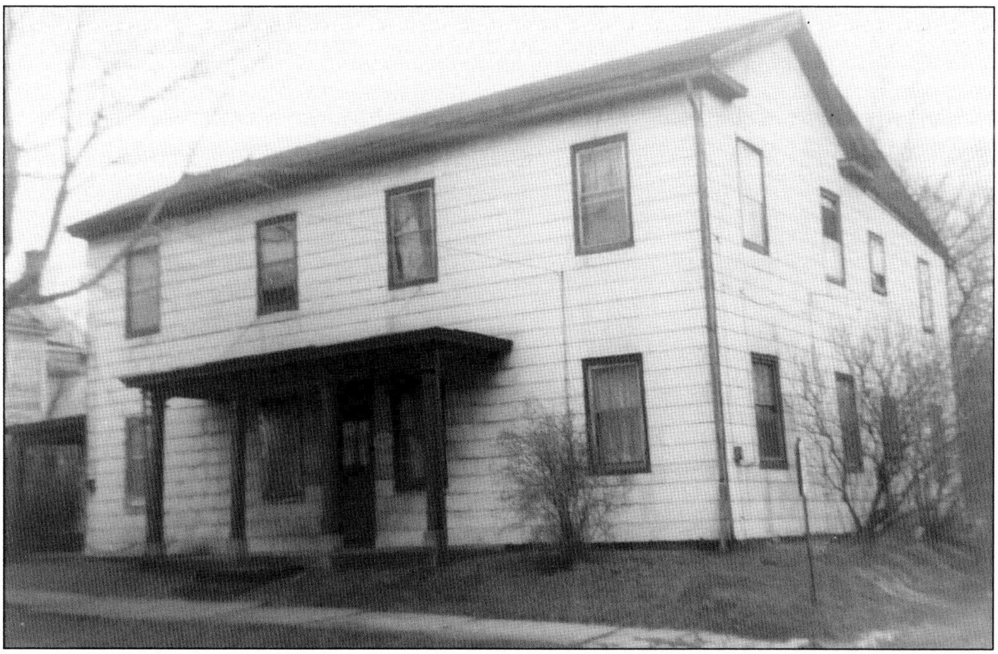

Liberty Hall, built in 1840, located at 264 North Ellsworth Avenue. Originally it was Samuel Reynolds's carpenter shop, but its upstairs was also used as a meeting place for local abolitionists. The structure is constructed by notch-and-pin, with the beams cut by "up-and-down" saws powered by water.

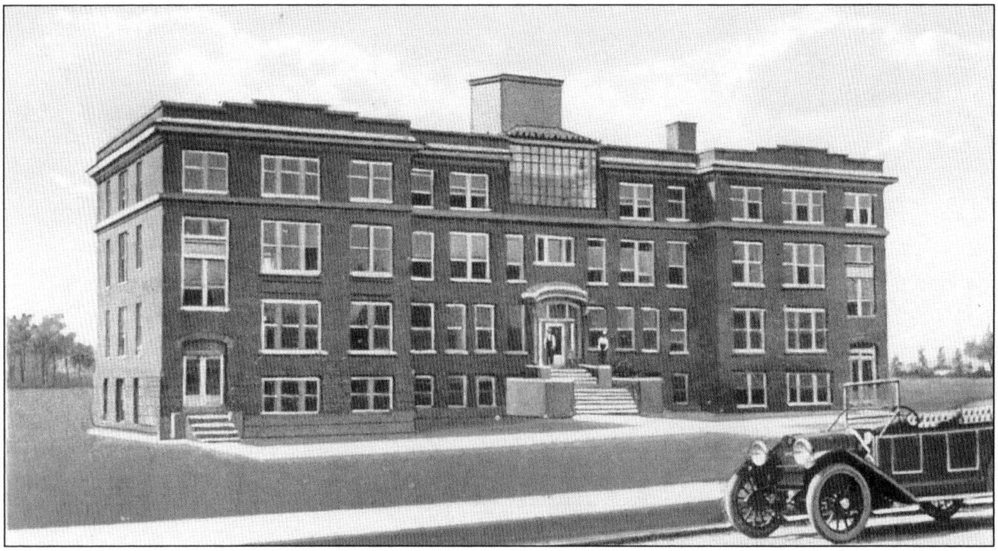

The Salem City Hospital as it looked when it was new in 1913. The building could accommodate 70 patients. In 1912 Salem residents were "crying out" in need of a hospital. Recognizing this need, W.H. Mullins, a prominent businessman, donated more than half the money needed to build the facility. Then, after it had been built, he equipped the operating room with the most costly instruments available.

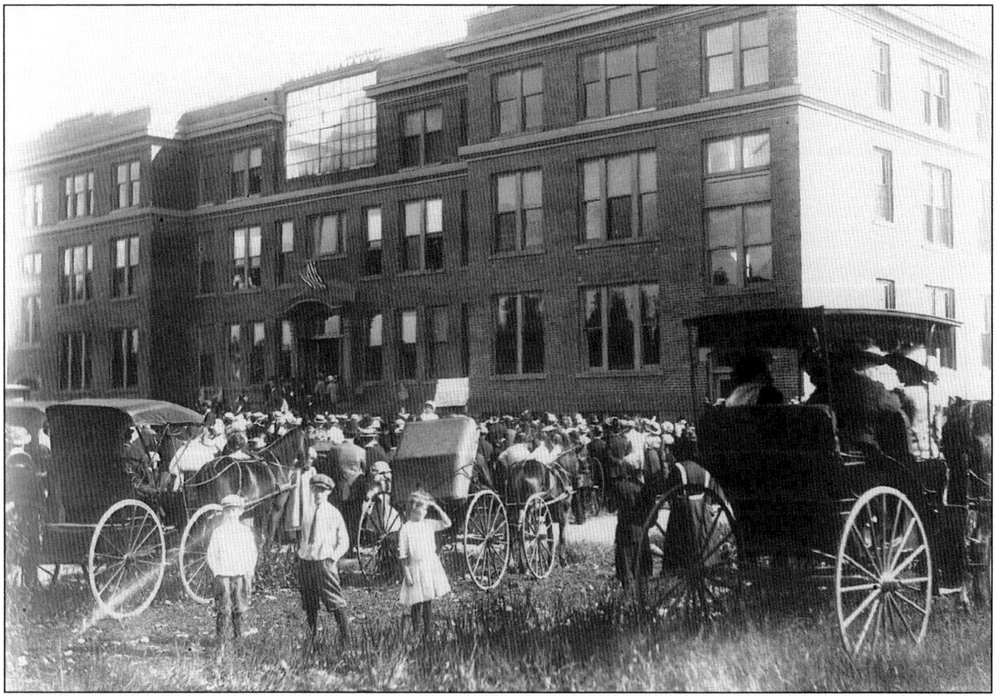

The dedication ceremonies for the Salem City Hospital, September 13, 1913. The driveway was filled with horse-drawn carriages. A horseshoe was buried directly under the front entrance to bring good luck to all the invalids. Within 24 hours after the dedication, two operations were scheduled and 13 patients admitted. A school of nursing was immediately established at the hospital.

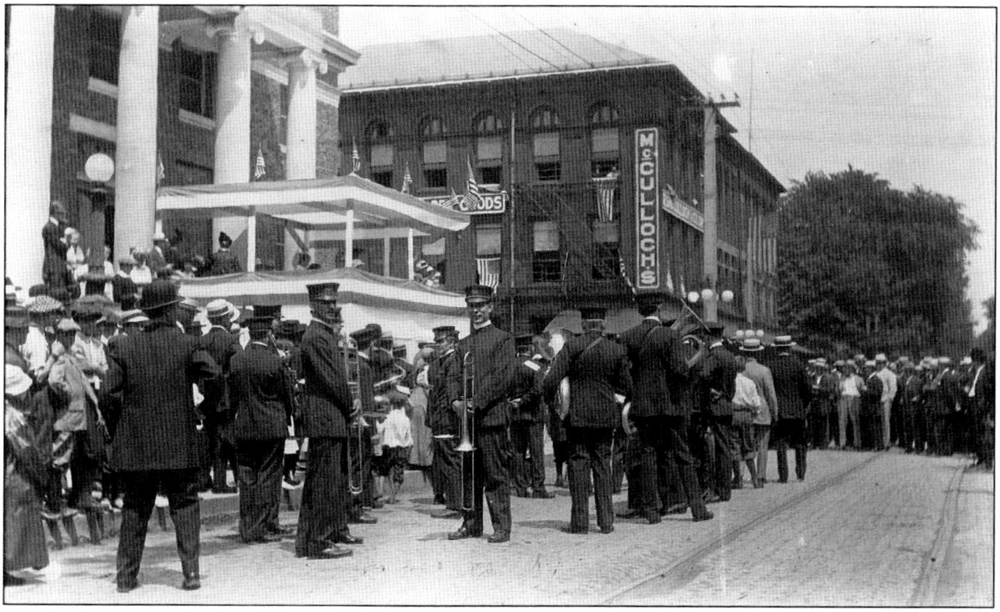

July 22, 1915, the date the post office (at left) was dedicated. Musicians in front are members of the Quaker City Band. The dedication ceremonies were recorded on motion picture film by Dr. H.W. Thompson. On this special day, the downtown was decked out in a bright array of flags, bunting, and other adornment. Merchants decorated their windows and store fronts.

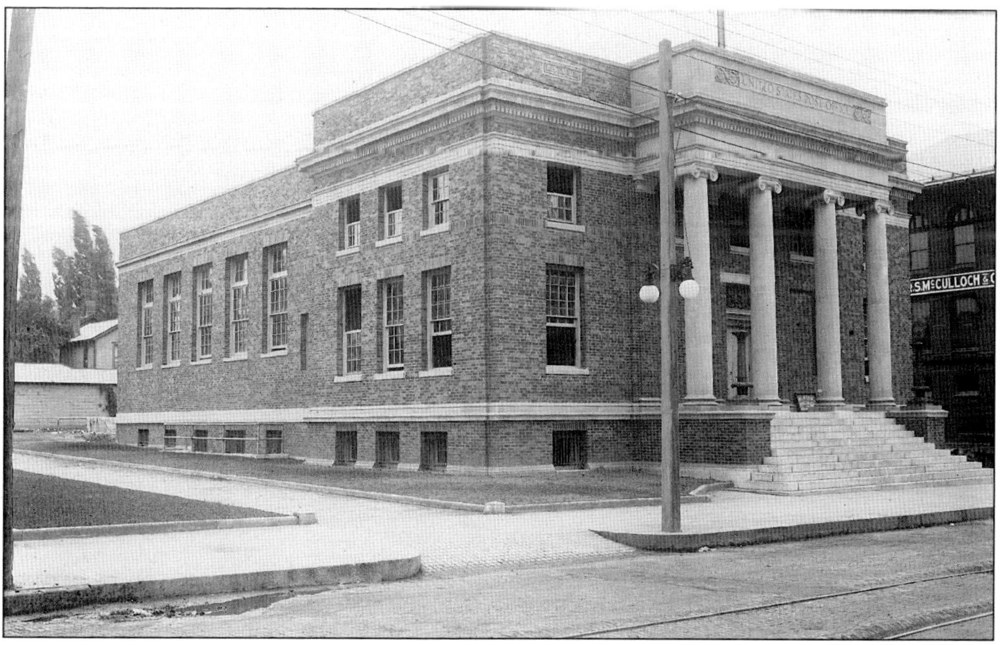

Salem's old post office in 1915, recently completed and ready for occupancy. It stood on the northwest corner of East State Street and North Lincoln Avenue, and was a grand-looking building of which Salem residents could be proud. Its colonial pillars and wide granite steps provided a feeling of grandeur for all who entered the front doors.

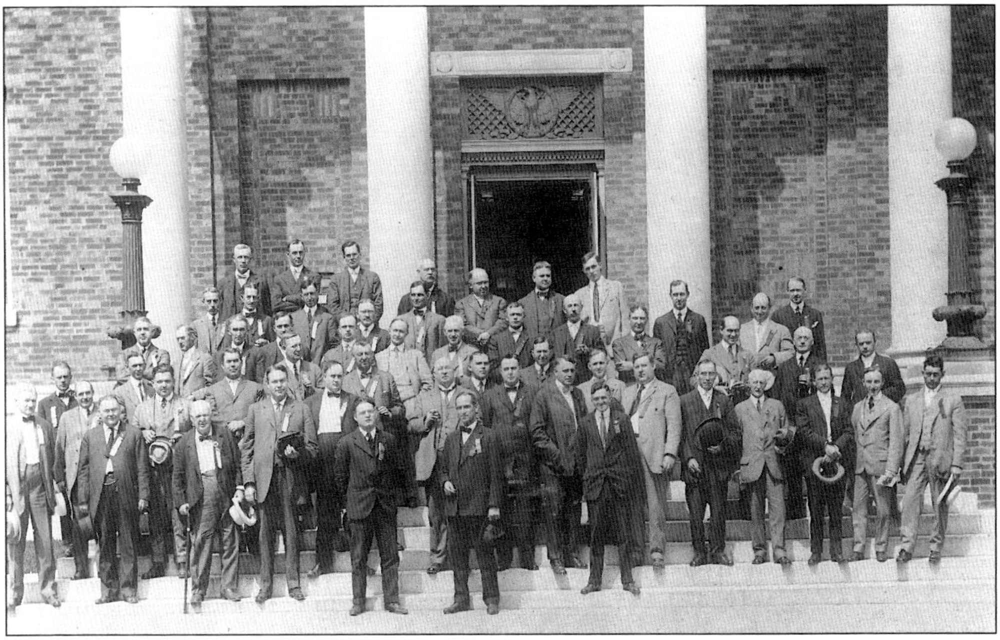

City officials in front of the new post office in 1915. The concrete eagle emblem above the doorway is now preserved in the south wall of the Salem Historical Museum. In 1962, when the building was razed, the granite steps were moved to the front of the Salem Public Library.

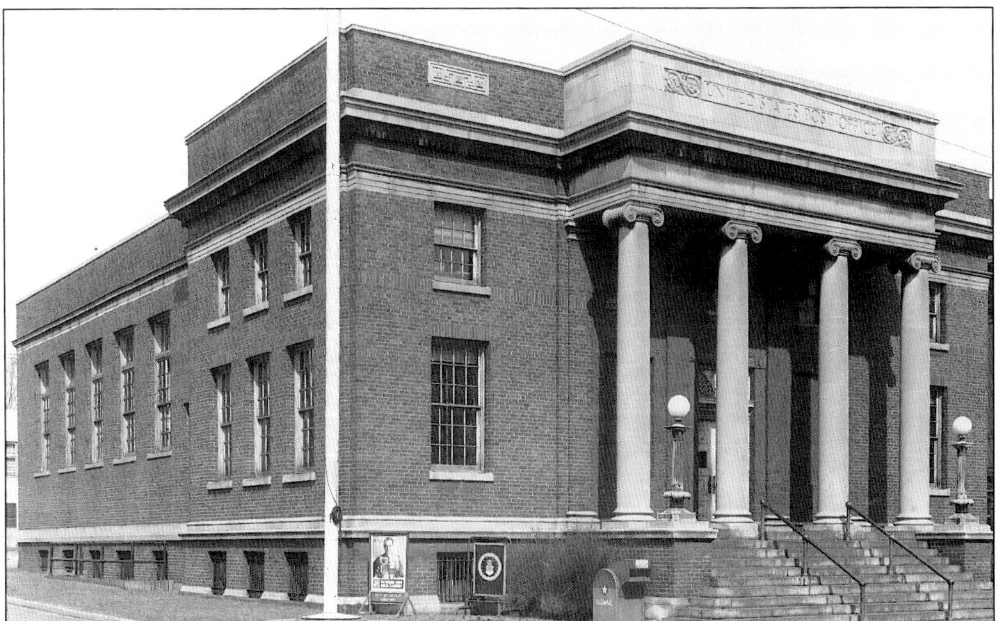

Another view of the post office, which stood for only 47 years, from 1915 to 1962. Young ladies being initiated into the Maids High School Club in the 1940s were required to scrub the steps with a toothbrush. Many Salem boys were recruited into military service on the second floor.

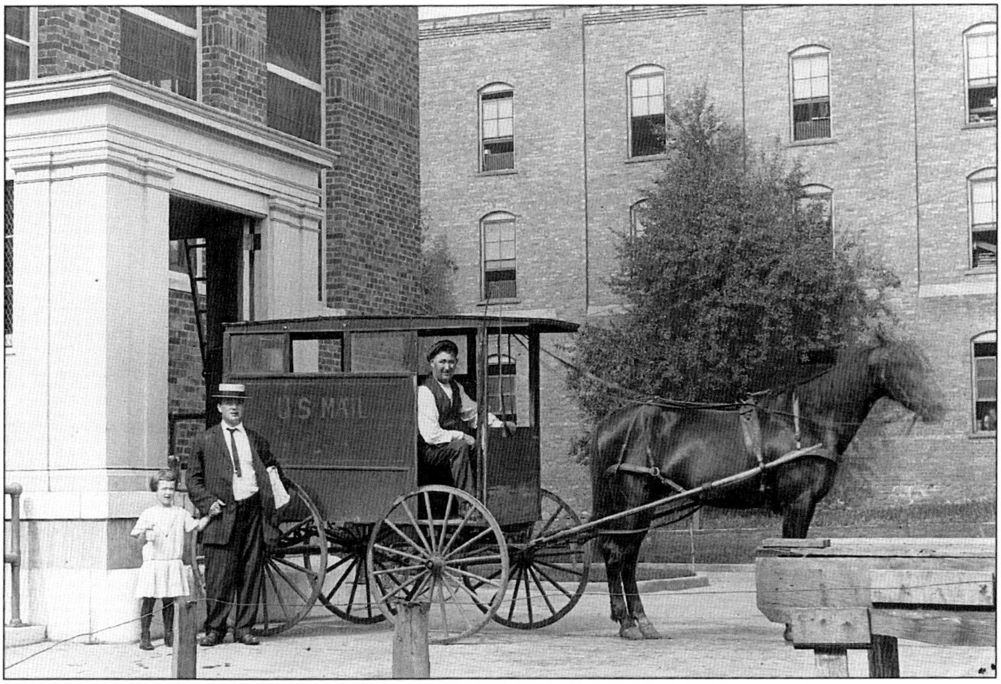

Jens Peter Jensen (the mail carrier in the wagon) and friends. When Salem's post office was built in 1915, rural mail was still being delivered by horse and wagon.

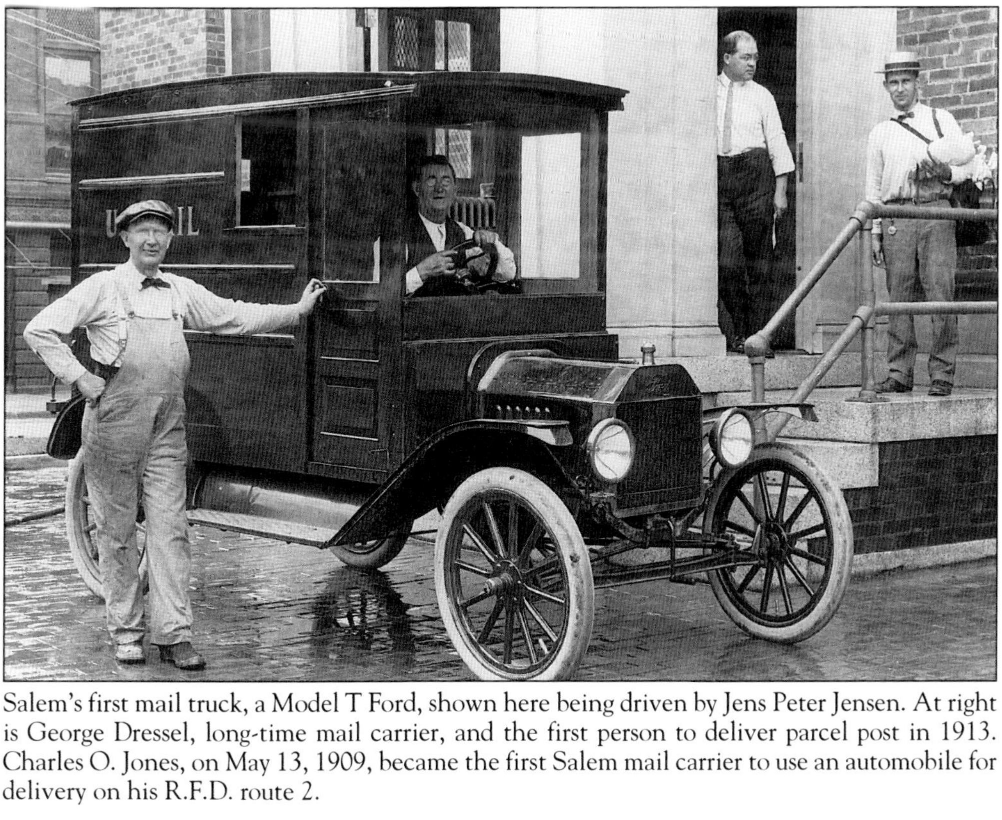

Salem's first mail truck, a Model T Ford, shown here being driven by Jens Peter Jensen. At right is George Dressel, long-time mail carrier, and the first person to deliver parcel post in 1913. Charles O. Jones, on May 13, 1909, became the first Salem mail carrier to use an automobile for delivery on his R.F.D. route 2.

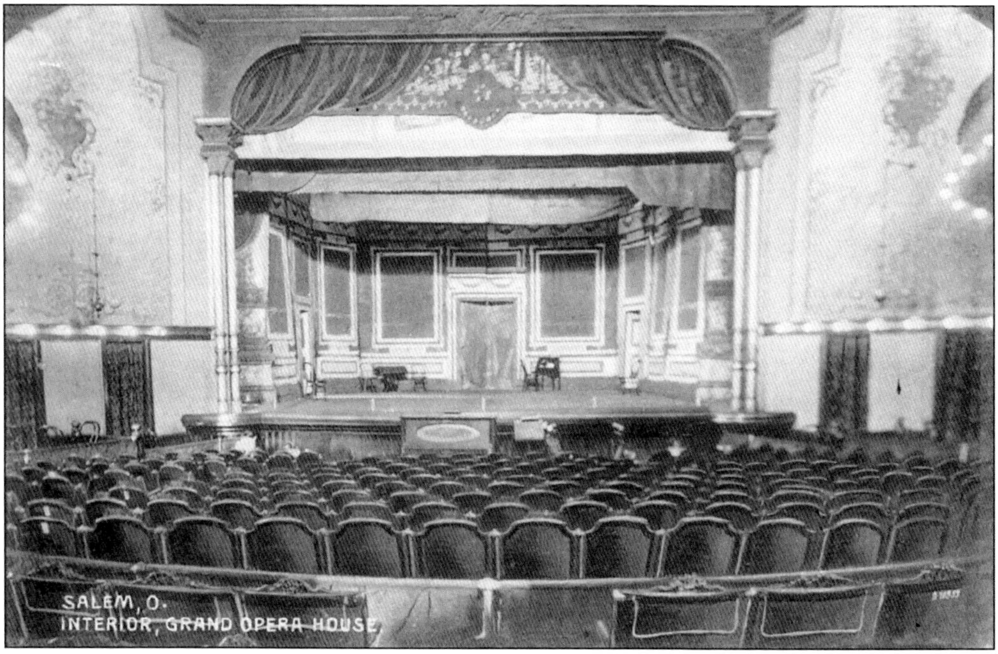

The interior of the old Grand Opera House, which opened October 10, 1890, with the production of Johann Strauss Jr.'s masterpiece, *The Gypsy Baron*. An original program from that performance is preserved at the Salem Historical Museum. The theater was designed for live stage plays and musicals. It was demolished in 1969.

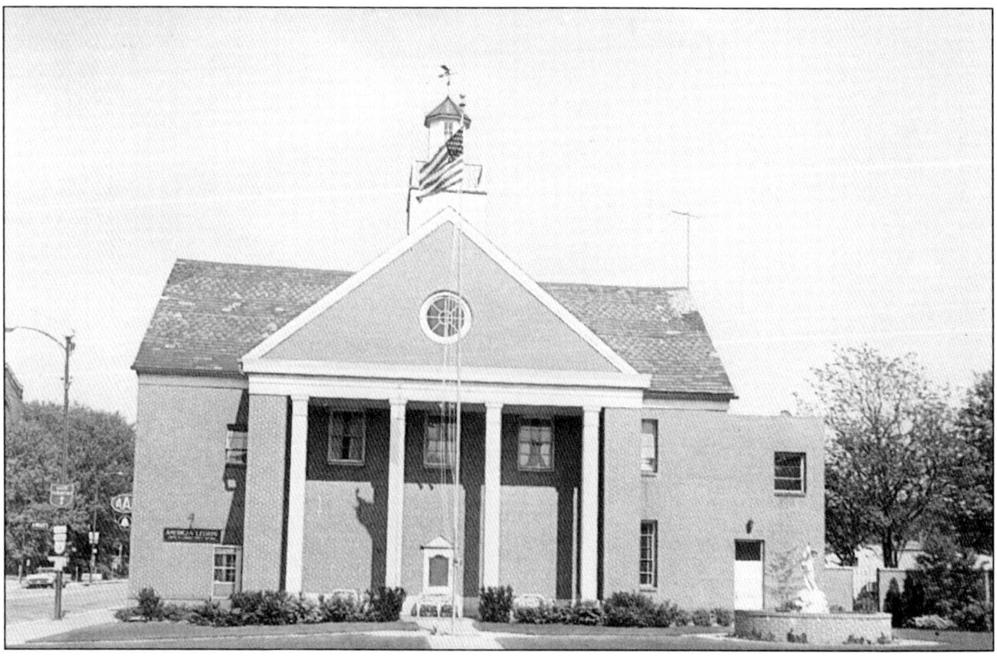

The Village Green, located on the southeast corner of East State Street and South Lincoln Avenue. It was dedicated in 1956 during Salem's Sesquicentennial in honor of local war veterans. Part of the building was renovated from what remained of the old First Baptist Church after the 1947 fire.

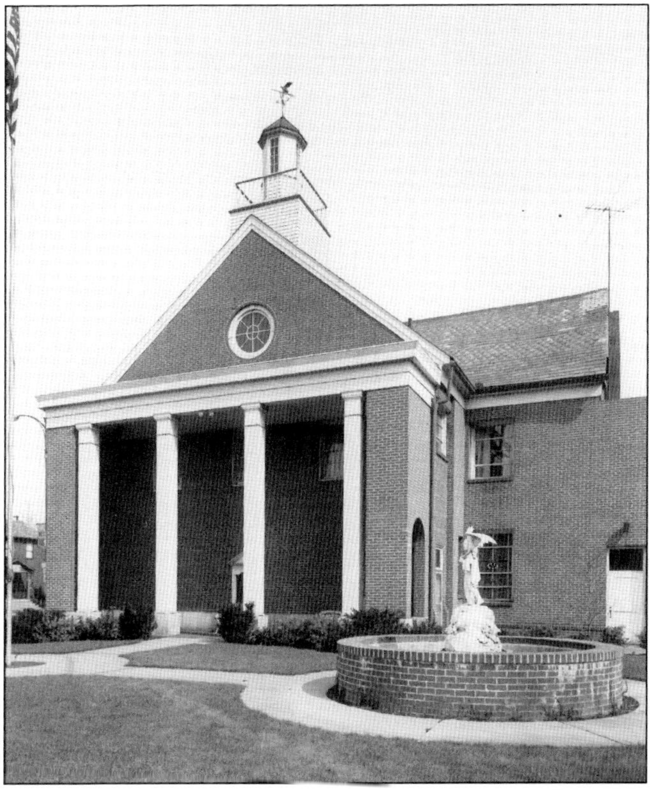

Salem's Village Green. The area includes the Chamber of Commerce Building, a historic fountain, and a war memorial that honors all veterans, living and deceased, of World War II and the Korean and Vietnam conflicts. The chamber of commerce fosters and promotes the advancement of the commercial, financial, industrial, and civic interests of the Salem area.

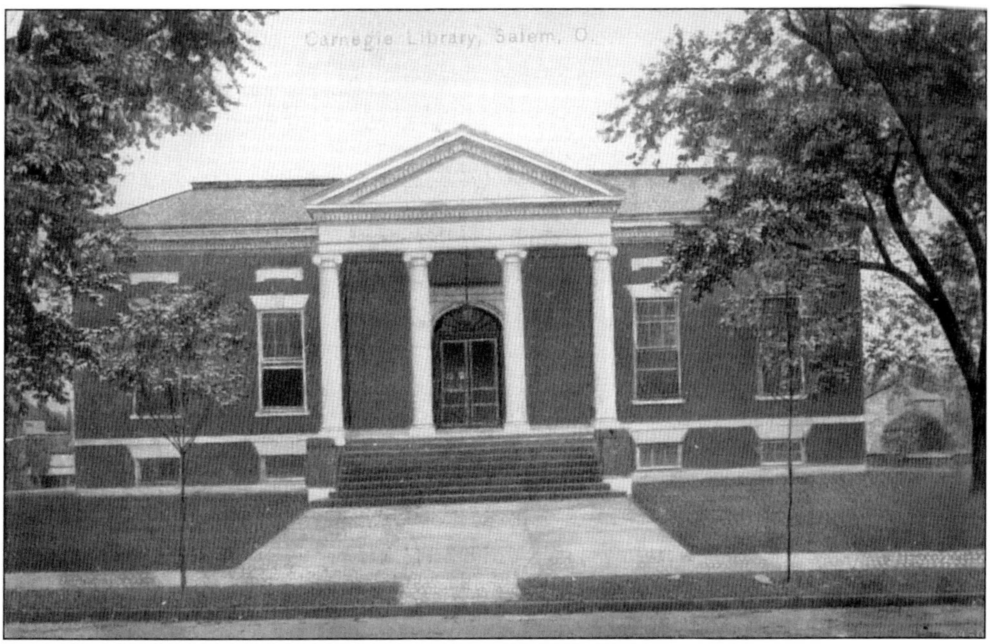

The Salem Public Library, dedicated August 31, 1905. Colonial in design, the structure cost $20,000, which was donated by Andrew Carnegie. His name appears in front. Mrs. Ashbel Carey (Helen Smith) had a lot to do with establishing the library. Her efforts began in 1895. She was also the first librarian of this new facility, serving from 1905 to 1920.

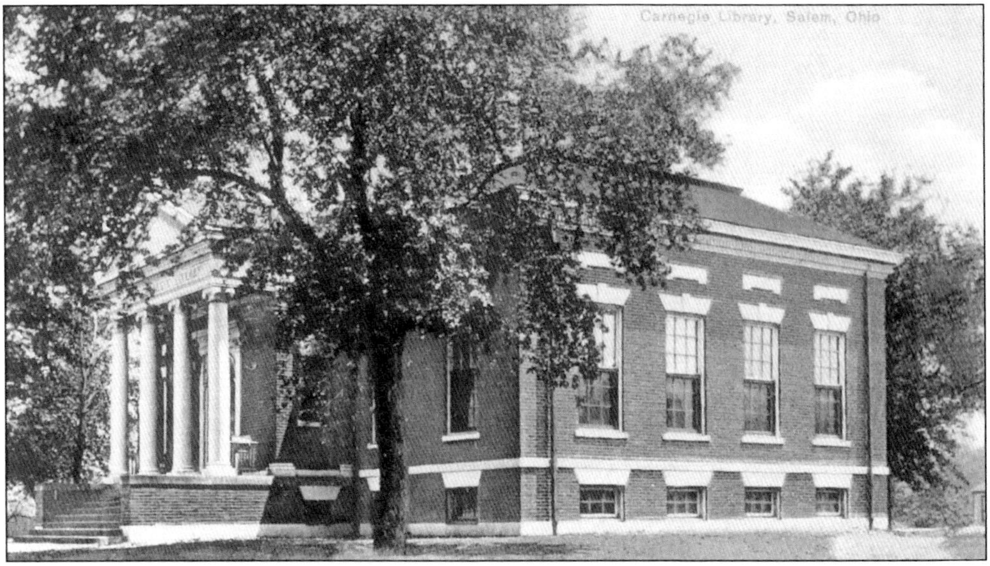

Another view of the Salem Public Library. The first library in Salem was in existence as early as 1814. It was called the Salem Library Company and had 50 stockholders, most of them Quakers. They each paid $3 per share in three installments of $1 each. Fifty cents was charged for each additional year of use. Dr. Benjamin Stanton (Salem's first physician) was the first appointed librarian on September 13, 1823.

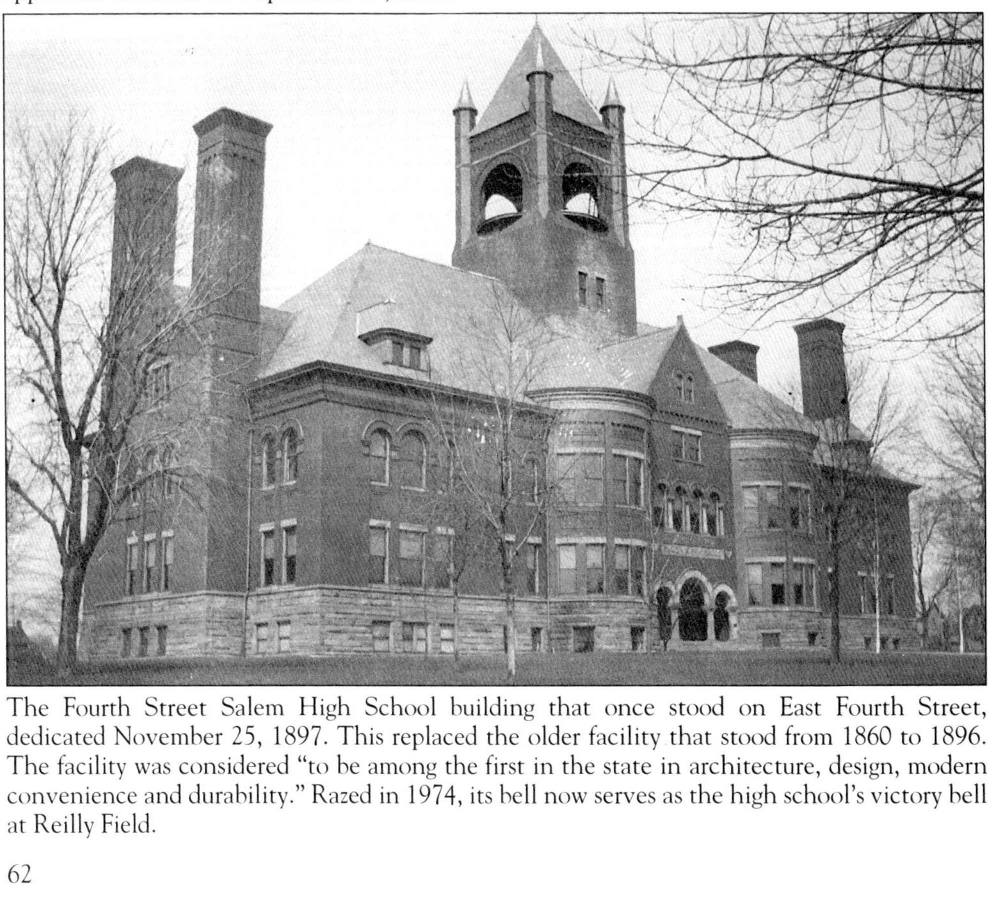

The Fourth Street Salem High School building that once stood on East Fourth Street, dedicated November 25, 1897. This replaced the older facility that stood from 1860 to 1896. The facility was considered "to be among the first in the state in architecture, design, modern convenience and durability." Razed in 1974, its bell now serves as the high school's victory bell at Reilly Field.

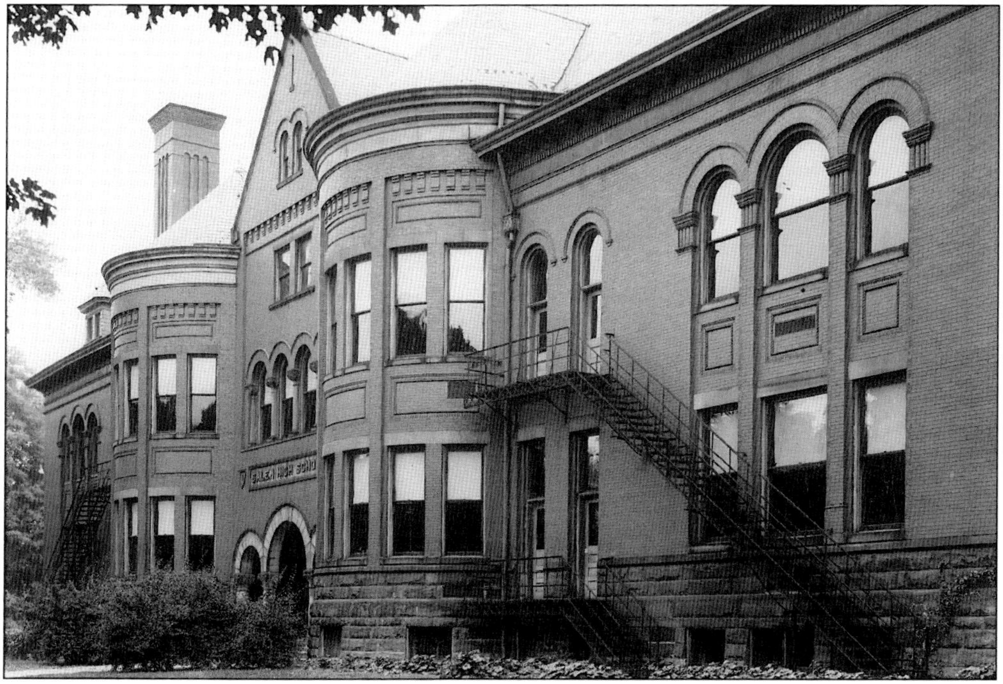

The Fourth Street School in 1940, serving as a facility for grades one through eight. A separate high school had been built in 1917. The Fourth Street School was one of Salem's most memorable structures—perhaps the grandest and most impressive building ever erected. Memories relate to the grandiose staircase, windowed rotunda, fire drills, orchestra, pole swings, recess bell, marble tournaments, and glass ink wells.

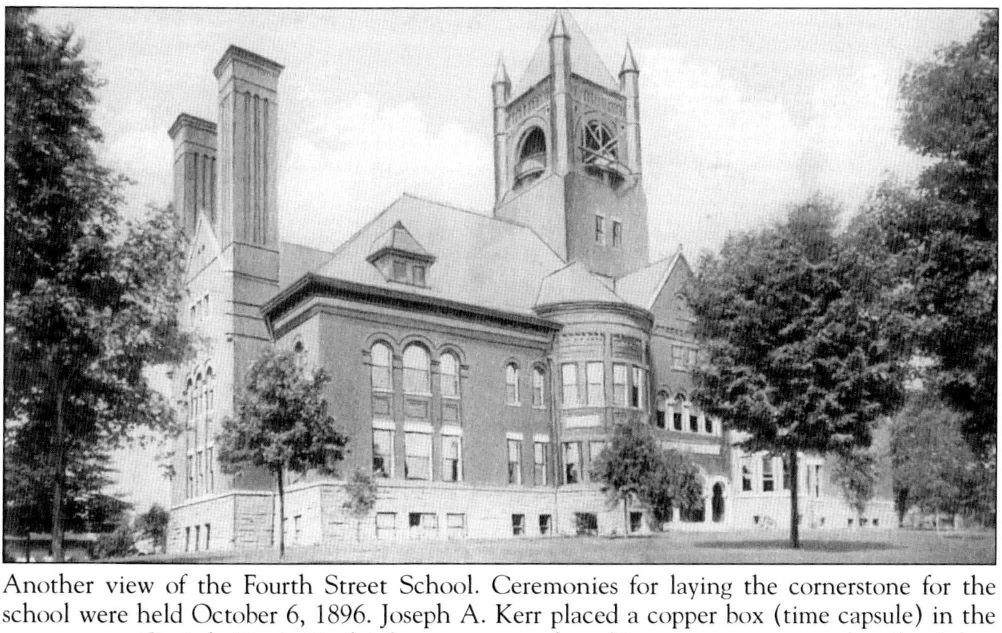

Another view of the Fourth Street School. Ceremonies for laying the cornerstone for the school were held October 6, 1896. Joseph A. Kerr placed a copper box (time capsule) in the cornerstone. On July 22, 1974, this box was opened, and its contents preserved at the Salem Historical Museum. The huge chimneys at each end of the building were part of the original toilet system. Air currents through them helped to carry away odors.

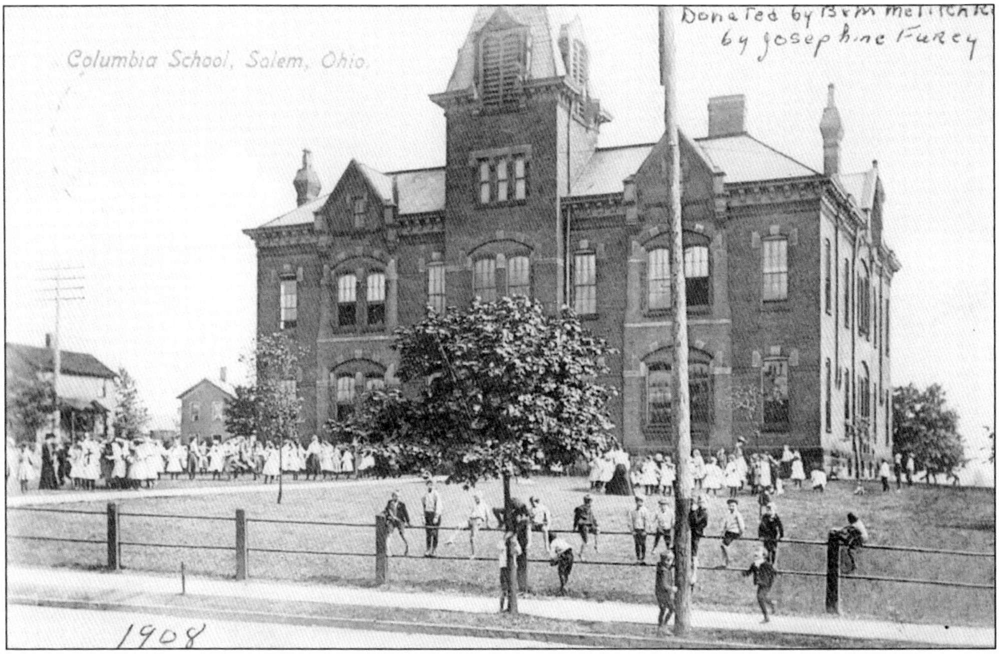

The Columbia Street School, once located on the southwest corner of Columbia Street and South Lundy Avenue, built in 1881 and razed in 1953. The bell from its tower is preserved at the Salem Historical Museum. Booker T. Washington spoke on the front lawn June 22, 1906. Chautauquas were held on the playground in the 1920s.

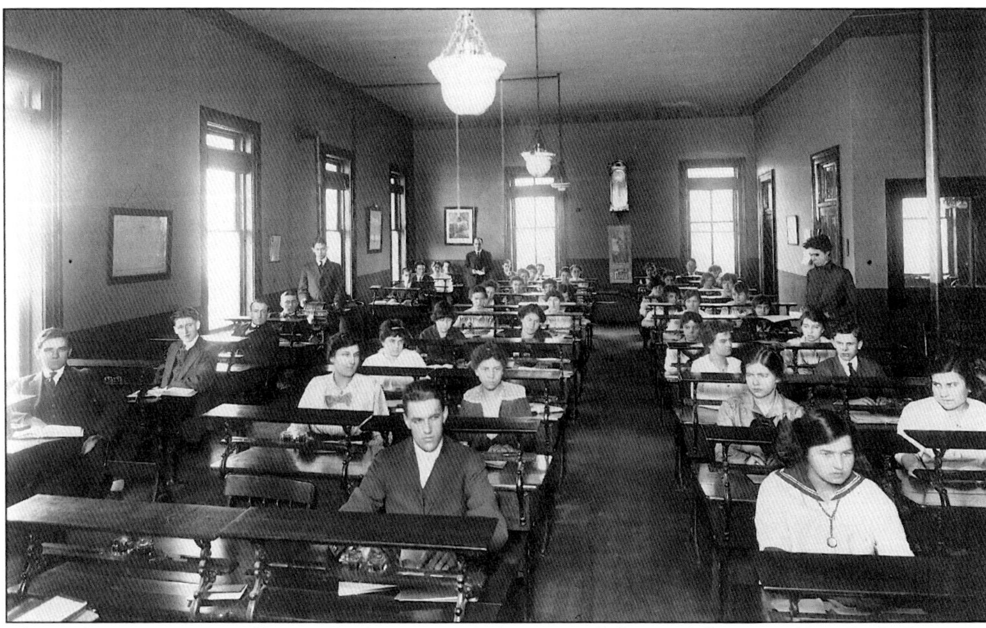

The Salem Business College, which occupied the second floor of the Trimble Block for many years. This school was organized in 1894 by J.W. Butcher and H.T. Edmeston of Cleveland. It was sold to W.H. Matthews in 1896. Students were taught typing, shorthand, and business skills. Teacher Ella Beeson (at right) took over when Mr. Matthews (rear) retired in 1923. Franklin Wells became administrator in 1929.

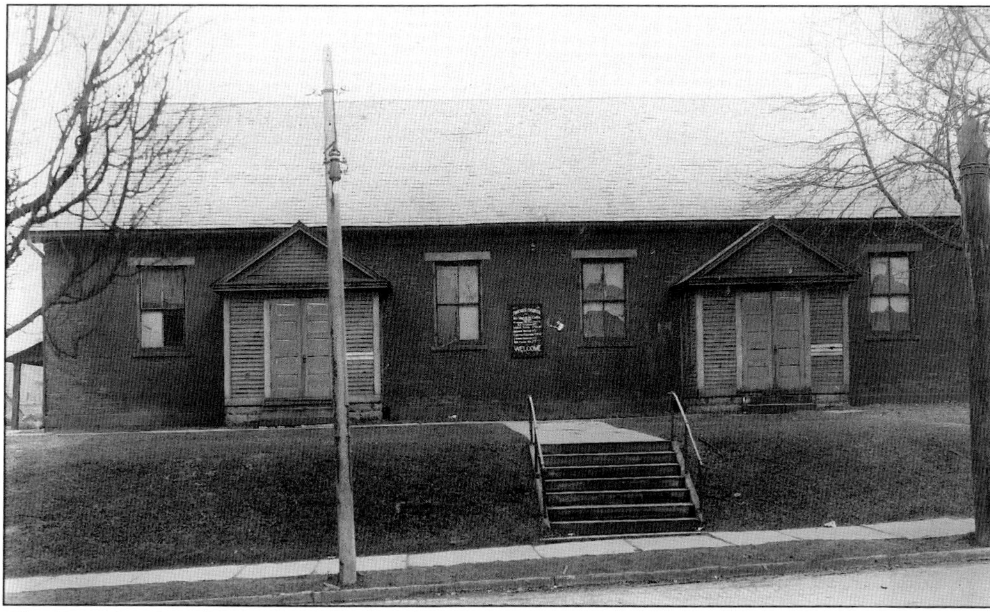

The Friends Church on Dry (East Pershing) Street, first used on July 27, 1845. It was utilized until 1924, when it was remodeled into a $26,000 brick facility. A part of this old building was preserved and used for Sunday school purposes. The new building was dedicated January 5, 1925. It was used until 1963, when a new church building was constructed at 1028 Jennings Avenue.

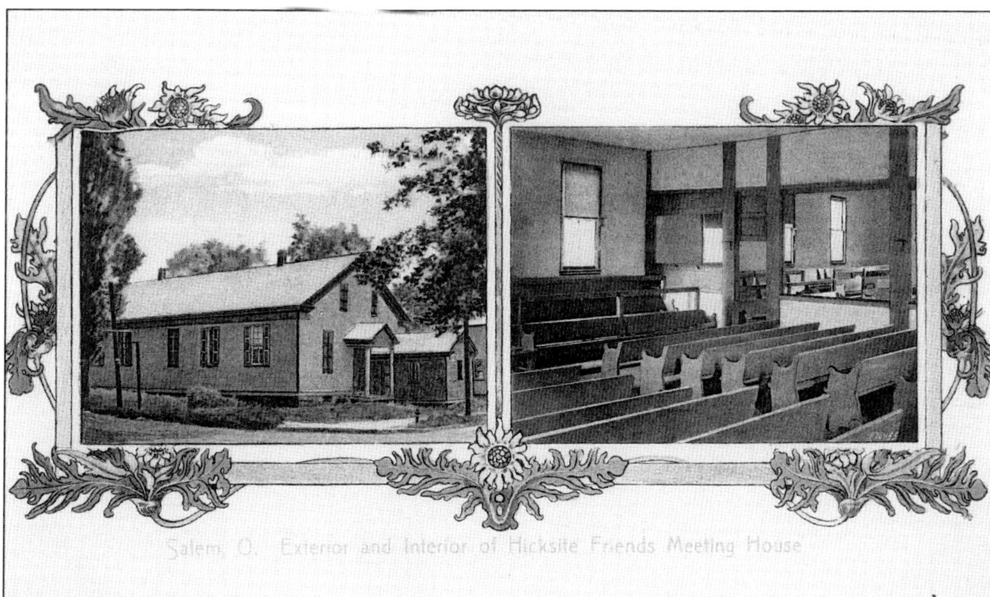

The meeting house that once stood on the southeast corner of Green (Second) Street and North Ellsworth Avenue, built in 1835 by the Hicksite Society of Friends. The Hicksites separated from the Orthodox Society of Friends in 1828 and organized a separate branch, named for Elias Hicks. This building is where the first Women's Suffrage convention in Ohio was held April 19–20, 1850. Abolitionists also met there to vigorously denounce human slavery.

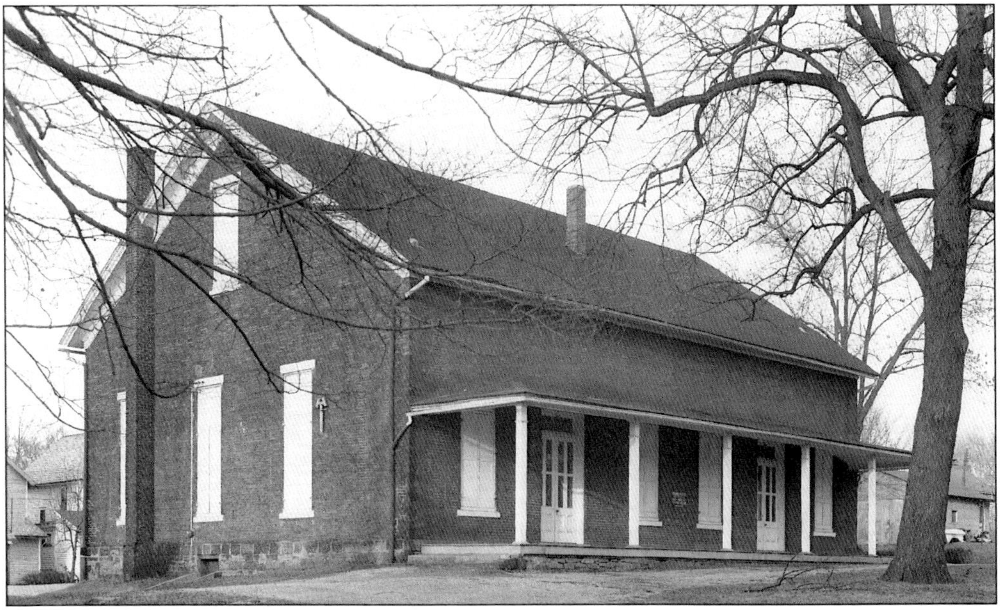

The Wilbur Friends Meeting House, erected in 1871, located at 350 East Sixth Street. The Quakers meet for worship without set form. They avoid liturgies and rites that might interfere with direct guidance of the Holy Spirit (Inner Light). They sit quietly, meditating and waiting for the Spirit of the Lord to move upon someone's heart. The person so moved stands up and speaks.

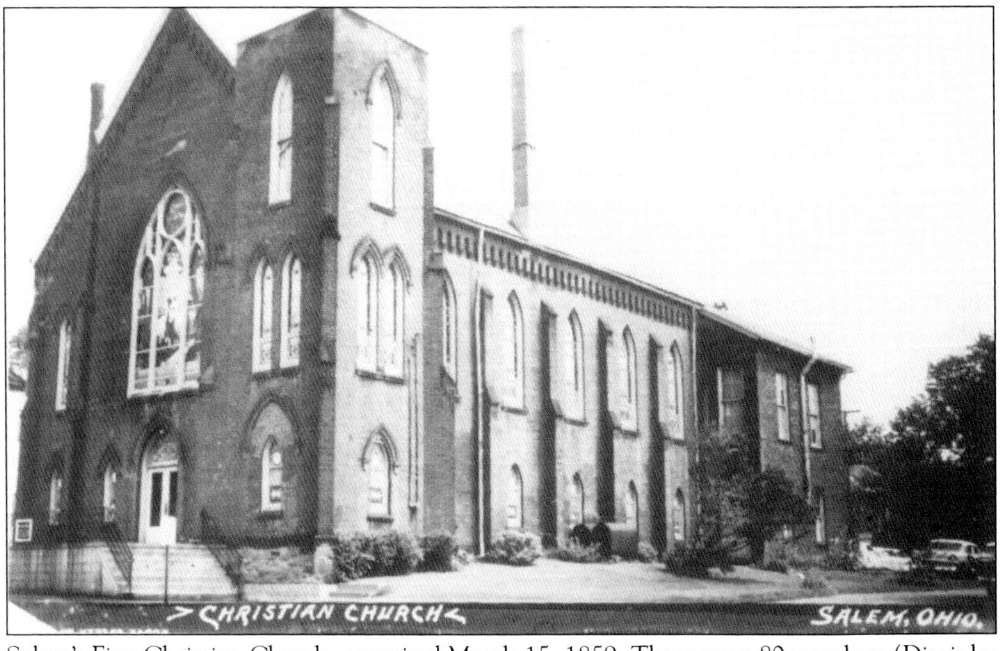

Salem's First Christian Church, organized March 15, 1859. There were 80 members (Disciples of Christ). This brick church, which once stood at 246 North Ellsworth Avenue, was dedicated in 1871. James A. Garfield spoke here in 1873 before he became President of the United States. The building was razed in 1959, and the congregation moved into a new facility at 1151 East Sixth Street.

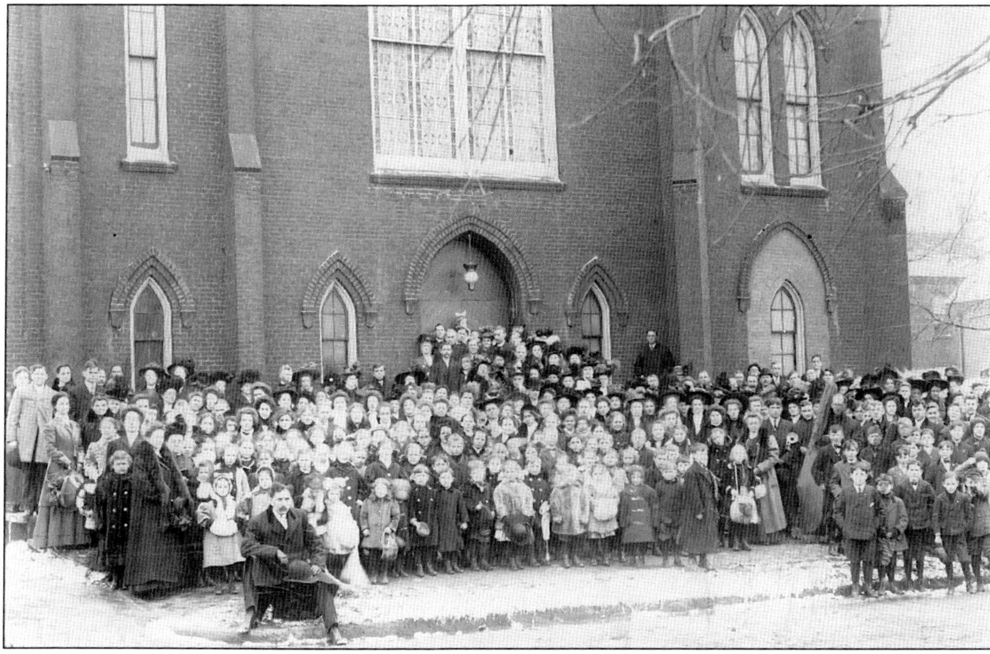

Members of the First Christian Church in front of their house of worship on North Ellsworth Avenue in 1907. Note the long dresses and coats. Two years later, on March 8, 1909, the church celebrated its 50th anniversary. The church had 31 of the most beautiful and memorable windows in town. Each was named for a special member of the congregation.

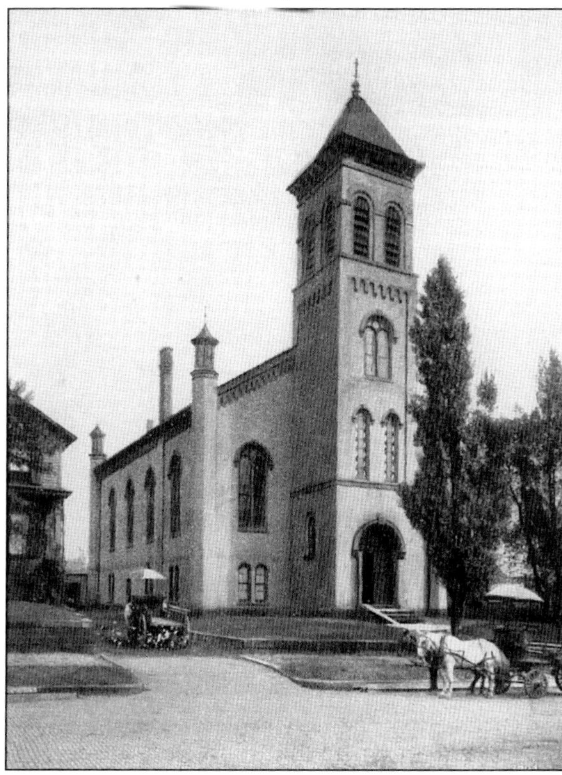

The First United Methodist Church at 244 South Broadway Avenue, built in 1858. In 1902 the spire of this church, 200 feet above ground, was still the highest structure in the city. The ornament surmounting the spire was a wooden affair, of which a ball 2 feet in diameter was the principal part. This ball was made by the Sharp, Davis, and Bonsall Company.

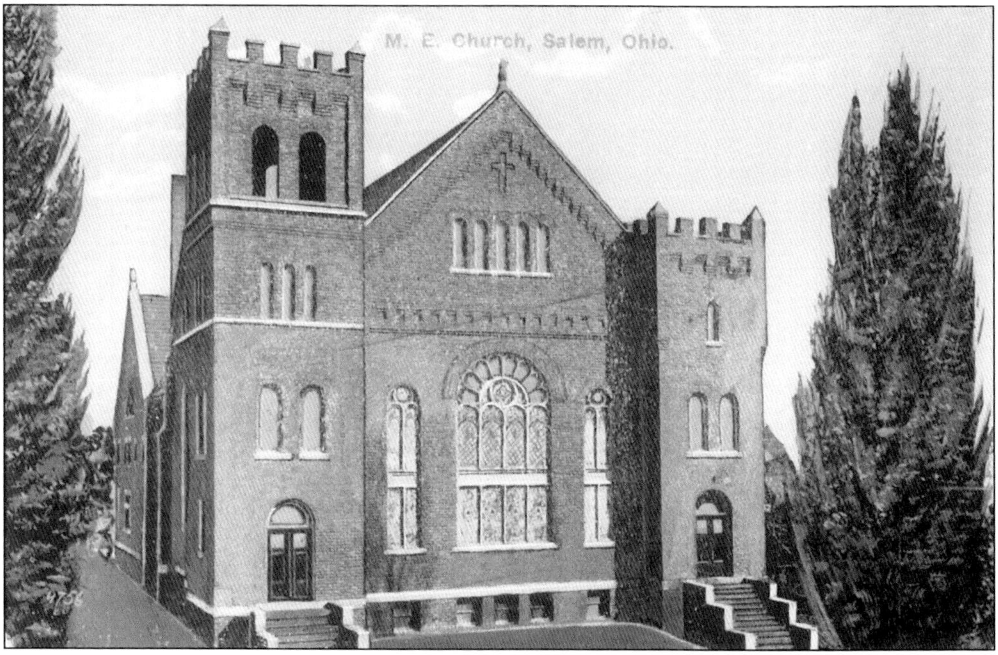

The present First United Methodist Church building, located at 244 South Broadway Avenue, dedicated April 2, 1911. Its cornerstone at the northwest corner, laid July 14, 1910, contained a copper box (a gift of Salem Hardware), inside of which were placed a copy of the Discipline of the Church, a hymnal, current copies of church periodicals, and some Salem papers.

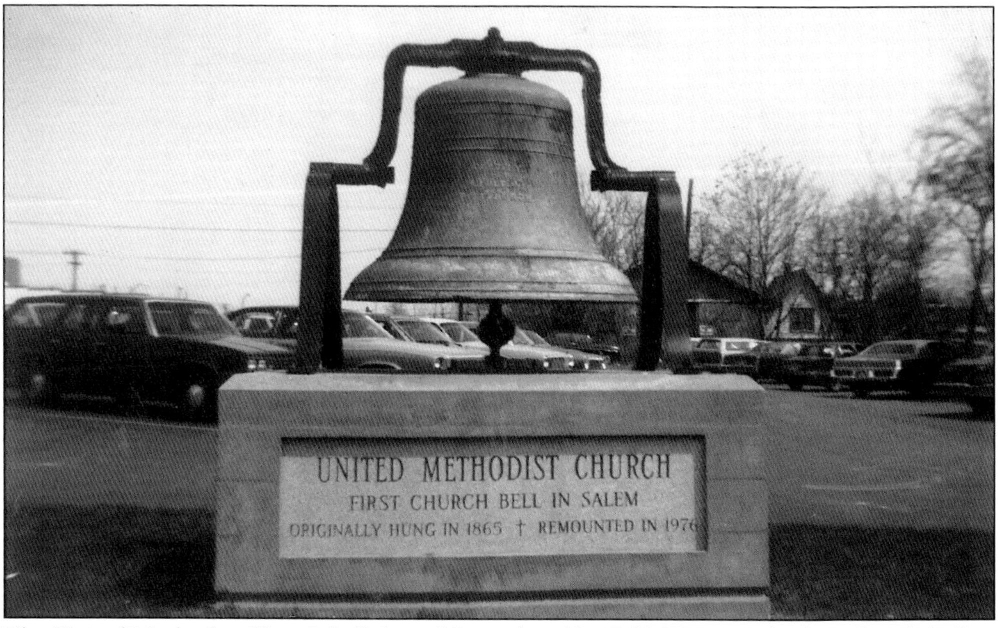

The United Methodist Church bell, hung November 10, 1865. This was the first church bell in the first steeple in Salem. Cast by the A. Fulton Company of Pittsburgh, Pennsylvania, the bell weighs 1,200 pounds and cost $480. In 1976 it was mounted and preserved next to the church on South Broadway Avenue. Methodism came to Salem around 1820 when John Flitcraft arrived from New Jersey.

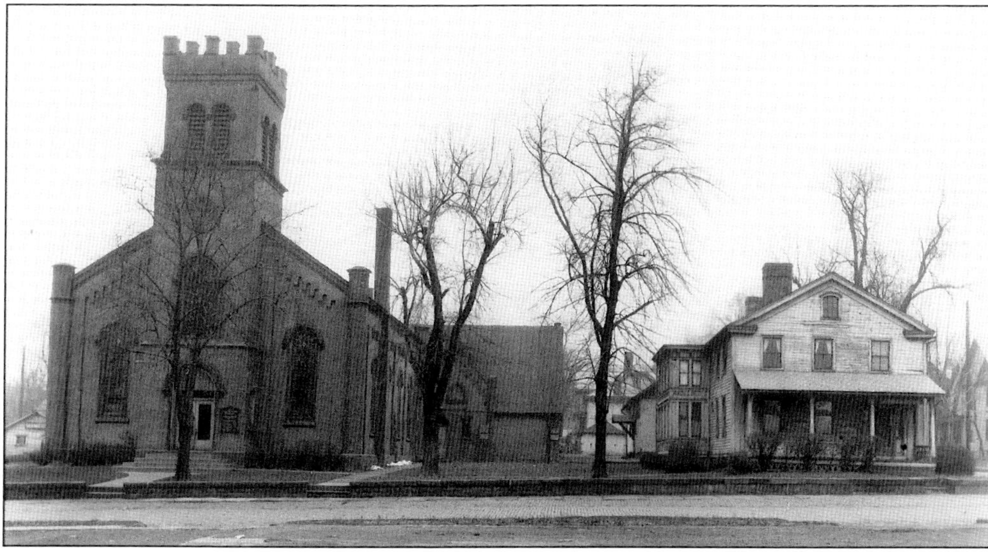

A 1936 photo showing the First Presbyterian Church on East Second Street. The house was being used as the primary building and parish house. Earlier it was the home of J. Twing Brooks, a prominent Salem attorney and official of the Pennsylvania Railroad, who constructed numerous downtown buildings. The Presbyterians were the fourth denomination to organize in Salem. This church building was constructed in 1860, and has been expanded several times.

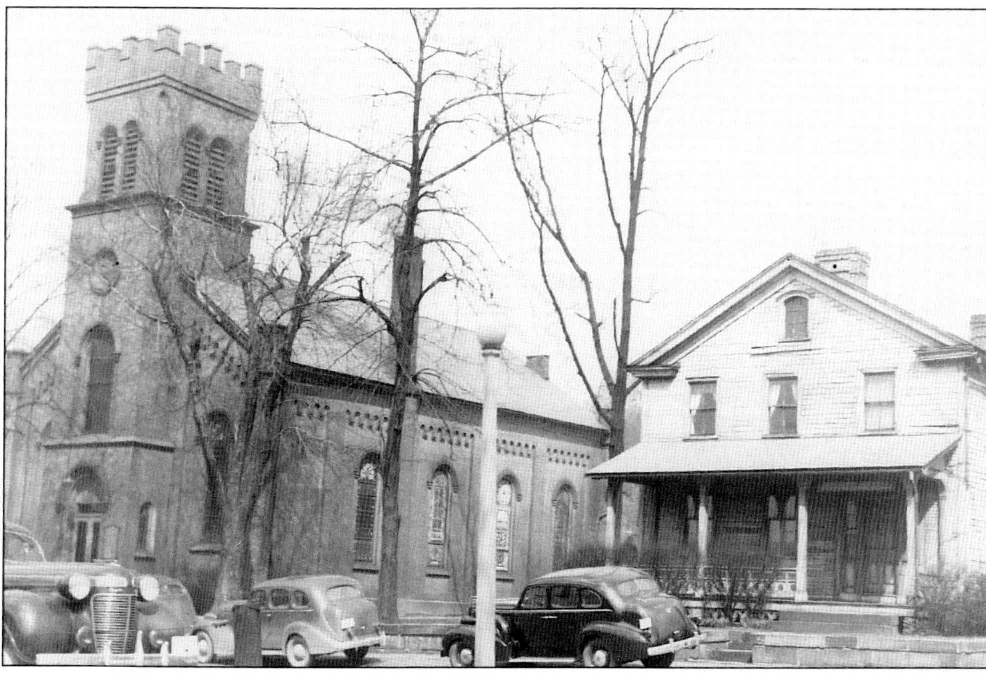

Another 1936 view of the Presbyterian church. In 1938, two years after this photo was taken, the church sanctuary was remodeled and the corner house razed to make room for an educational wing. The 1860 building still stands today, at the same location where the first church, a frame structure, was completed in 1842. It all began when several families gathered in John Campbell's Harness Shop on West State Street in 1830. They organized as a church in 1832.

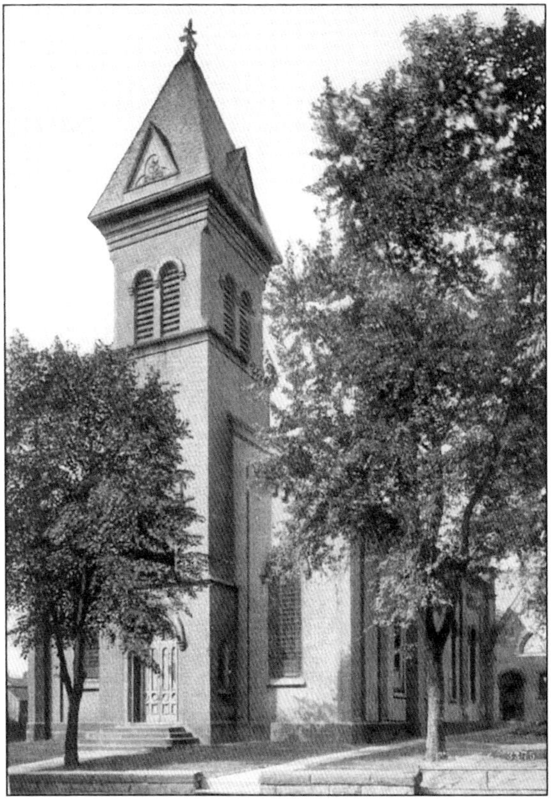

The First Presbyterian Church, dedicated in 1861. Money for it was raised in various ways, including the renting of pews for $125 each. In 1880 Carl Barckhoff installed Salem's first pipe organ in the church. This was before he established his organ factory on Vine Avenue. Salem once had two organ factories.

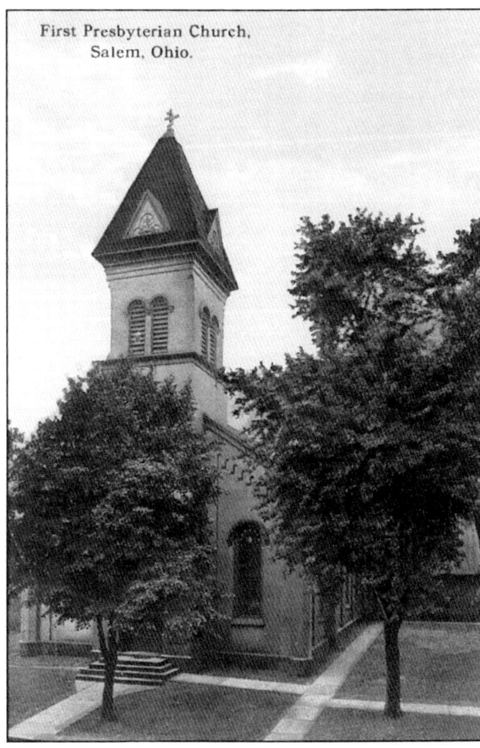

The First Presbyterian Church. The old stone wall, with its pyramid cornerstone, was installed in the 1830s and remains today in front of the Presbyterian church. Robert Hannay and two Hinchcliff brothers cut all the stone and hauled it by ox cart. The congregation of this church has grown to become one of the largest in Salem.

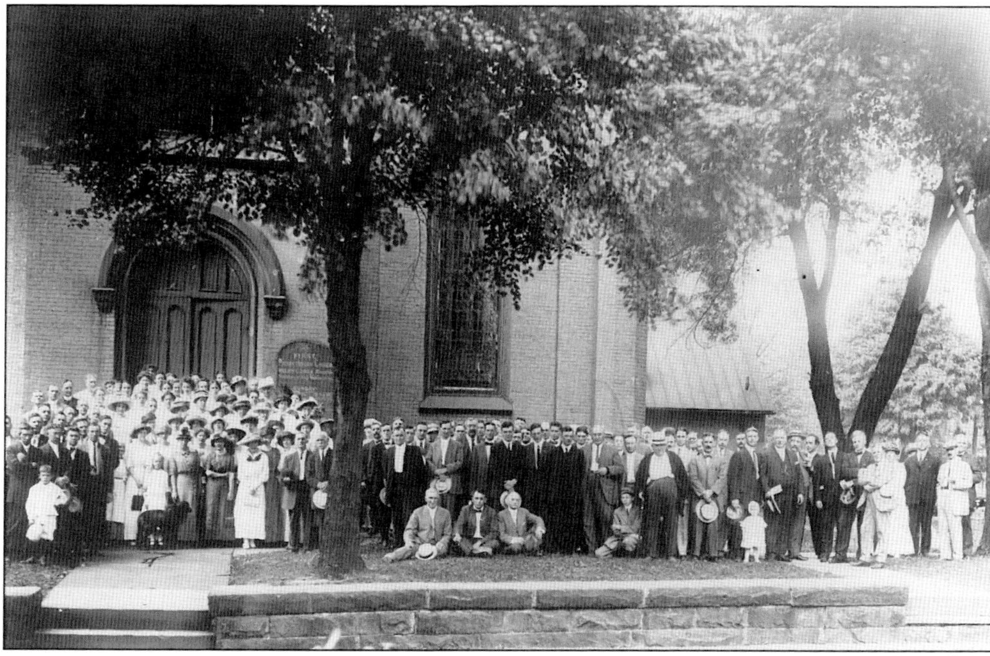

Members of Salem's First Presbyterian Church on East Second Street in a group photo from around 1920. Note their fine dress and the beautiful hats worn by the women. Most of the men had removed their straw hats.

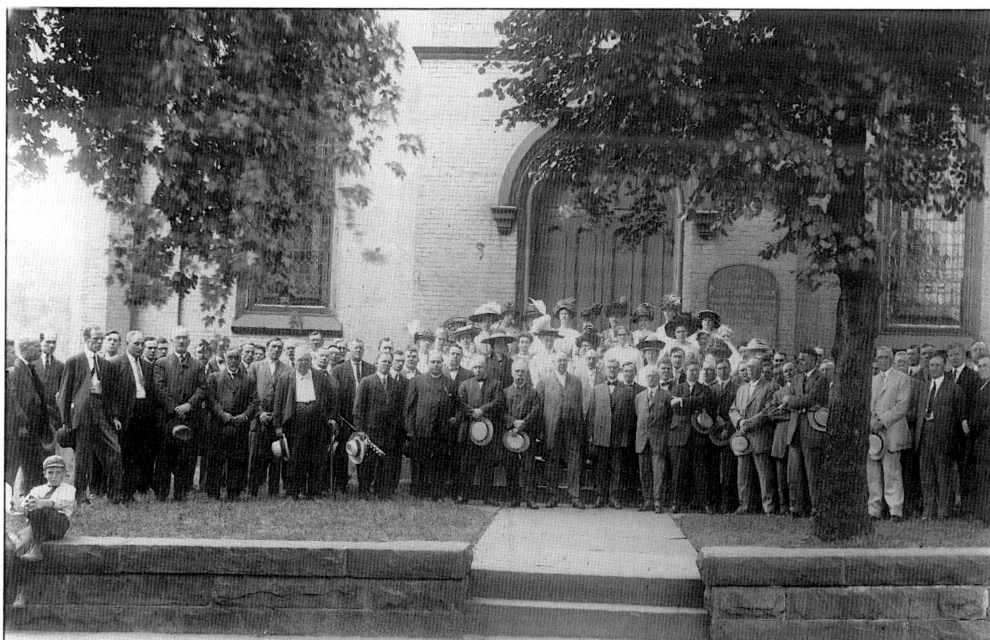

Members of the congregation of the First Presbyterian Church. In the early years of this century, many of Salem's prominent businessmen attended the First Presbyterian Church. In this photo are people with such well-known names as Grove, Metzger, Dunn, Carlisle, Deming, Koll, Pow, and Atchison. Note the large decorated hats worn by the women. The church still stands today, although greatly remodeled.

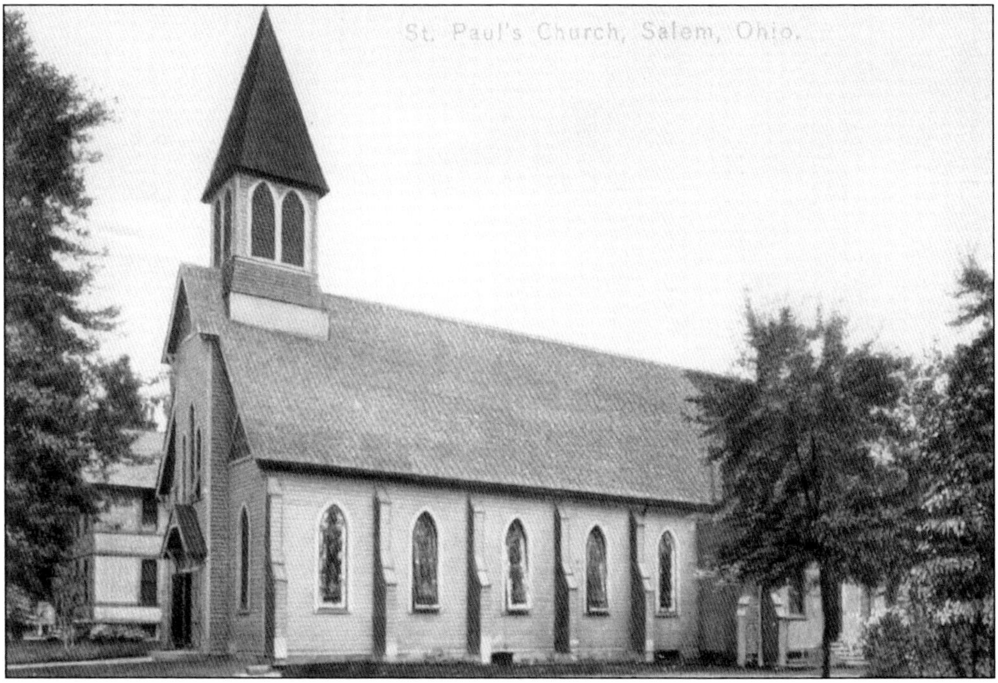

Salem's old Saint Paul's Catholic Church, located at 961 East State Street. Built in 1881, this building was replaced in 1930. Mass was celebrated here for the first time on November 27, 1887. Father Clement H. Treiber was the first resident pastor. Prior to the church being built, meetings were held in homes and in the old town hall. Father Lindesmith said the first mass in Salem on January 22, 1869.

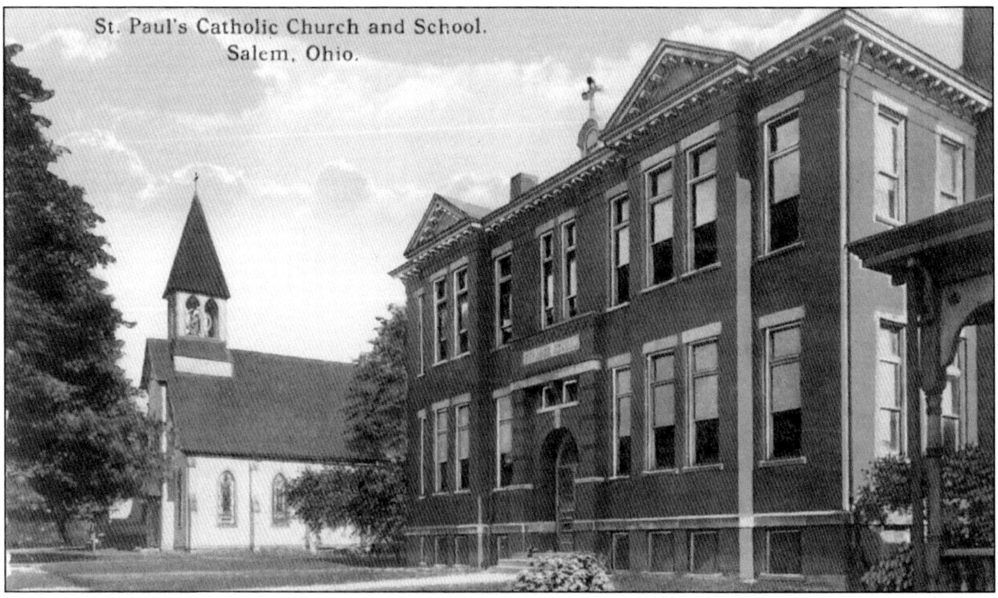

Saint Paul's School, once located at 901 East State Street, dedicated September 20, 1904. It cost $12,000. The curriculum was almost identical with that of Salem public schools. Sisters Foley and McCarthy were in charge. Teachers occupied an old house behind the school from 1904 to 1924. The building was razed in 1954 and replaced with a new facility.

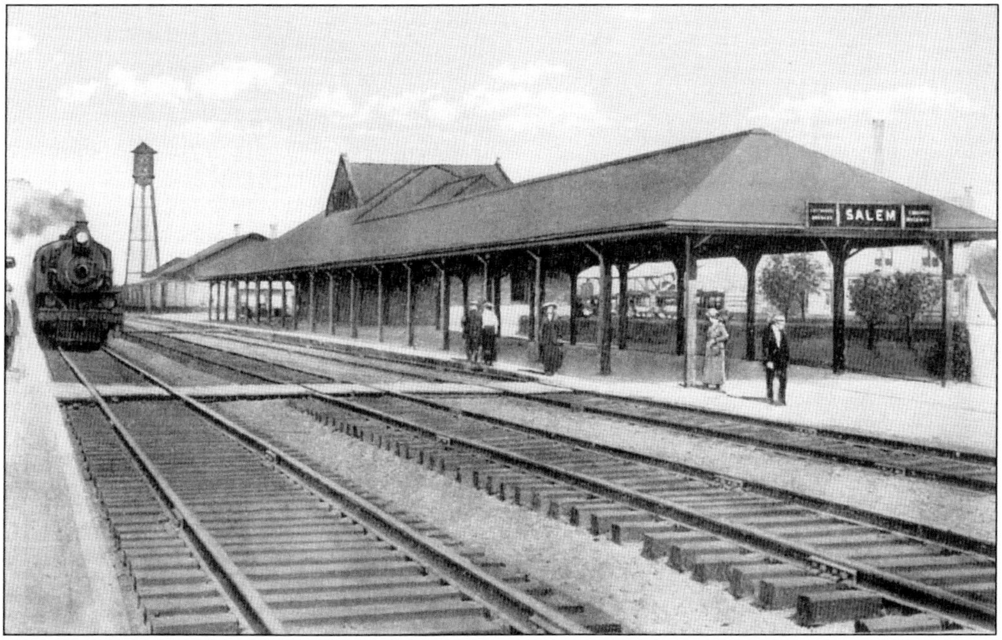

An artist's drawing of the Pennsylvania Railroad Depot, showing a train arriving from the west. In the background is the Mullins Manufacturing Company water tower. The first passenger car arrived in Salem on November 27, 1851, pulled by an engine called "The Beaver." This depot was destroyed by a train wreck on July 31, 1997.

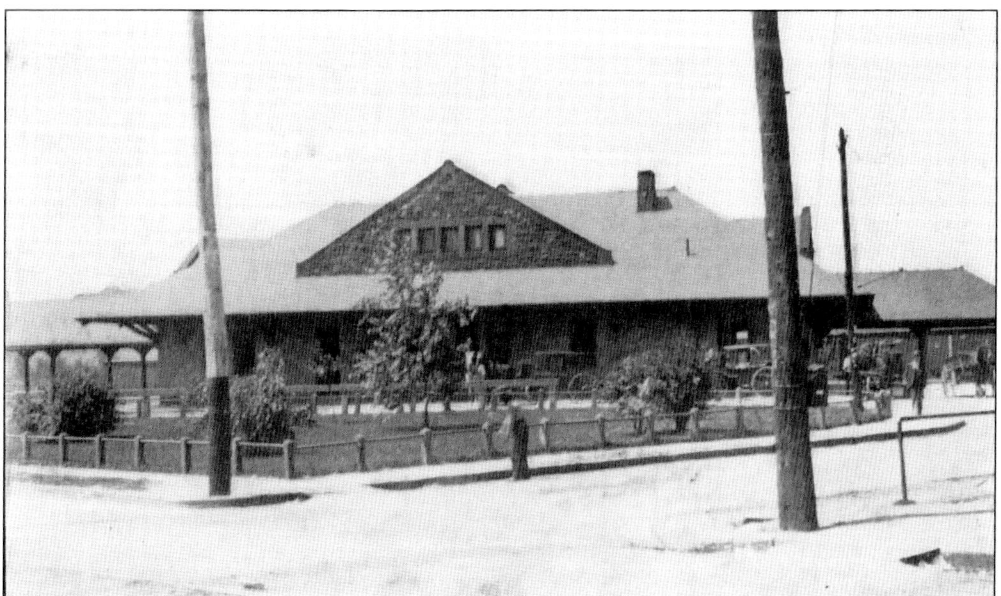

The Pennsylvania Railroad Depot, built in 1893. So handsome was this station that a photo of it was exhibited at the 1893 Columbian Exposition in Chicago. Brownstone for the structure came from a quarry near Beaver Falls, Pennsylvania. This photo was taken in 1907.

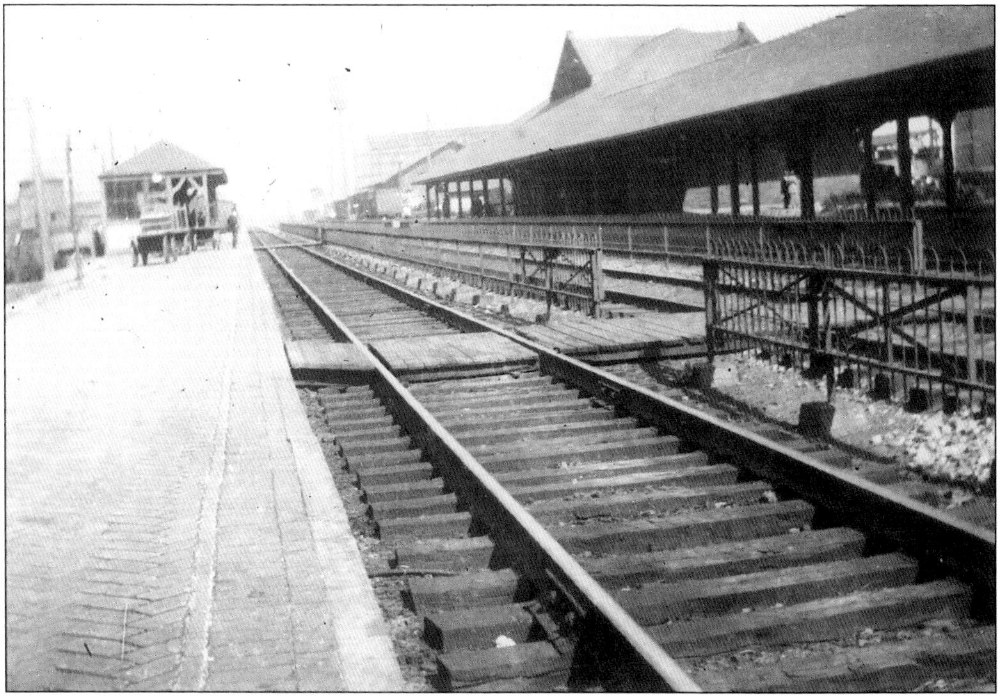

Another view of the railroad depot. At one time there were 32 passenger trains passing through Salem every day. They had names such as the Golden Triangle, Broadway Limited, Trailblazer, Manhattan Limited, Detroit Red Arrow, General, Admiral, and Pennsylvania Flyer. Families would often gather here in the evening to see the huge steam locomotives stop or roar through town.

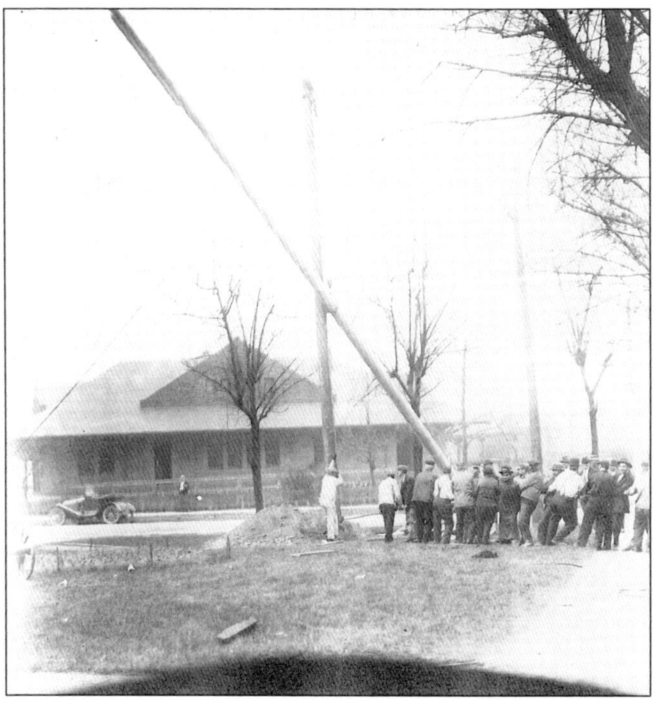

An early 1900s photo of workers installing telephone poles in front of the Pennsylvania Railroad Depot on South Ellsworth Avenue. As late as 1955, visiting railroad officials were amazed that a little town like Salem had a stone building, while so many other larger communities still had frame depots. During World War II thousands of military troops passed through this station. Trains carried men to points of embarkation.

Four

Business and Industry

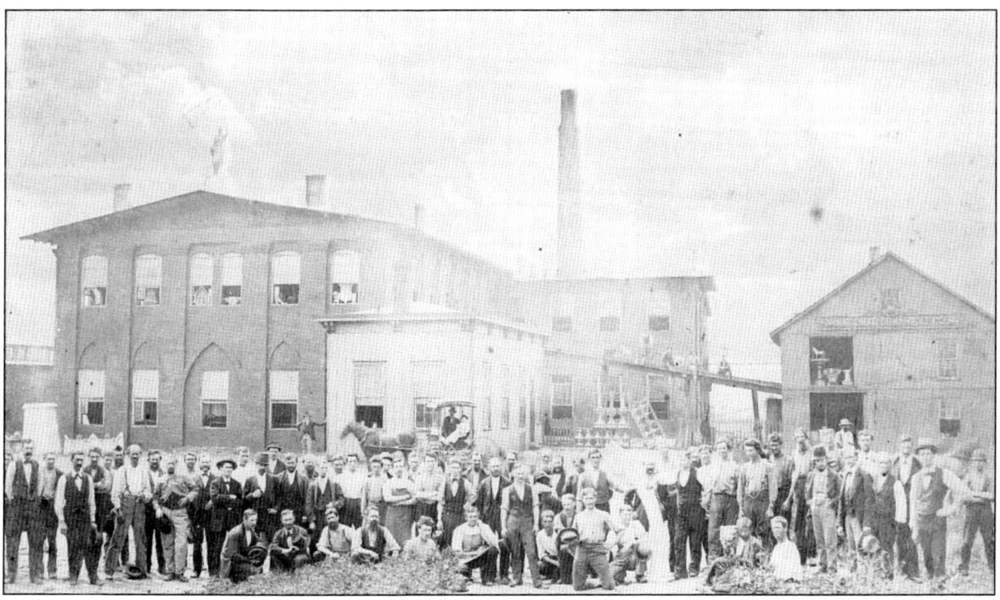

The Kittridge Cornice Works, the predecessor of the Mullins Manufacturing Company. This 1875 photo shows the owners and employees at the plant on South Ellsworth Avenue, displaying stamped metal work for buildings at the Centennial Exposition held in Philadelphia in 1876. The owners were Anson Kittridge, William Clark, J.T. Brooks, and Joseph Fawcett. Alphons and Hubert Pelzer were the designers for this firm.

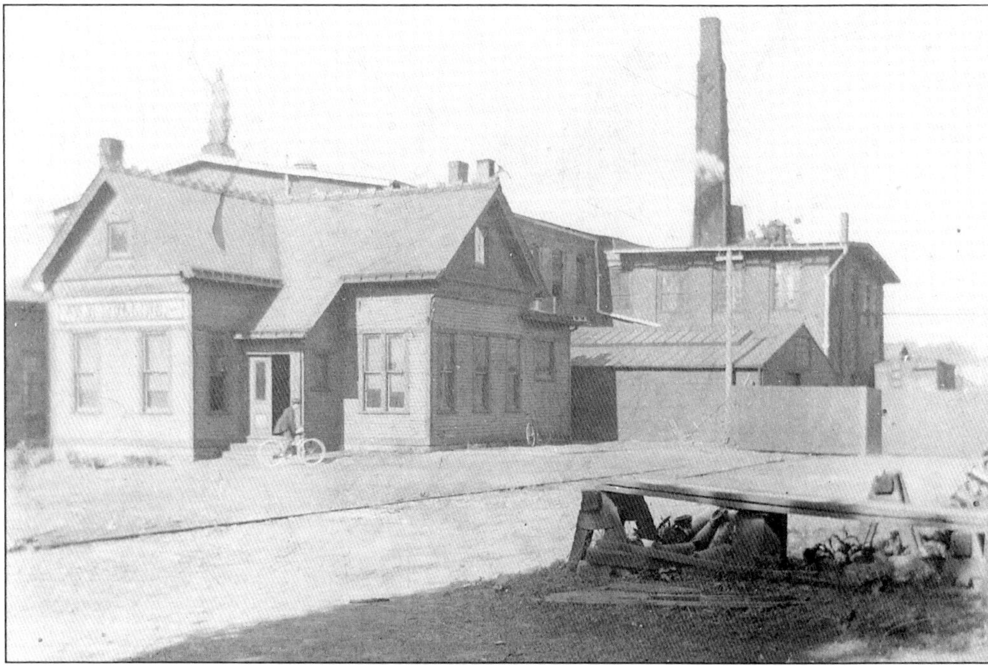

The original Mullins firm. In 1890 W.H. Mullins bought out Thomas H. Bakewell and the firm became "W.H. Mullins." He had 100 workers, was heavily in debt, and a depression was on the way. Mr. Mullins began as a clerk in the Pittsburgh office of the Pennsylvania Railroad. He came to Salem in 1882 and bought the statuary firm.

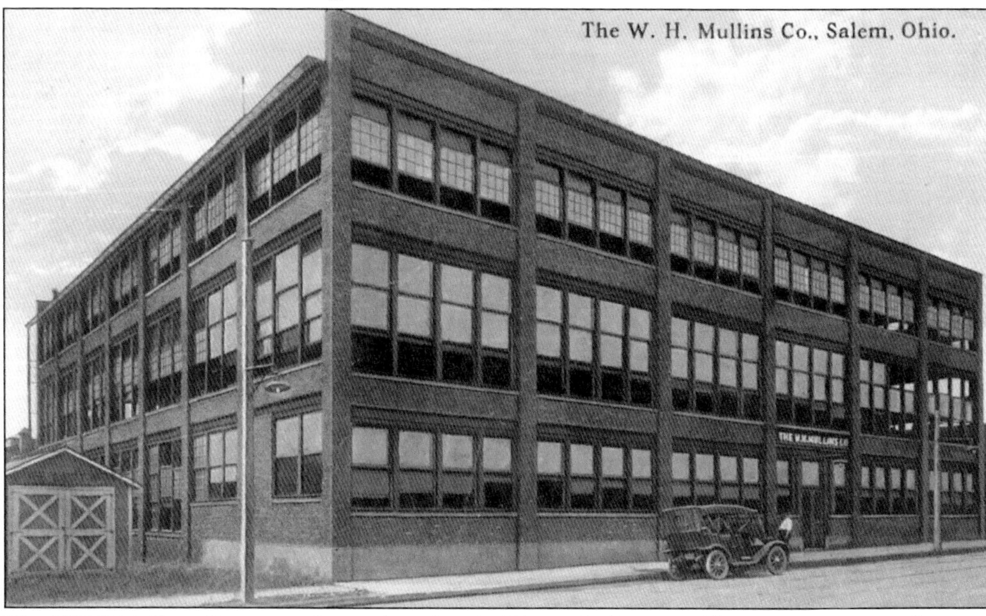

The W.H. Mullins Company, located on South Ellsworth Avenue. The company manufactured a large variety of products, including architectural ornaments, auto parts and trailers, boats, store fronts, metal ceilings, tile roofing, kitchen equipment, shells and casings, signs, washing machine tubs, weather vanes, and window frames. These products meant jobs for thousands of people. W.H. Mullins did for Salem what Henry Ford did for Detroit.

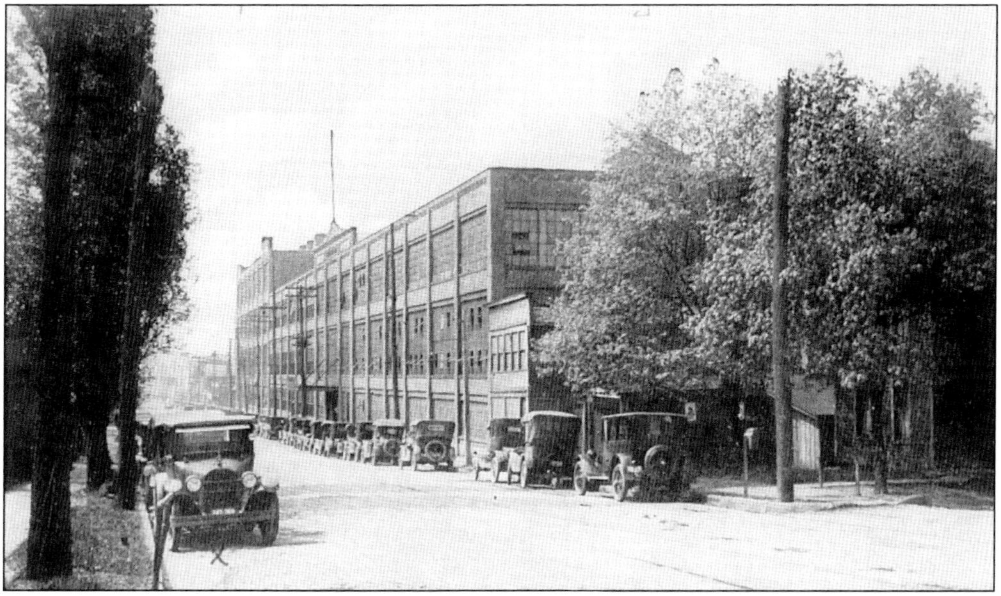

The Mullins Body Corporation, c. 1925. Mullins began making hot-stamped body parts in 1904 with the production of the first steel body for the Pope-Toledo Automobile Company. During the years 1906 to 1925 the company made body stampings for the Peerless, the Franklin aluminum car, Winton, Stearns Knight and Royal, Jewel, and Welsh. Fenders and parts for the Pierce-Arrow and Cadillac were made from 1910 to 1937.

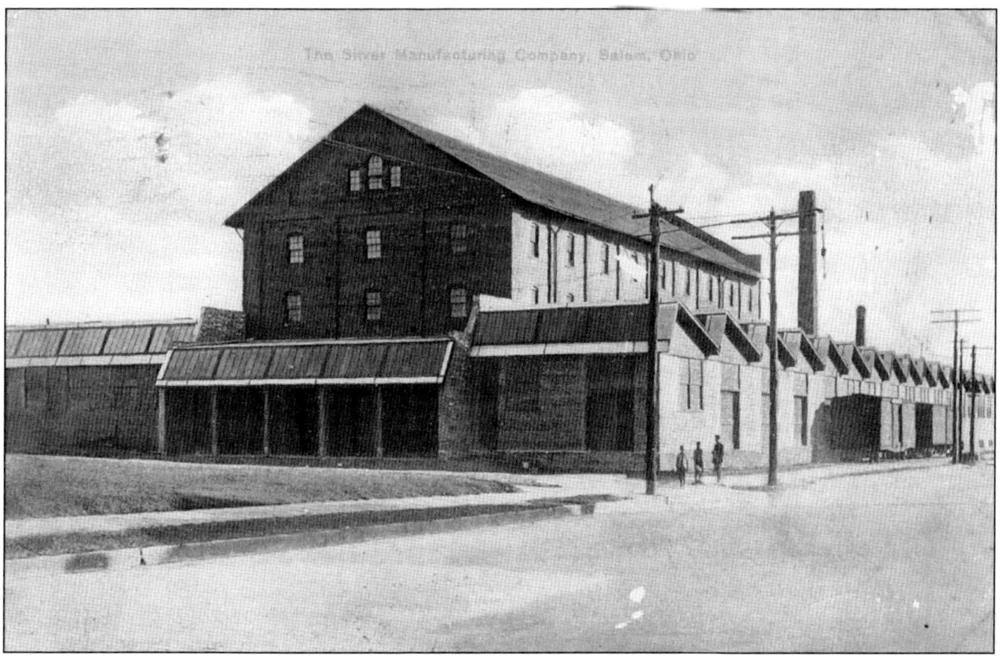

The Silver Manufacturing Company, a major firm in Salem at the turn of the century. It manufactured a wide variety of products—machines for contractors, woodworkers, butchers, machinists, and patternmakers. Feed cutters and fodder shredders were produced for farmers. Mullins took over the property in 1925.

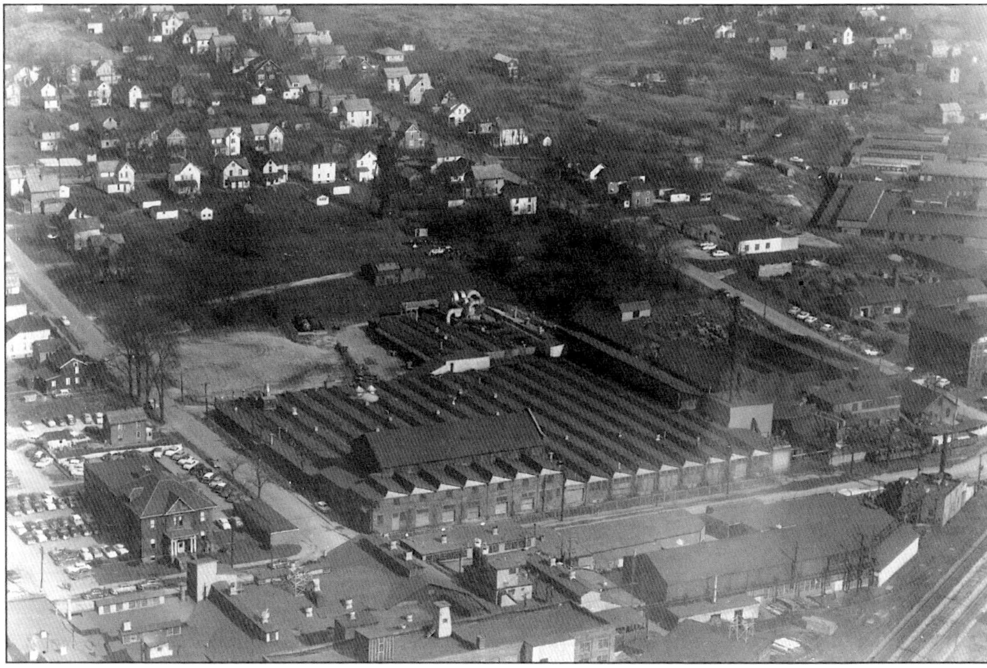

Mullins's Plant 3 in a 1956 aerial photo. Produced were such products as radiator covers, cabinets, military equipment, shelving, and trays. Originally, the facility was used by the Silver Manufacturing Company, maker of farm machinery. Mullins bought it in 1925. The two-story brick structure on the left once housed the offices of the Silver firm.

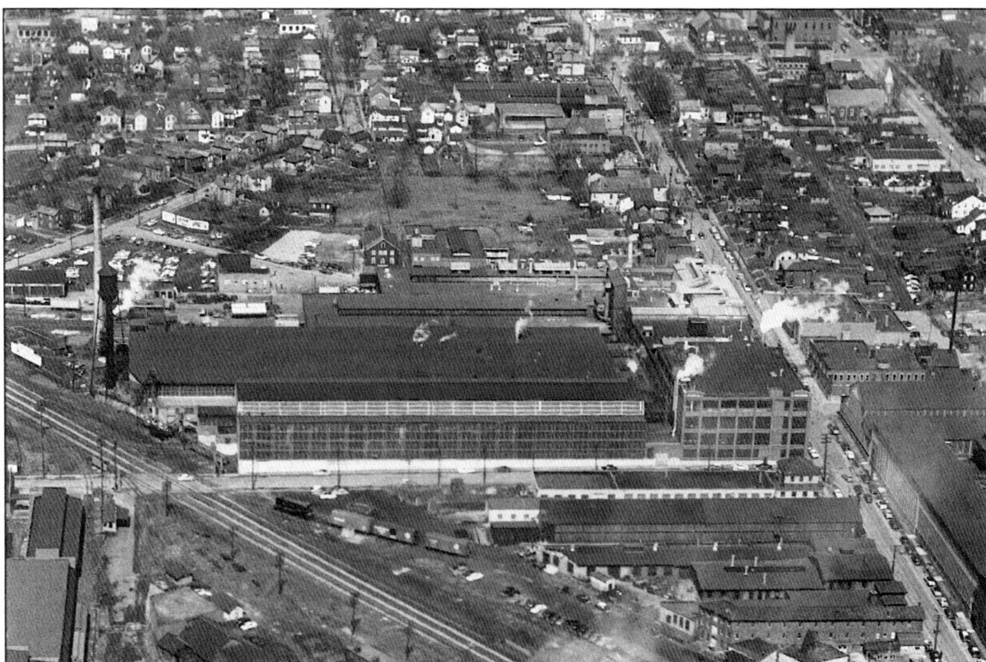

An aerial view (looking north) of the Mullins Manufacturing Company in 1956. The buildings are now used by the American Standard Company.

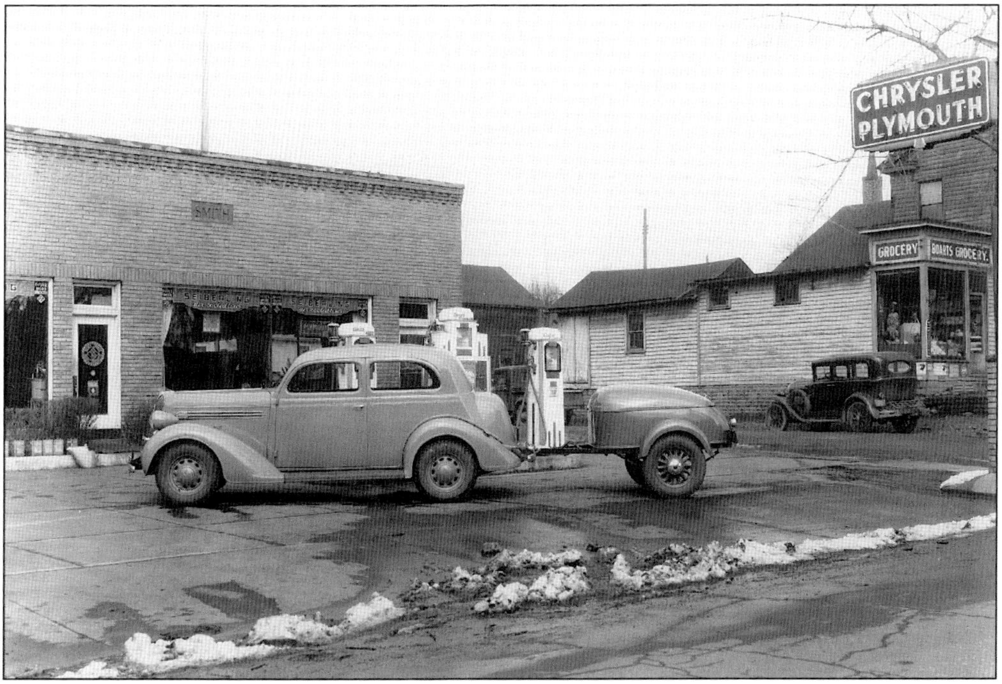

One of Joe Smith's new Plymouths pulling a Mullins Red Cap trailer in the late 1930s. The Mullins Manufacturing Company produced this trailer from 1936 to 1938. It was the only all-steel, two-wheel auto trailer on the market at the time. Selling for $119.50, it was an immediate hit with the public. Note the Canzol gasoline being sold at this garage. Boarts's mom-and-pop grocery is on the right.

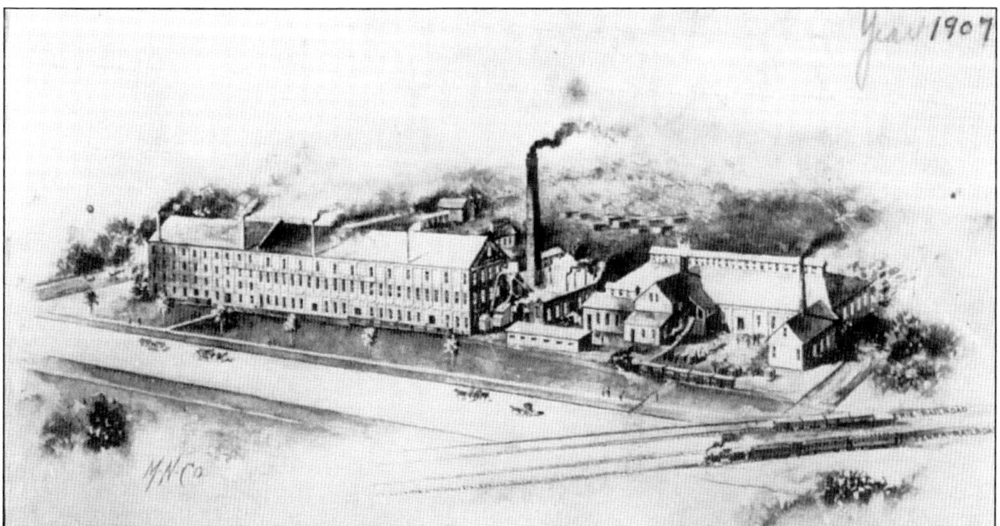

The Silver Manufacturing Company. The company began as the Silver and Dole Company in 1865, and became the Silver and Deming Company in 1874, which in turn divided into the Silver Manufacturing Company and the Deming Company. Silver manufactured cutting tools—saws, planes, drilling machines, sausage and lard-making machines, feed cutters, and other tools for all types of industries. Albert R. Silver was the founder.

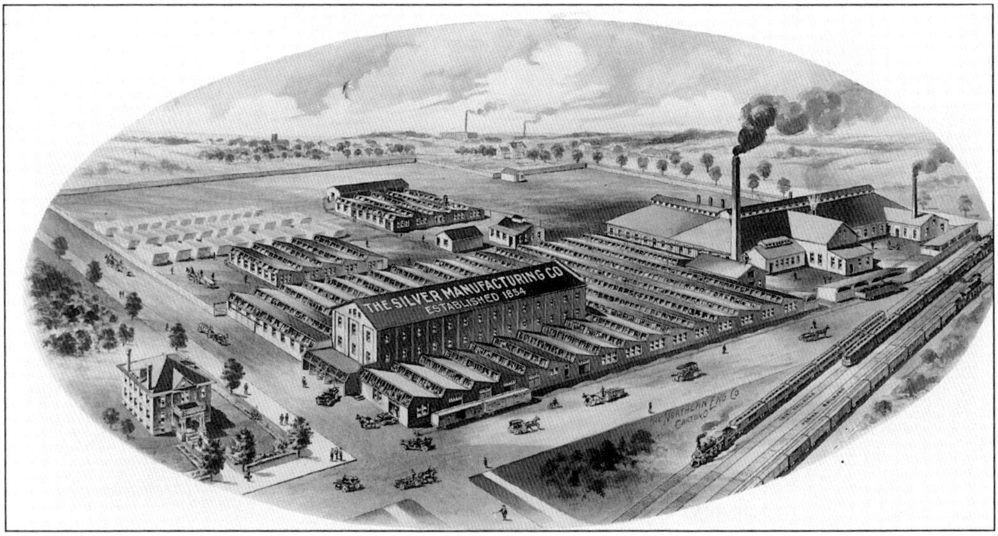

A 1907 drawing showing the Silver Manufacturing Company plant at the southeast corner of South Broadway Avenue and Perry Street, along with Silver's office building (at left). The buildings still stand today. Heirs of the Silver family sold the business in 1930, and all that remains today is the Industrial Paper Shredders Company at 707 South Ellsworth Avenue.

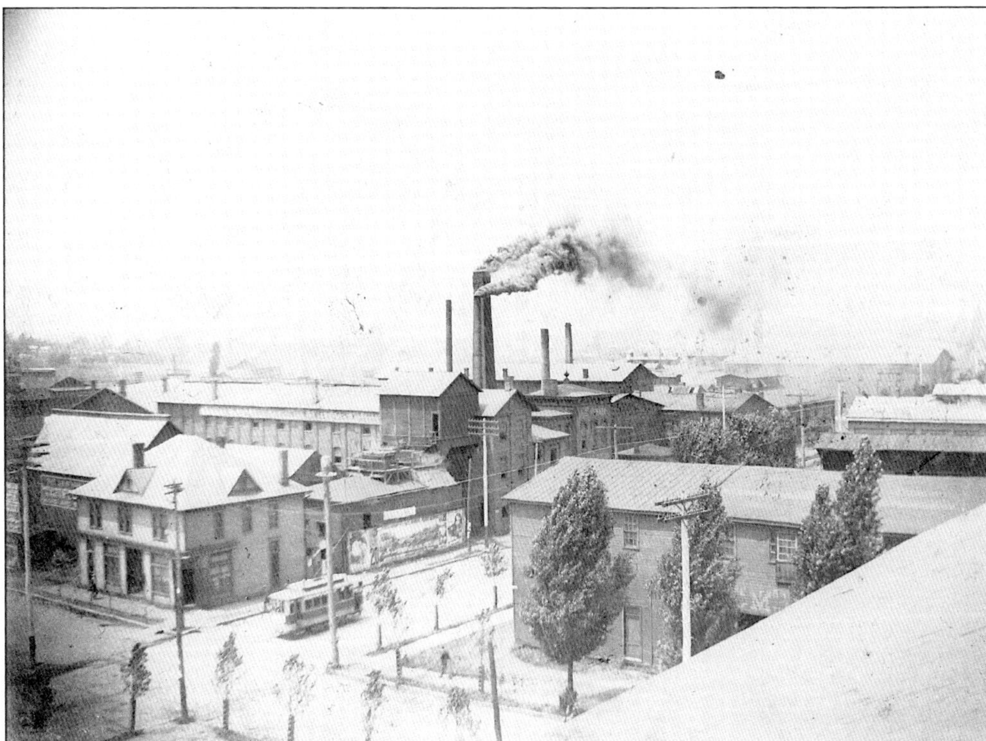

A Salem Electric Railway trolley car heading south down South Ellsworth Avenue past the Deming Company plant in the 1890s. Many workers rode the trolley to and from work. Only a few of these buildings still stand today.

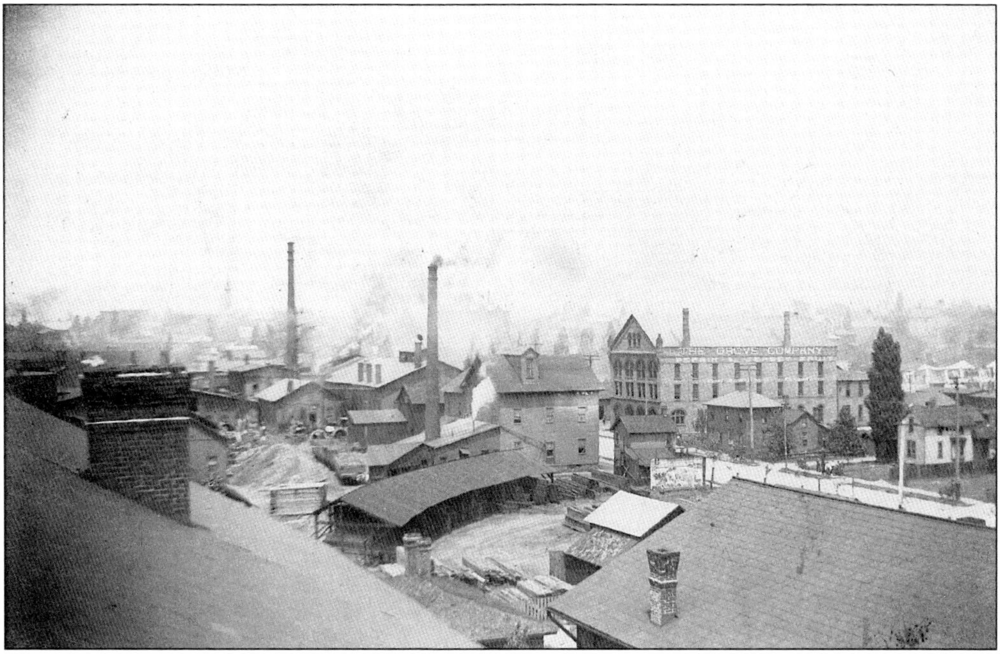

Another 1890s view of the Deming Company plant. The large building on the right is the Grove Chewing Gum Factory, which flourished before and after the turn of the century. It employed about 100 people and sold its 11 flavors of gum throughout the country.

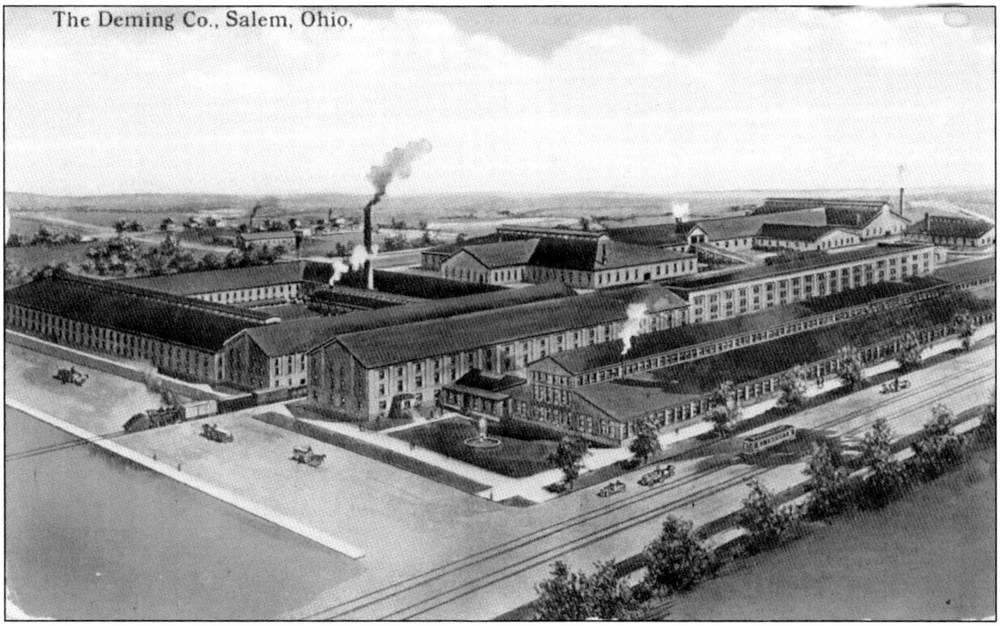

The Deming Co. John Deming came to Salem in 1862 and opened a grocery store. Levi Dole and Albert R. Silver were manufacturing tools for blacksmiths and wagon-makers, and Deming bought into the firm. In 1874 it became the Silver and Deming Manufacturing Company, and in 1890 the company divided into two separate firms. The Deming Company manufactures pumps of all sizes and capacities. Its headquarters remains in Salem today.

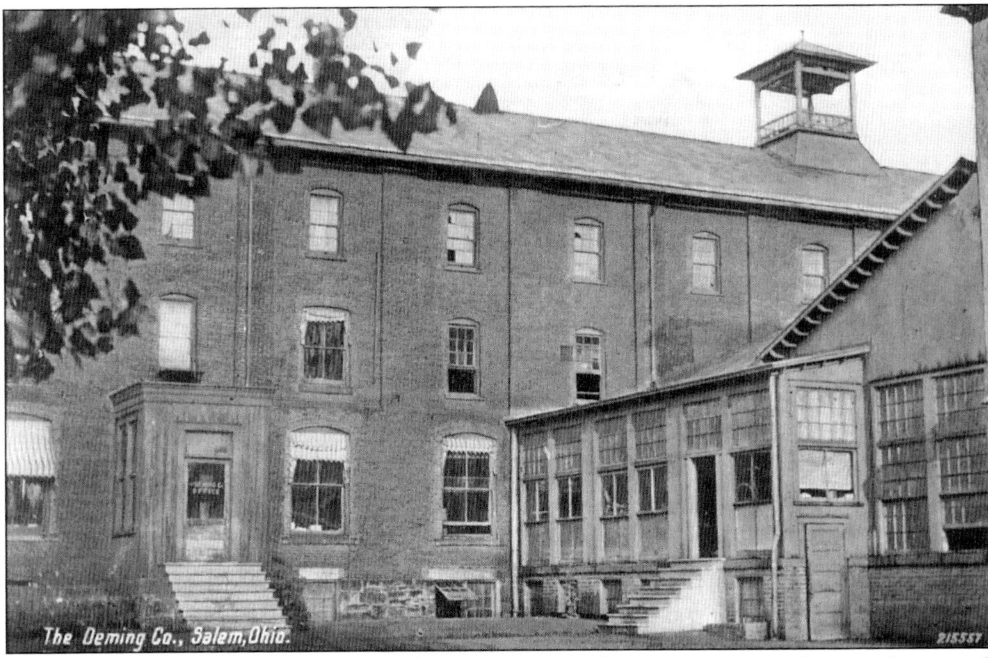

One of the old Deming Company buildings in Salem, located on Aetna Street, that is still standing. This is where the first hand- and windmill pumps were made in 1880. The Deming Company continues today as a leading manufacturer in the international market.

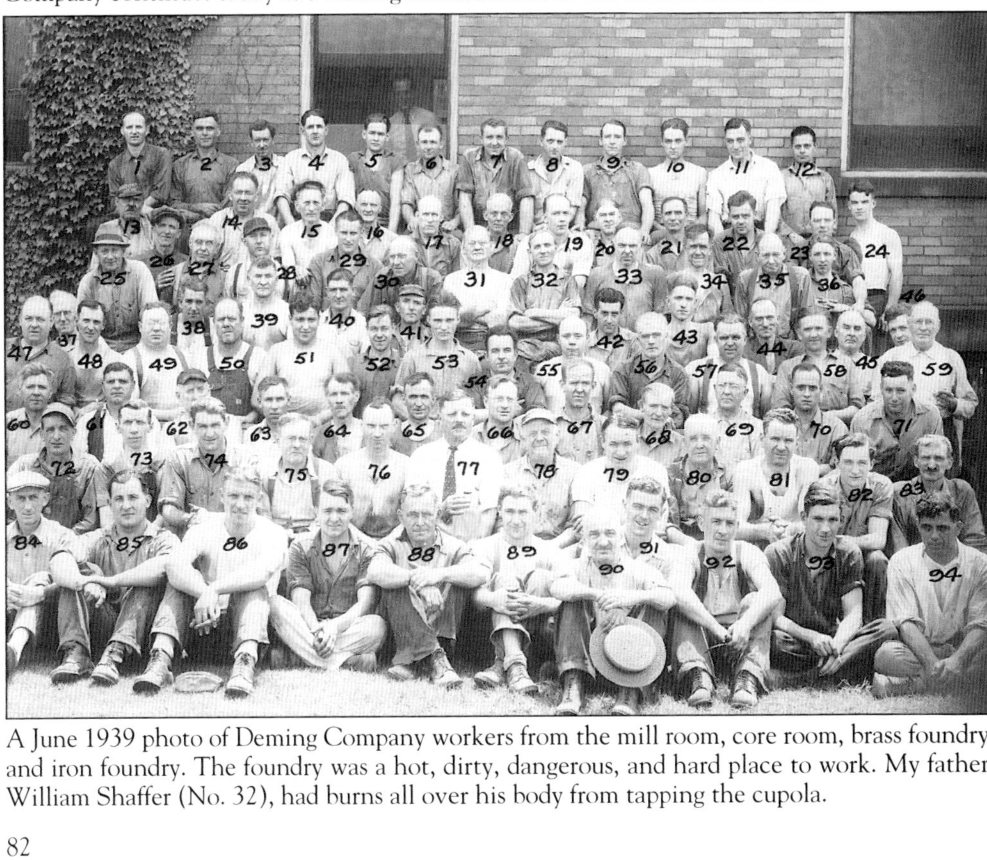

A June 1939 photo of Deming Company workers from the mill room, core room, brass foundry, and iron foundry. The foundry was a hot, dirty, dangerous, and hard place to work. My father, William Shaffer (No. 32), had burns all over his body from tapping the cupola.

Products of the Deming Co. Through the years, the Deming Company produced many different types of pumps that served a variety of needs. Hand- and windmill pumps were the first ones made in 1880. The illustrations shown here are from a catalog in the early 1900s.

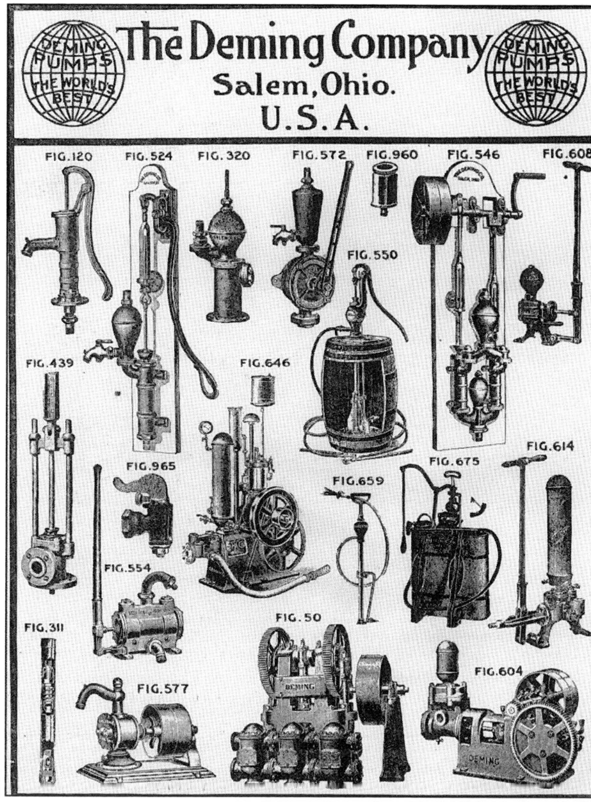

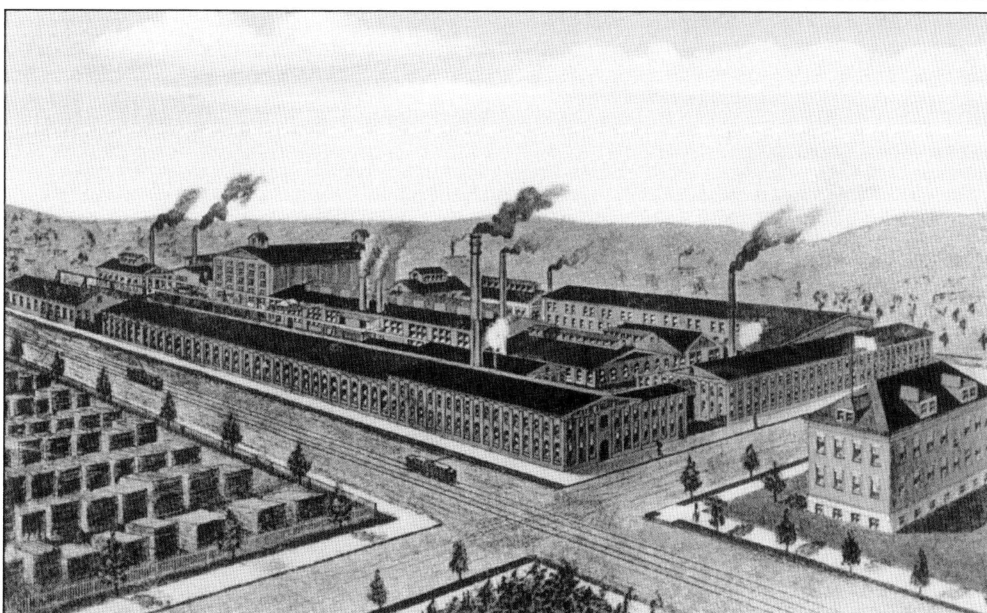

The Buckeye Engine Works, Salem's first major industrial enterprise. It operated for 69 years, from 1851 to 1920, manufacturing steam engines. In 1920 its buildings were sold to the E.W. Bliss Company. This view is looking southwest toward the intersection of Franklin Street and South Broadway Avenue. At right is the company's office building. Note the trolley car.

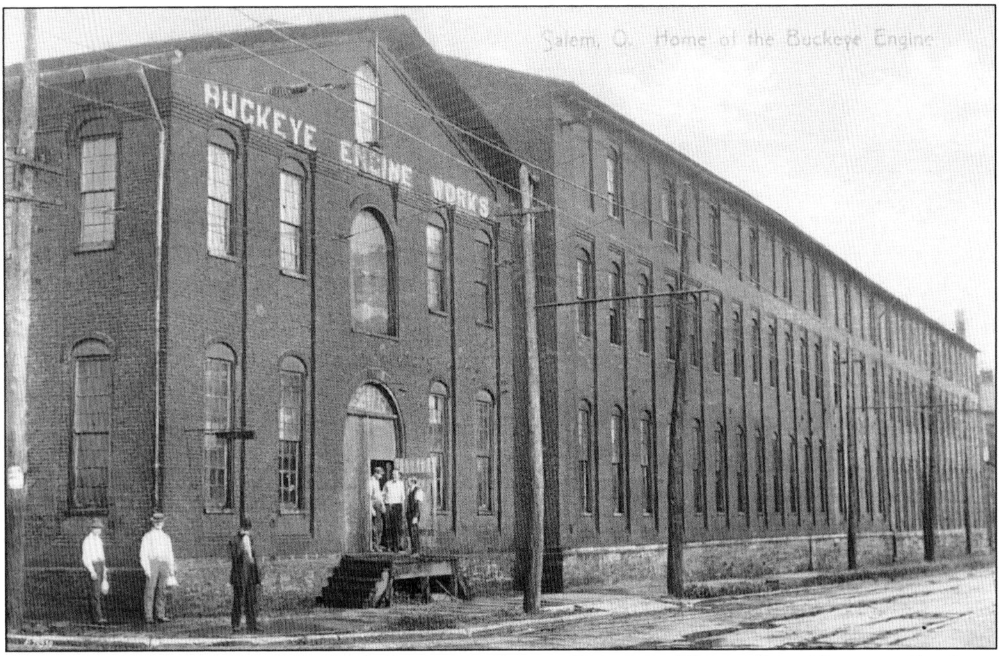

The Buckeye Engine Works, which began as Sharps, Davis, and Bonsall and became Buckeye in 1871. Its buildings covered about 4 acres. Buckeye engines had broad applications and were sold throughout the world. Older residents remember the plant's 4 p.m. whistle. It gave the daily weather report.

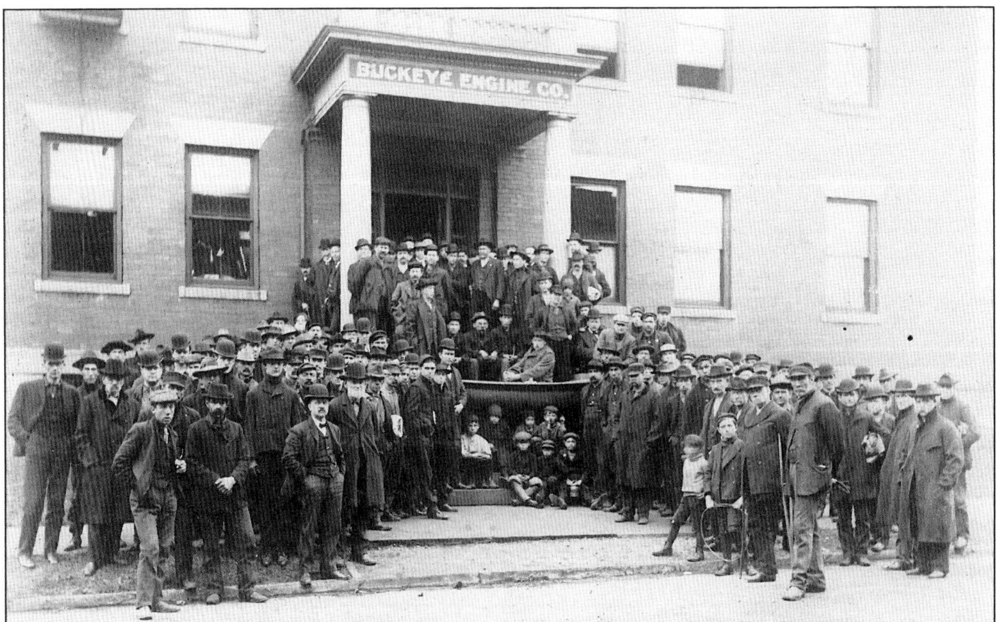

A group photo taken at the turn of the century in front of the Buckeye Engine Company office building, once located on Franklin Street. It was razed in 1989. Buckeye steam engines were sold to water-pumping stations, mining firms, and for large industrial mobile units. Power for the 1893 Columbian Exposition in Chicago was provided by a Buckeye engine.

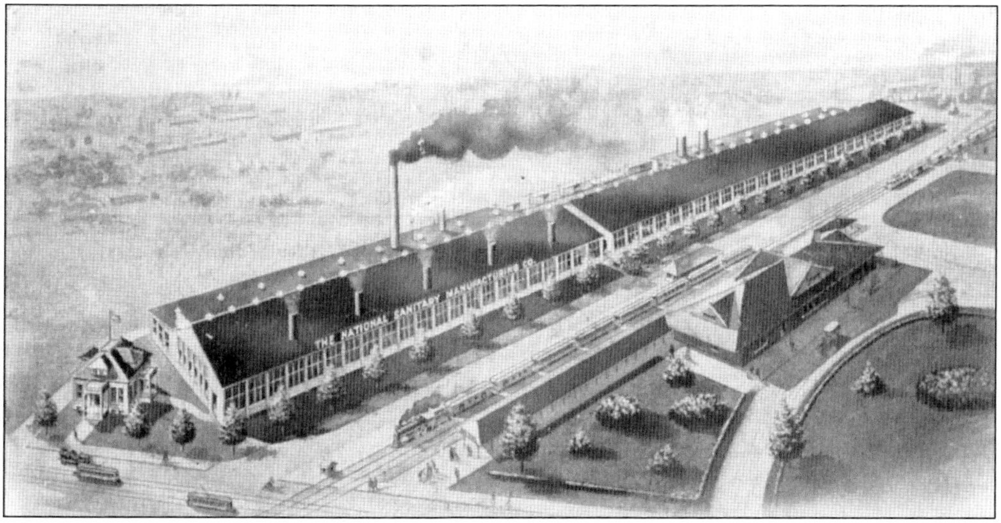

The National Sanitary Manufacturing Company plant, built in 1908. In 1928 it became part of the Eljer Company, a manufacturer of cast-iron plumbing fixtures and the inventor of the famous round china closet tank, which was the forerunner of all china tanks. Eljer still operates in this facility and is an important asset to Salem's economy.

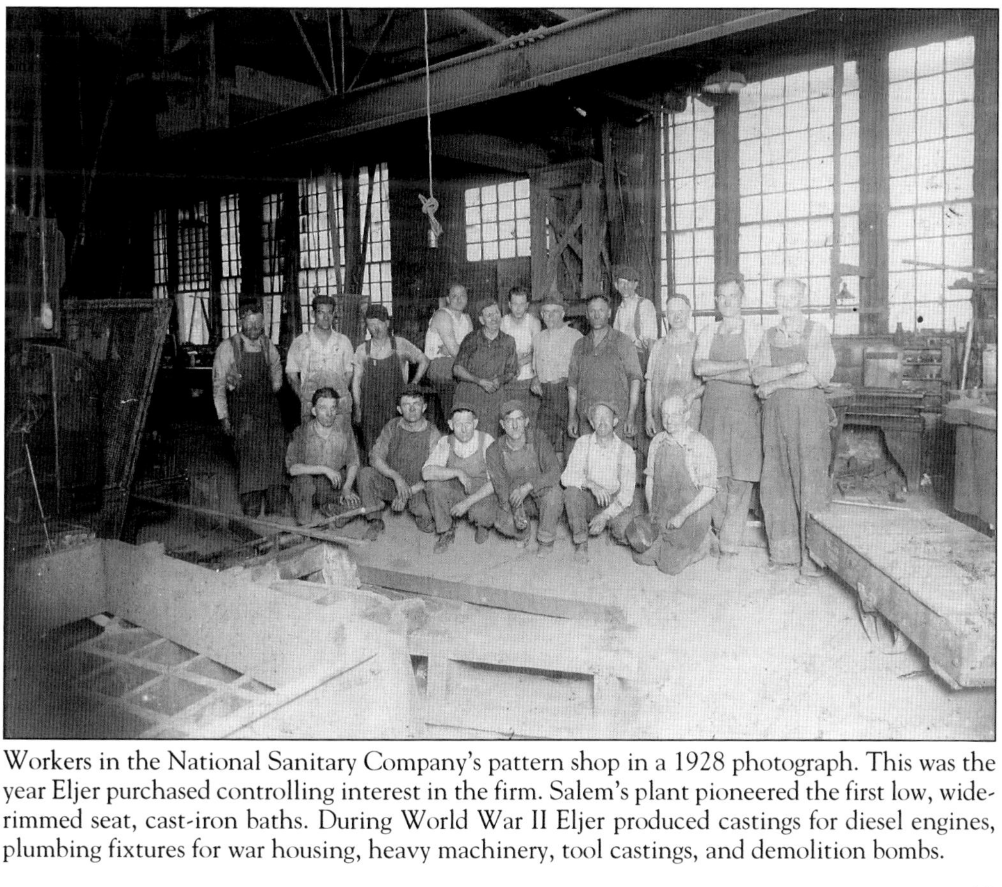

Workers in the National Sanitary Company's pattern shop in a 1928 photograph. This was the year Eljer purchased controlling interest in the firm. Salem's plant pioneered the first low, wide-rimmed seat, cast-iron baths. During World War II Eljer produced castings for diesel engines, plumbing fixtures for war housing, heavy machinery, tool castings, and demolition bombs.

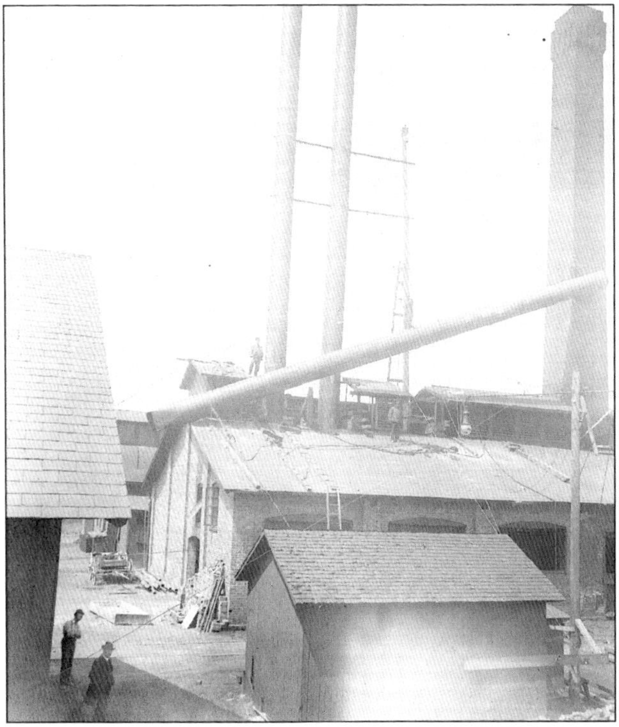

A 1902 view of the American Steel and Wire Company plant (Nail Mill) on Mill (Mullins) Street. Organized in 1884, the firm was a large producer of wire nails—2,600 kegs of nails per day. It closed February 28, 1929, and moved to Cleveland. Some of its red brick buildings are still standing. The Eljer Company purchased the buildings around 1940.

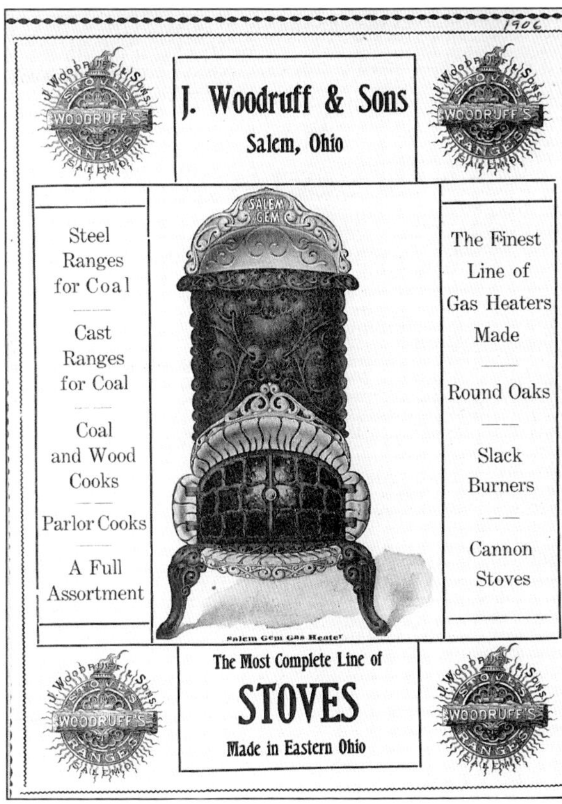

J. Woodruff and Sons stoves. In the latter half of the 19th century there were several stove manufacturing firms in Salem. One of the largest was J. Woodruff and Sons. James M. Woodruff started out with the Snyder, Woodruff, and Company, and in 1870 took it over under his own name. Woodruff stoves were beautifully designed. There were over 130 different sizes and varieties of stoves. The illustration shown is from 1906.

The Victor Stove Company, the successor to King, Gee, and Company, which was founded in 1867. This firm produced over 120 styles and sizes of stoves, all made in Salem under the name of the Victor Stove Company. The plant, located in two buildings on South Ellsworth Avenue, discontinued operations in 1925. Stoves shown in the illustration are dated 1906.

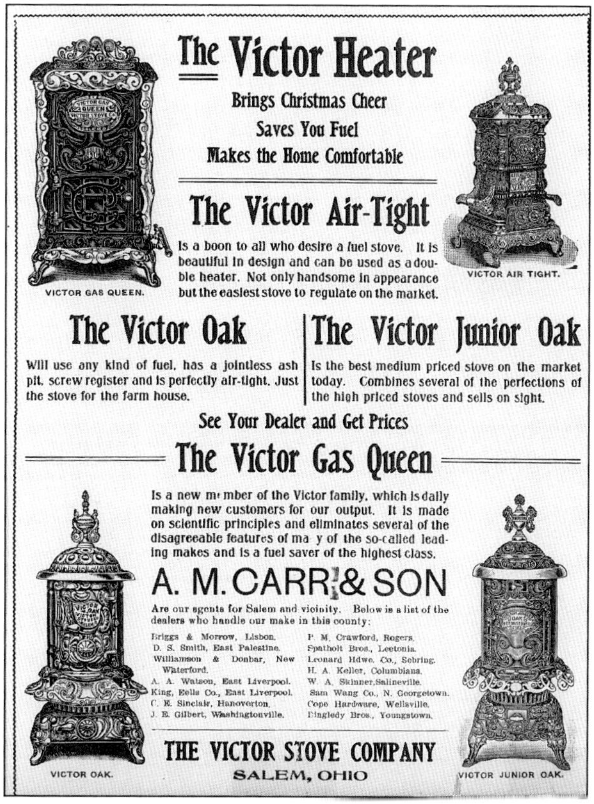

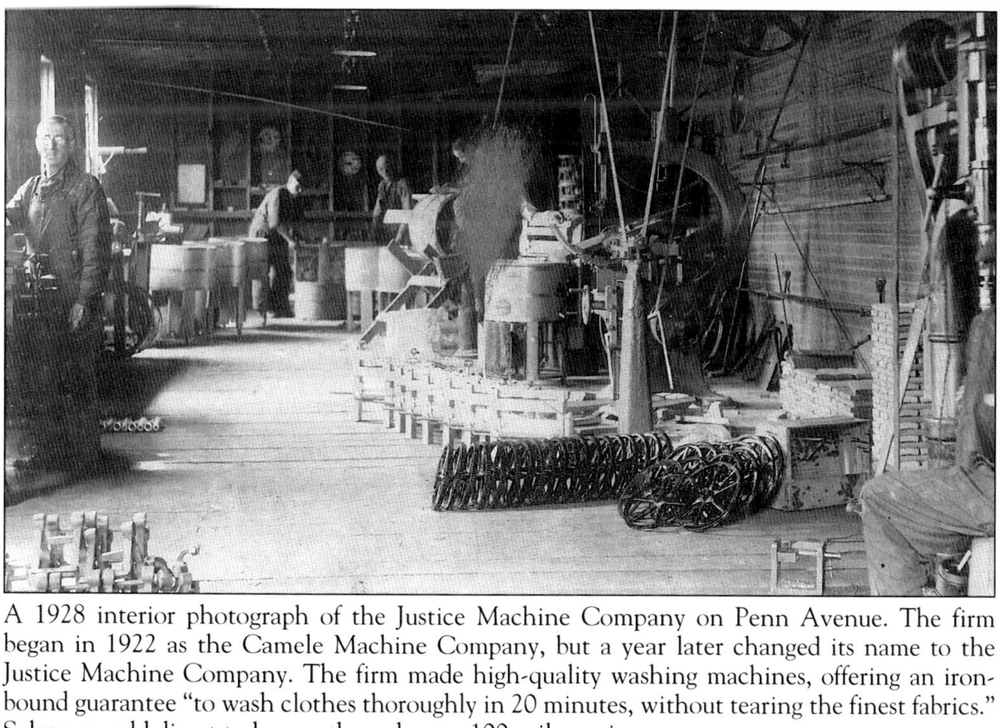

A 1928 interior photograph of the Justice Machine Company on Penn Avenue. The firm began in 1922 as the Camele Machine Company, but a year later changed its name to the Justice Machine Company. The firm made high-quality washing machines, offering an iron-bound guarantee "to wash clothes thoroughly in 20 minutes, without tearing the finest fabrics." Salesmen sold direct to homes throughout a 100-mile territory.

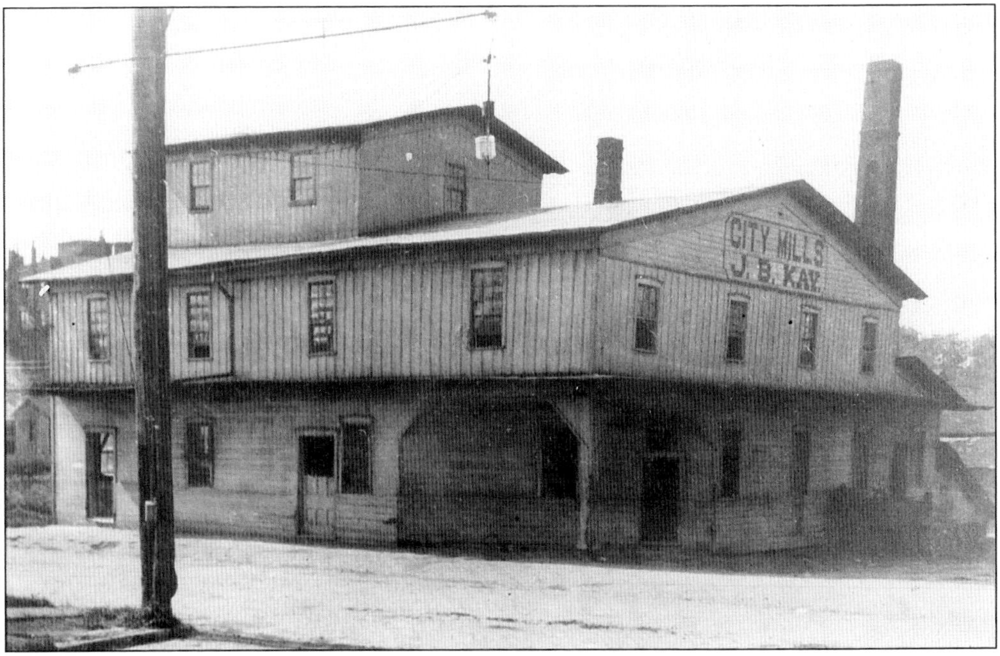

The City Mills, once located on the northwest corner of East Pershing Street and Penn Avenue. In 1877 it was known as the Salem Flour Mills, operated by F.P. Van Syoc. In 1889 it became the City Mills under the ownership of W.P. Stanley, and in 1891 J.B. Kay took it over. The structure was dismantled in 1907 and the wood used to build the Globe Auditorium, which stood until a fire destroyed it in 1917.

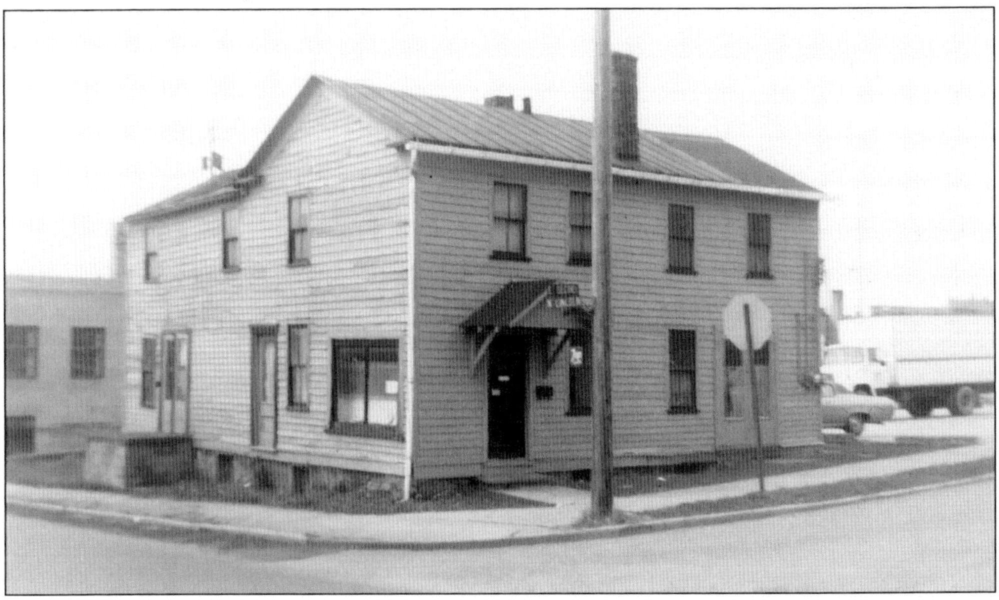

Roy W. Harris's Print Shop, which once occupied the southwest corner of North Lincoln Avenue and East Second Street. Across from the old Salem High School, it had a little school supply store where students could buy tablets, pencils, notebooks, and candy. Roy was the son of Jesse Wright Harris, one of Salem's early printers, who worked in the office of the *Anti-Slavery Bugle*.

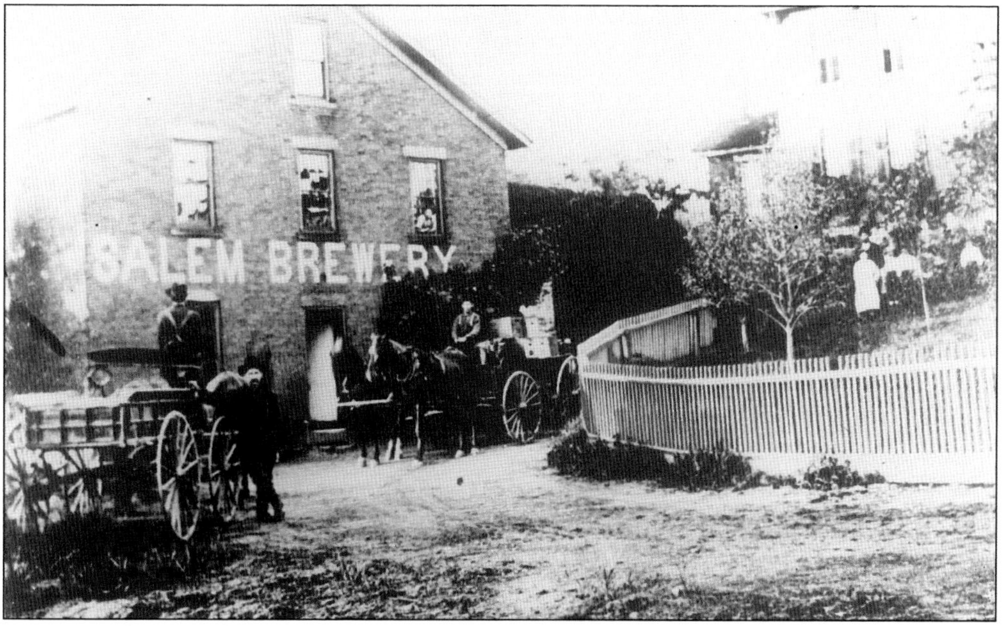

A *c*. 1900 photograph of the Salem Brewery. Located at 448 Franklin Street, it was owned and operated by the L. Schlather Brewing Company of Cleveland. Gustav Zelle and a Mr. Moff were involved in the business, which operated from 1898 to 1905. The building still stands today, now being used as an apartment residence.

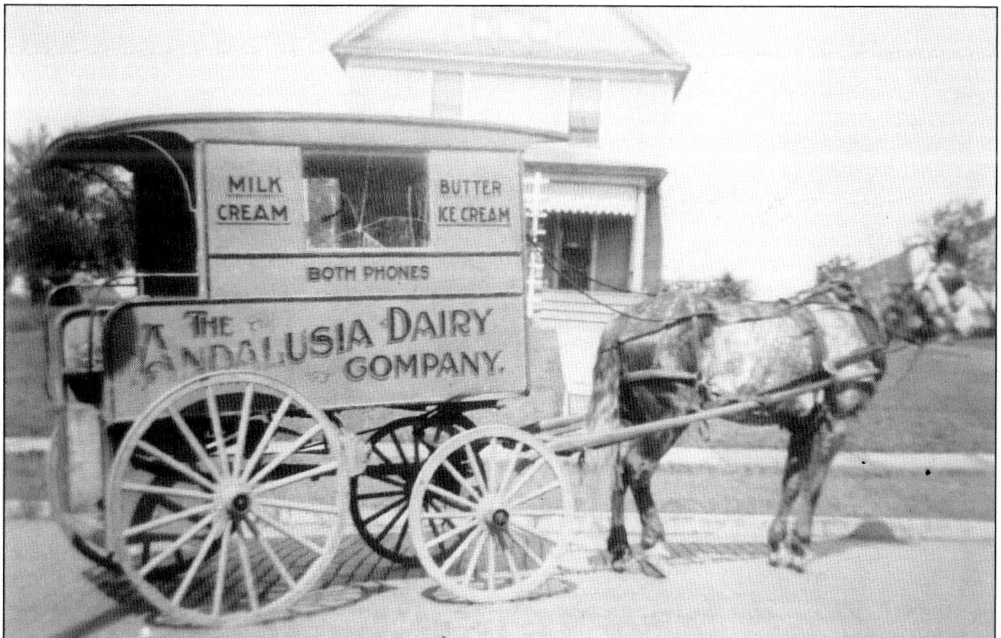

The Andalusia Dairy, one of the longest lasting among the many locally owned dairies that once served the Salem area. It operated for over 60 years, from 1897 to the early 1960s. In 1897 J. Twing Brooks, who had a herd of prize Jersey cattle and needed an outlet for his milk, got together with four other men and formed the company. It began on a farm, and in 1907 moved to South Ellsworth Avenue.

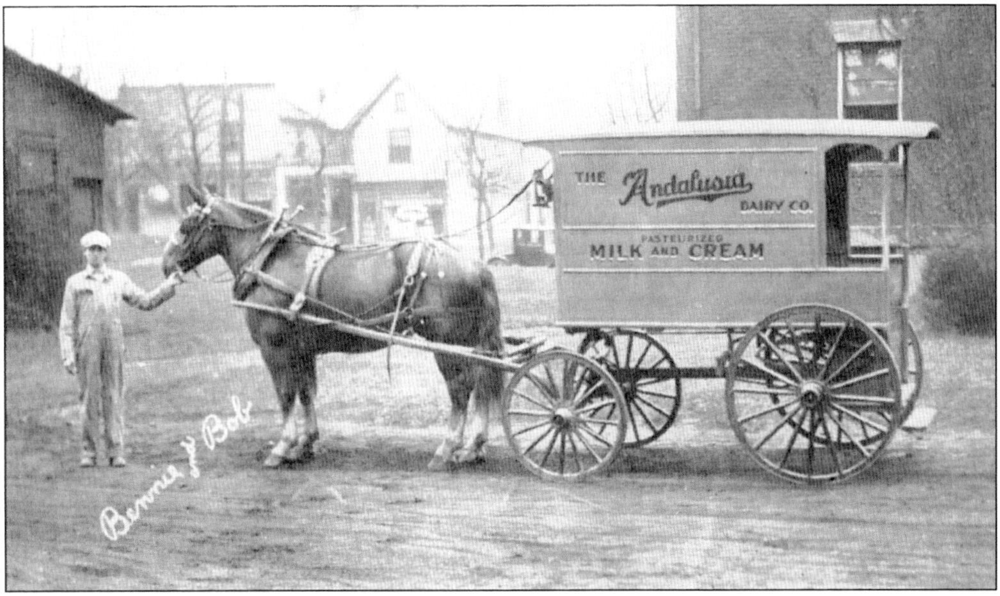

A 1931 photo of Ben Ware Sr. with his horse "Bob" harnessed to an Andalusia Dairy milk wagon. The well-trained horses used for this job knew the milk routes by heart. Milkmen would put eight glass bottles of milk in their carriers and run across backyards with bottles jingling, while the horses kept going to meet them at a given location down the street.

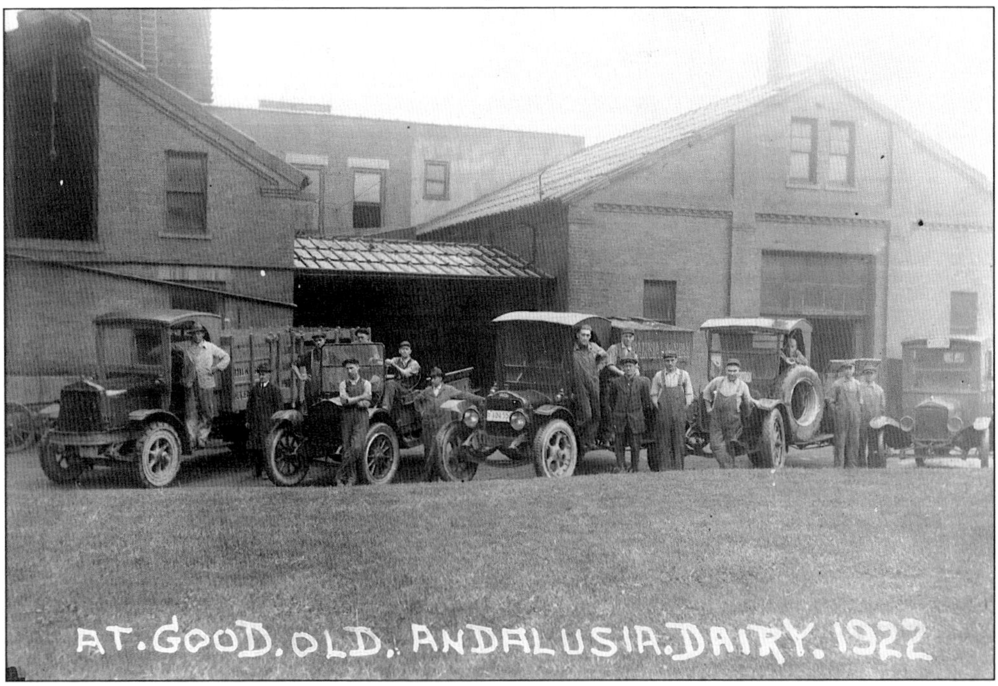

A 1922 photo of Andalusia drivers and trucks taken at the back of the dairy on South Ellsworth Avenue. Among those shown are Art Herron, George Rogers, Jesse Black, Lee Hollinger, Fred Minamyer, Jim Herron, Ray Beck and Harry Bichsel. An early customer of this dairy was the Pennsylvania Railroad. When the trains stopped in Salem, Pullman cars were supplied with milk, cream, and butter for their diners.

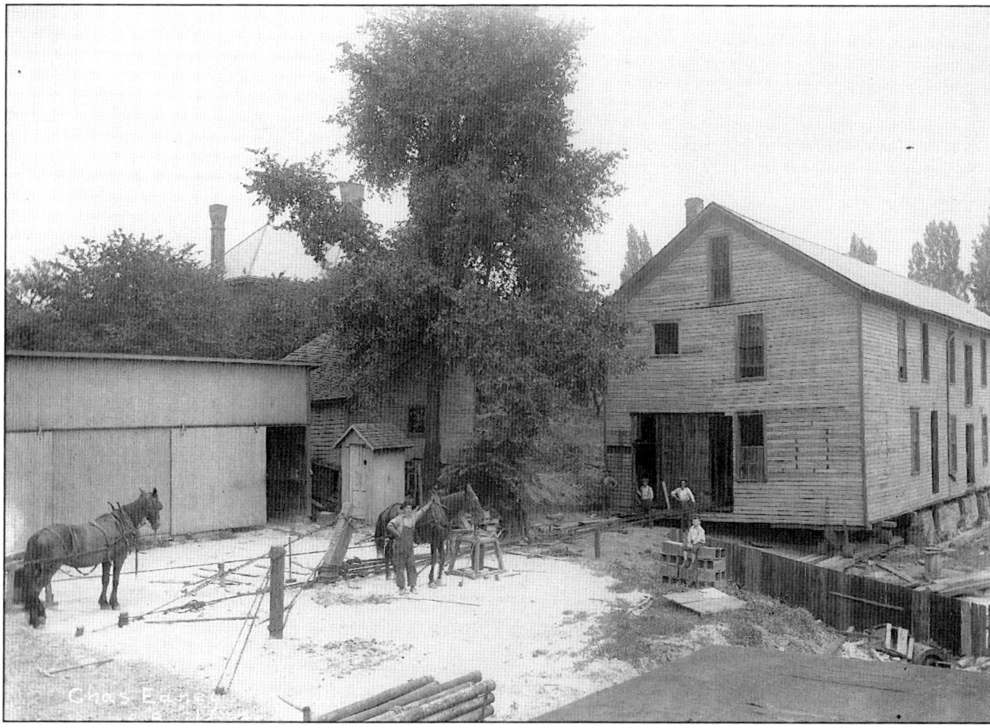

Charles Edney, who was in the business of moving buildings in the late 1800s. He is shown here working on one of his projects. Note the elaborate system of pulleys, and the outhouse.

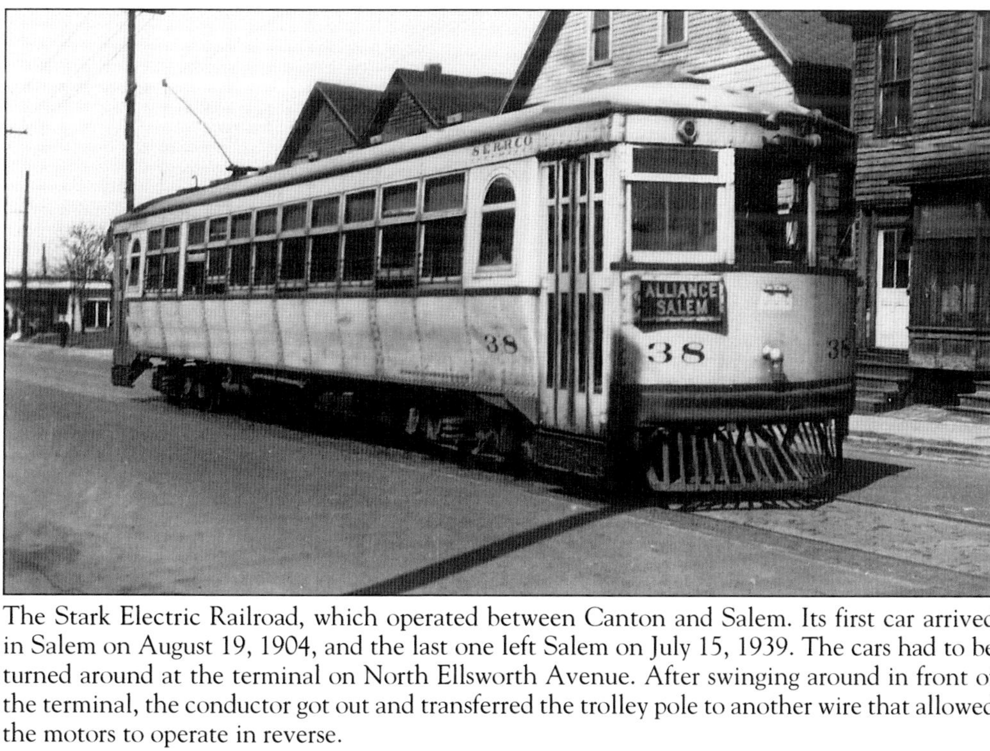

The Stark Electric Railroad, which operated between Canton and Salem. Its first car arrived in Salem on August 19, 1904, and the last one left Salem on July 15, 1939. The cars had to be turned around at the terminal on North Ellsworth Avenue. After swinging around in front of the terminal, the conductor got out and transferred the trolley pole to another wire that allowed the motors to operate in reverse.

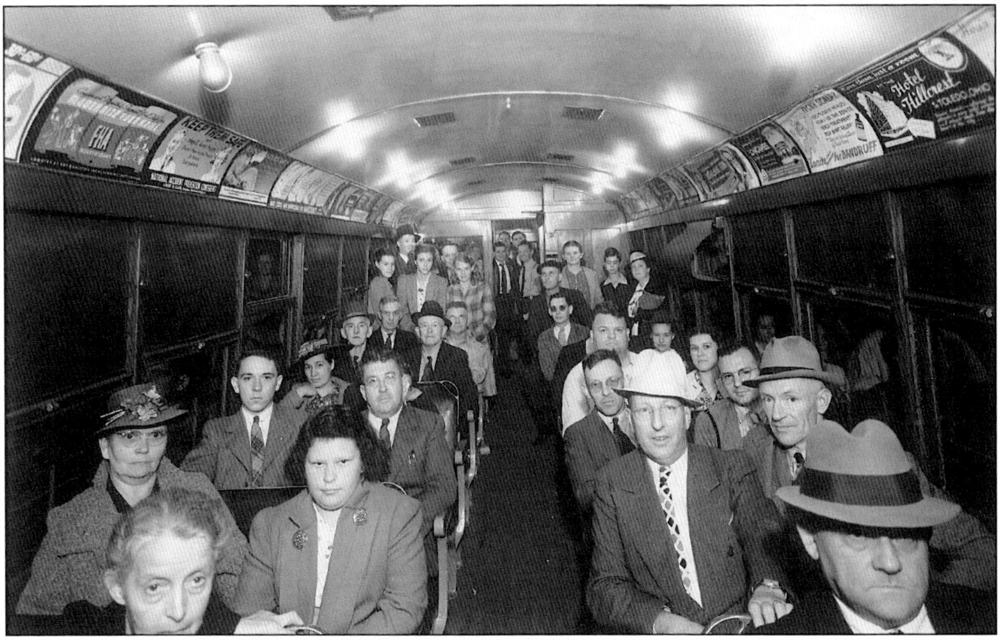

A rare view inside a Stark Electric Railroad car. A sign inside reads: "Do Not Talk to the Motorman While the Streetcar is in Motion." The inter-urban was a popular way of getting to the Country Club and nearby towns. Students commuted to Mount Union College and studied on the way. Some young people met their future spouses on the streetcar.

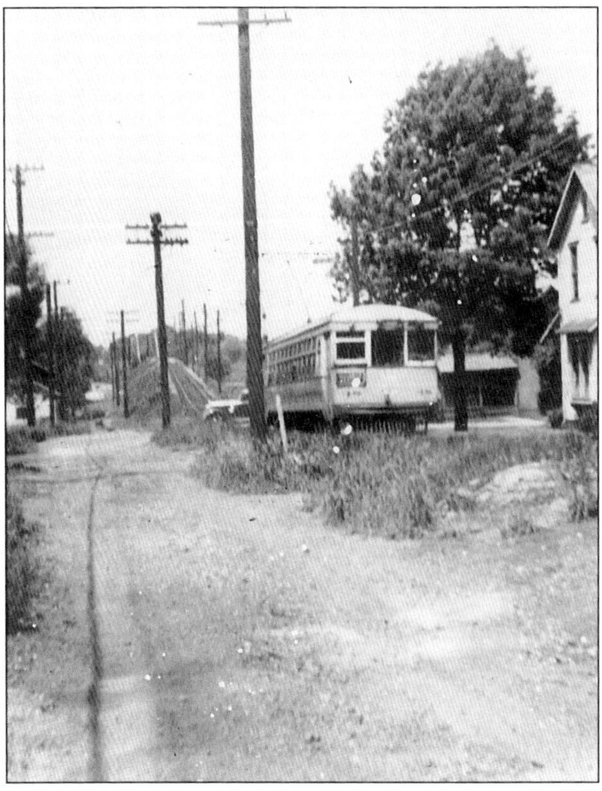

Stark Electric's inter-urban car 44 in the late 1930s. The car is coming from Alliance, and is shown heading for the Salem terminal after crossing the trestle over the Pennsylvania Railroad tracks. Buses took over after 1939.

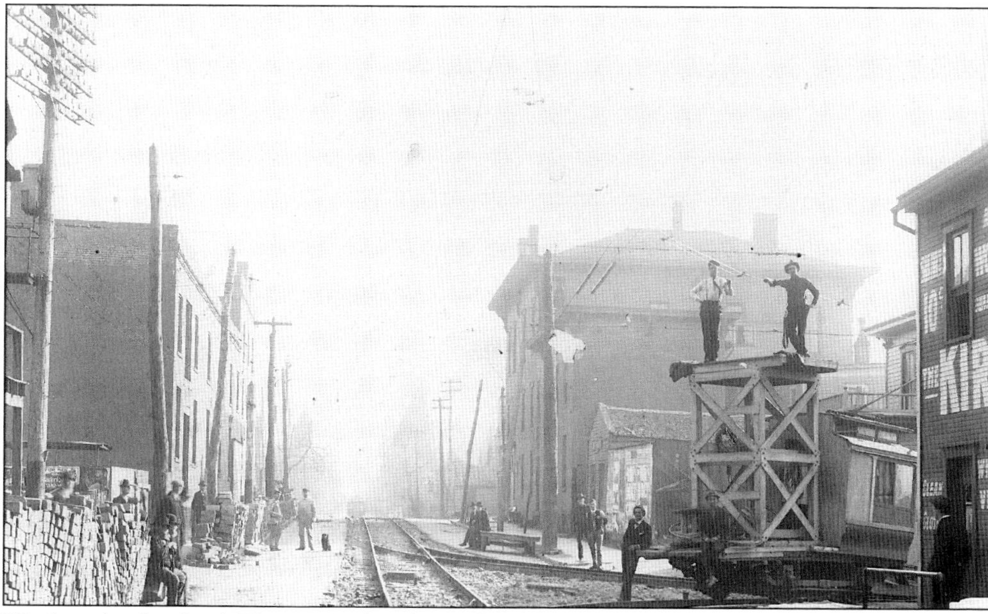

Workers for the Stark Electric Railroad installing track and electric wires in 1904 for its interurban line to Salem. Streets had to be torn up wherever track was laid. The track rested on thousands of wooden railroad ties. Stark Electric was called the "bachelor railroad" in the early days because its directors were bachelors.

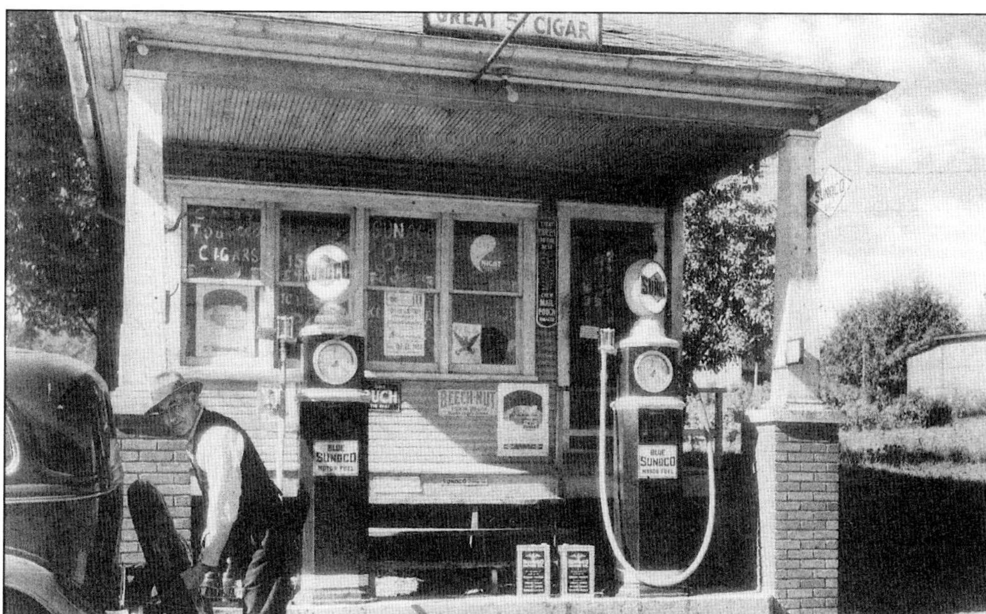

William H. Bradley's Sunoco Service Station on the Newgarden Road, in front of his home. The station operated from 1930 to 1940. It had a small grocery store that stocked a wide variety of penny candy. Note the 5¢ cigar sign. Both this building and the Bradley house are still standing.

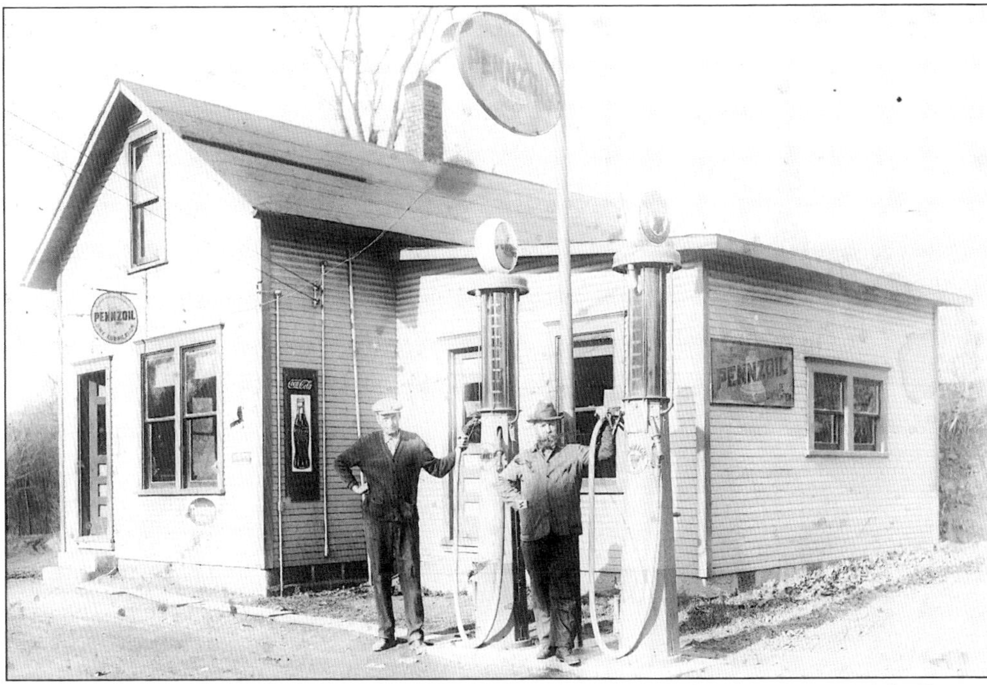

William Crooks and Frank Van Winkle in front of their Pennzoil gas station in Millville, just east of Salem. The photo was taken in the 1920s. By the 1930s there were a large number of stations in the Salem area—one on practically every corner. Familiar signs no longer with us include Shell, Texaco, Pure Oil, Phillips 66, Sinclair, Freedom, City Service, and Gulf.

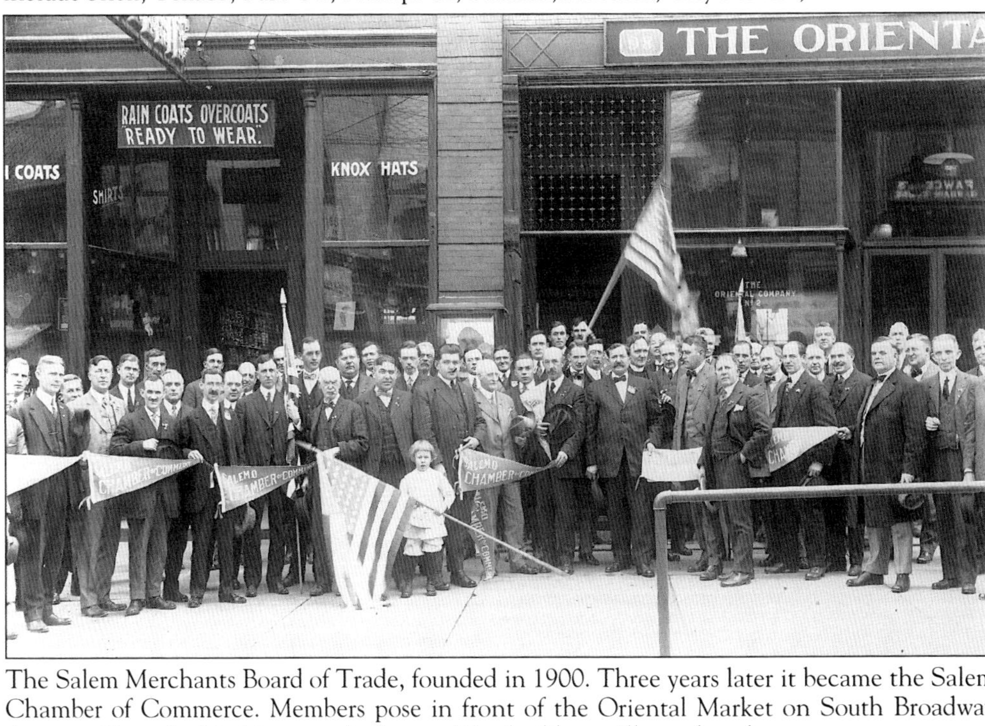

The Salem Merchants Board of Trade, founded in 1900. Three years later it became the Salem Chamber of Commerce. Members pose in front of the Oriental Market on South Broadway Avenue. Note the hitching post for horses. The building still stands today.

Five

People

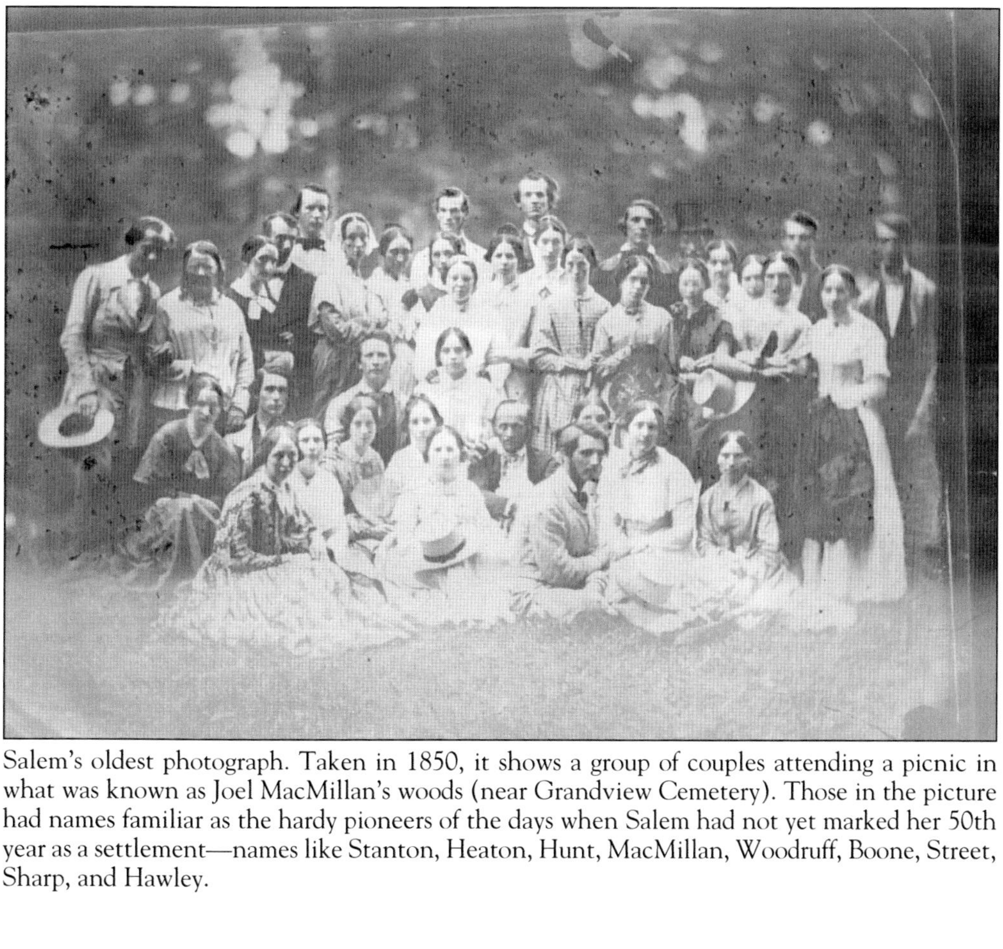

Salem's oldest photograph. Taken in 1850, it shows a group of couples attending a picnic in what was known as Joel MacMillan's woods (near Grandview Cemetery). Those in the picture had names familiar as the hardy pioneers of the days when Salem had not yet marked her 50th year as a settlement—names like Stanton, Heaton, Hunt, MacMillan, Woodruff, Boone, Street, Sharp, and Hawley.

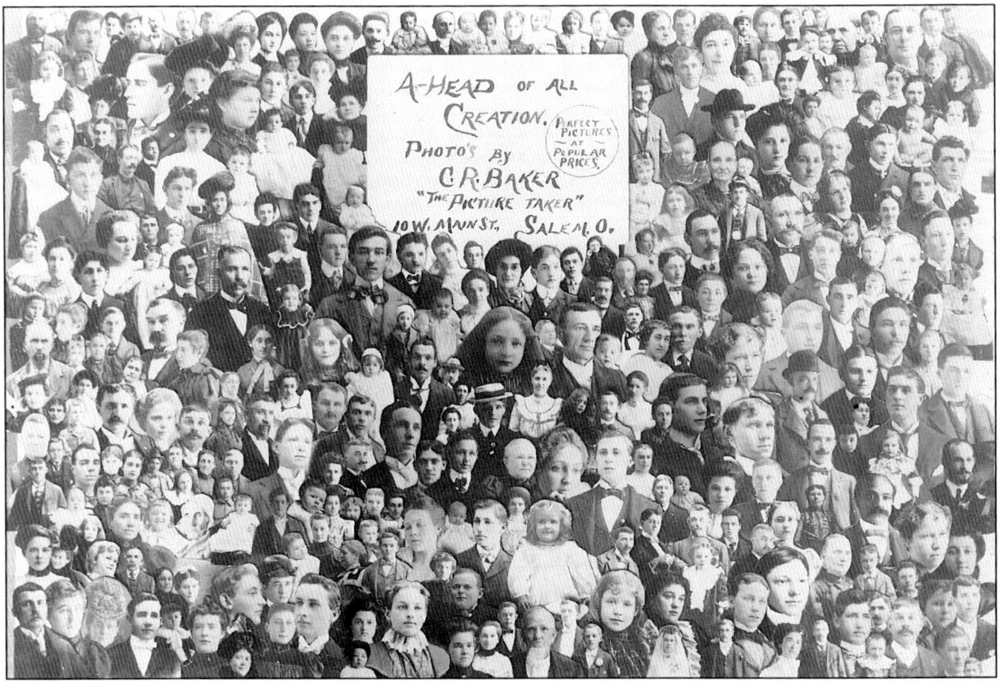

A composite layout of the hundreds of Salem people C.R. Baker photographed when he operated his studio on West State Street, shortly after the turn of the century. Mr. Baker was also Salem's first Ford dealer in 1906, and drove one of the first cars made by that company—a Model N. His wife was the first woman in northeastern Ohio to drive an automobile.

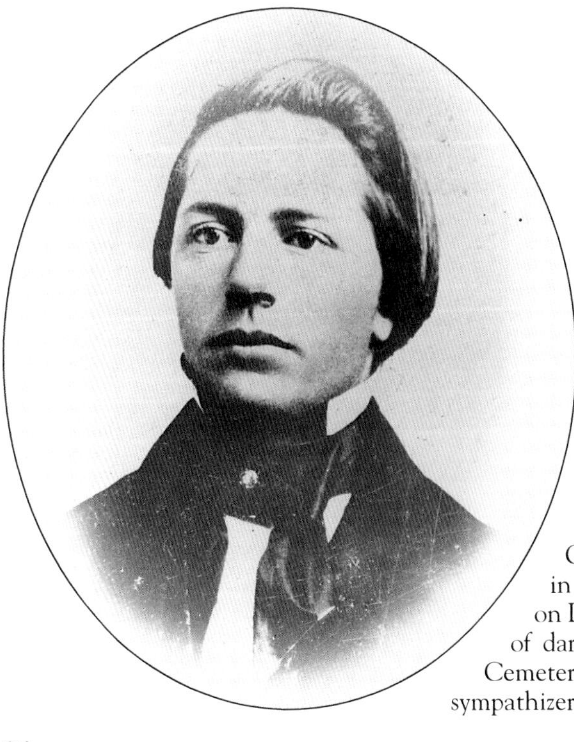

Edwin Coppoc, a Quaker and martyr to the anti-slavery cause. Coppoc followed John Brown in the Harpers Ferry raid in 1859 and was tried, condemned, and executed at Charles Town, Virginia. First interred in Winona, his body was moved to Salem on December 30, 1859. A tall, pointed shaft of dark sandstone marks his grave at Hope Cemetery. There was concern that pro-slavery sympathizers might remove the coffin.

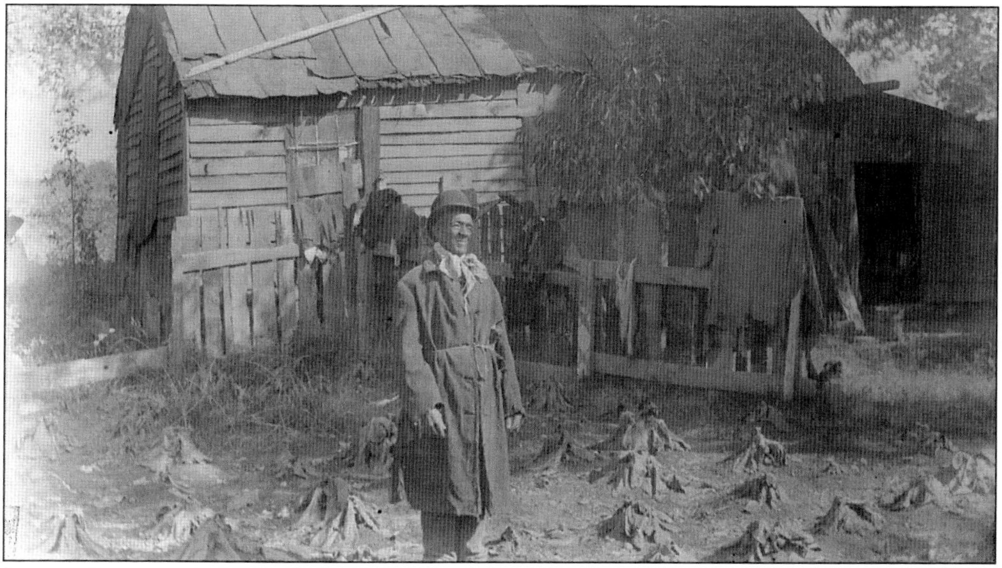

Strotter Brown, an ex-slave from Virginia, in front of his house on Elm Avenue. During the Civil War he furnished a Salemite with some of his fine, home-grown tobacco. After the war he rode into town on his white mare, Jenny, looking for his friend. He settled on a small plot of ground and began making baskets and raising tobacco and vegetables. His baskets are now collectibles.

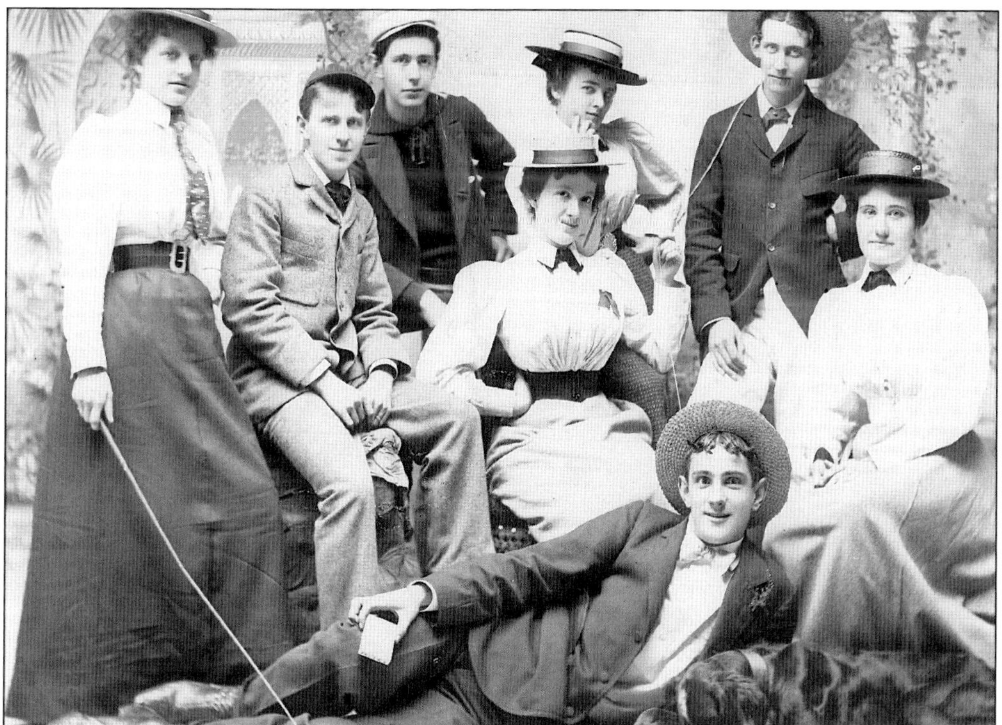

Theater performers on stage. All are beautifully dressed and well accustomed to appearing before camera. The photo was taken in the early 1900s by a professional photographer. Note the dog in front.

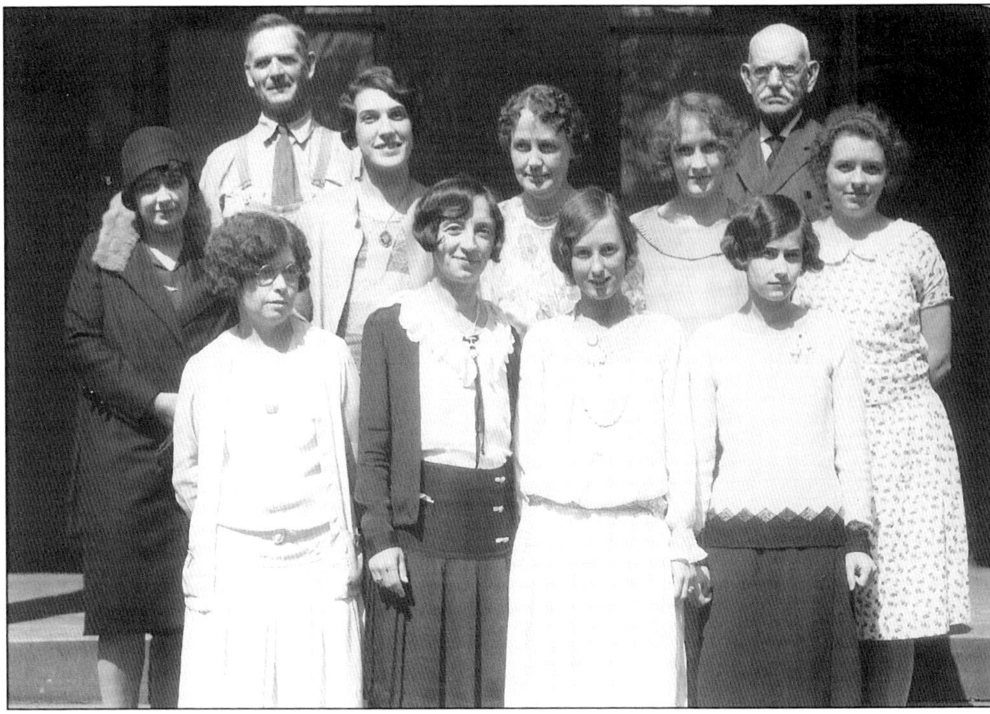

Elementary teachers of the Fourth Street School. The photo was taken October 28, 1929. From left to right, they are as follows: (front row) Miss Todd, Inez Hisler, Mary Yarwood, and Miss Houlin; (middle row) Miss Carnes, Miss Leipper, Miss Hoopes, Miss Floyd, and Miss Allen; (back row) Mr. Whinnery and Otto Juergens.

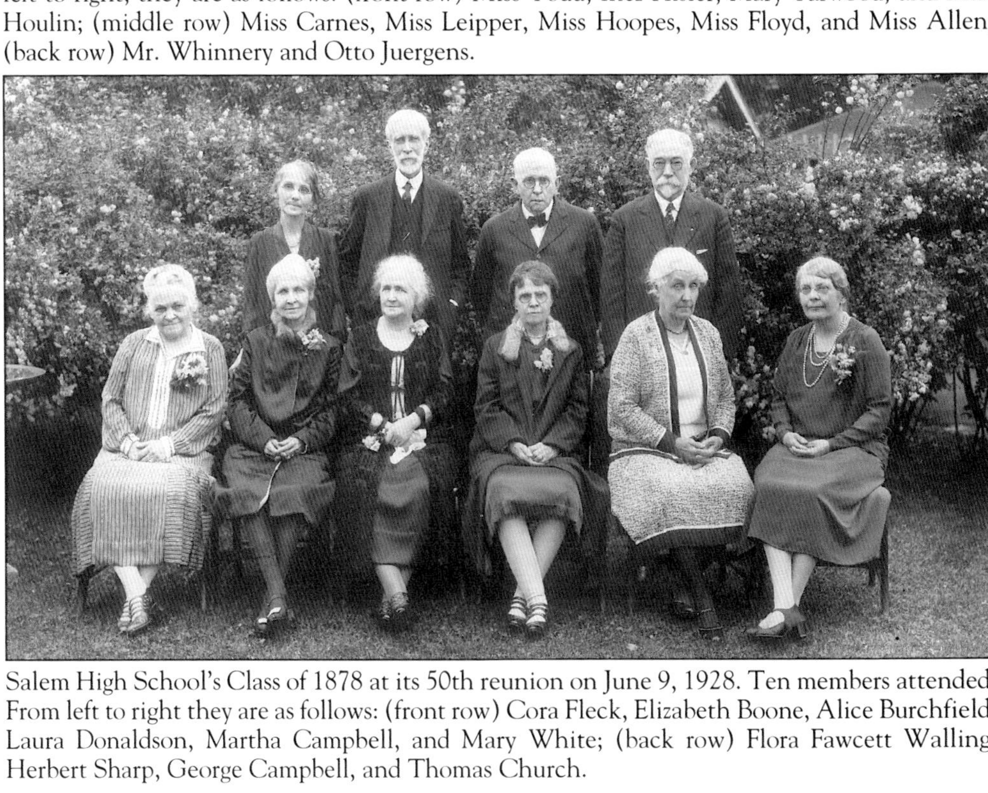

Salem High School's Class of 1878 at its 50th reunion on June 9, 1928. Ten members attended. From left to right they are as follows: (front row) Cora Fleck, Elizabeth Boone, Alice Burchfield, Laura Donaldson, Martha Campbell, and Mary White; (back row) Flora Fawcett Walling, Herbert Sharp, George Campbell, and Thomas Church.

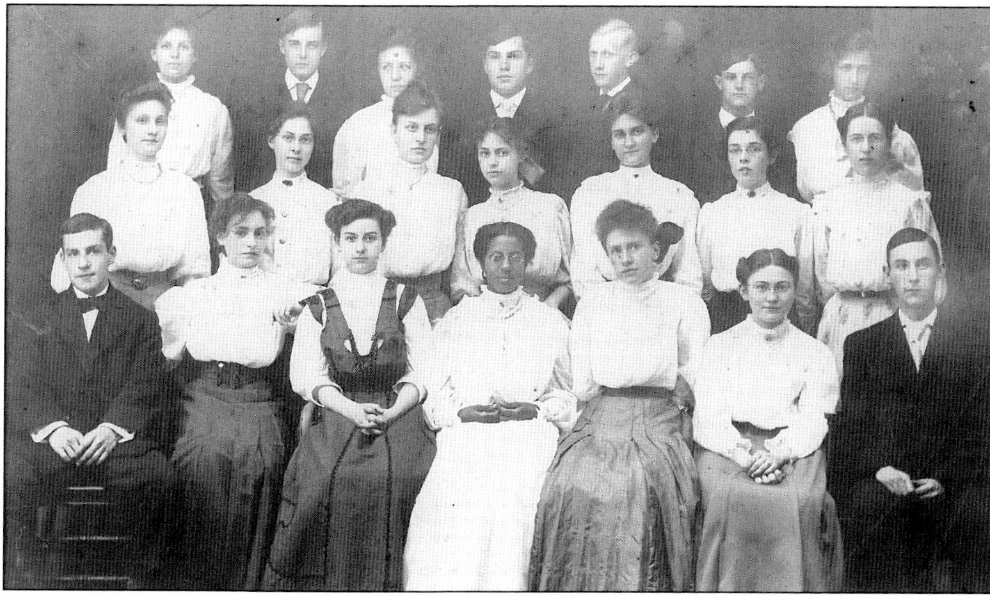

The Salem High School Class of 1906, consisting of 15 girls and 6 boys. There were only two girls in the first commencement June 15, 1865—Anna (Kuhn) Weaver and Lauretta Barnaby. The first male graduate was Willis Weaver in 1866. The first black student to graduate was Felix Williams in 1882.

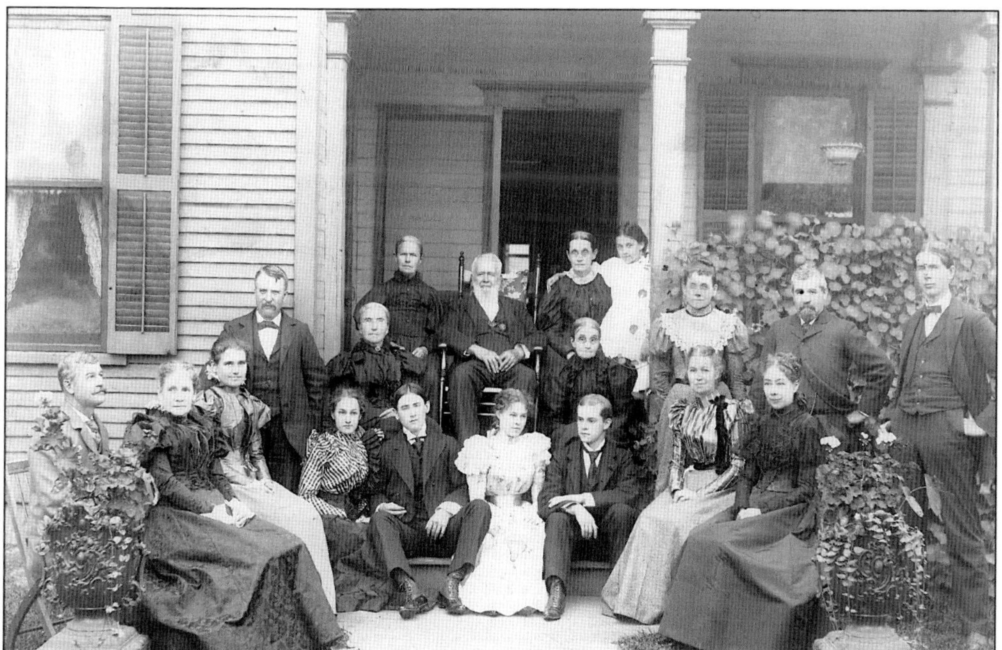

The James M. Woodruff family, a prominent one in Salem. James (in the chair) owned and operated the J. Woodruff and Sons stove manufacturing company. Born near Salem, New Jersey, in 1817, he came to Salem, Ohio, in 1836 and learned the blacksmith trade. In 1848 he joined in partnership with Isaac Snyder and they began making stoves. Mr. Woodruff eventually took over the firm.

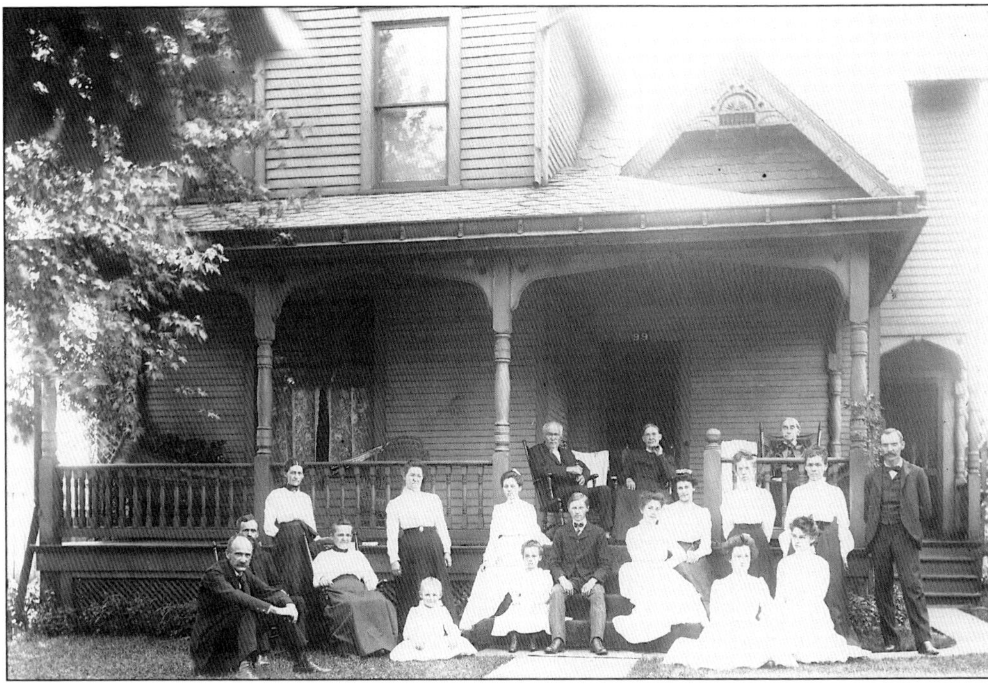

The Amos Steele family on the front porch of their home on Garfield (361 North Lincoln) Avenue in a turn-of-the-century scene. The house still stands today.

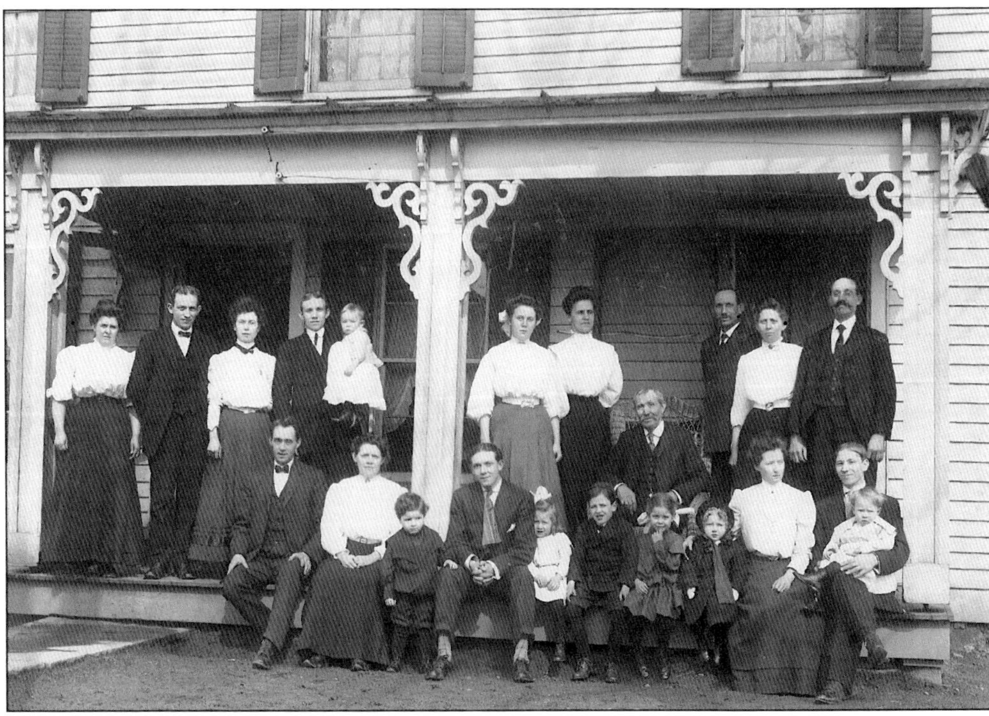

A 1908 photo of the Conrad Shaffer family. Conrad operated a dairy farm and grocery store. Part of the old store still stands today on the northwest corner of East State Street and Hawley Avenue.

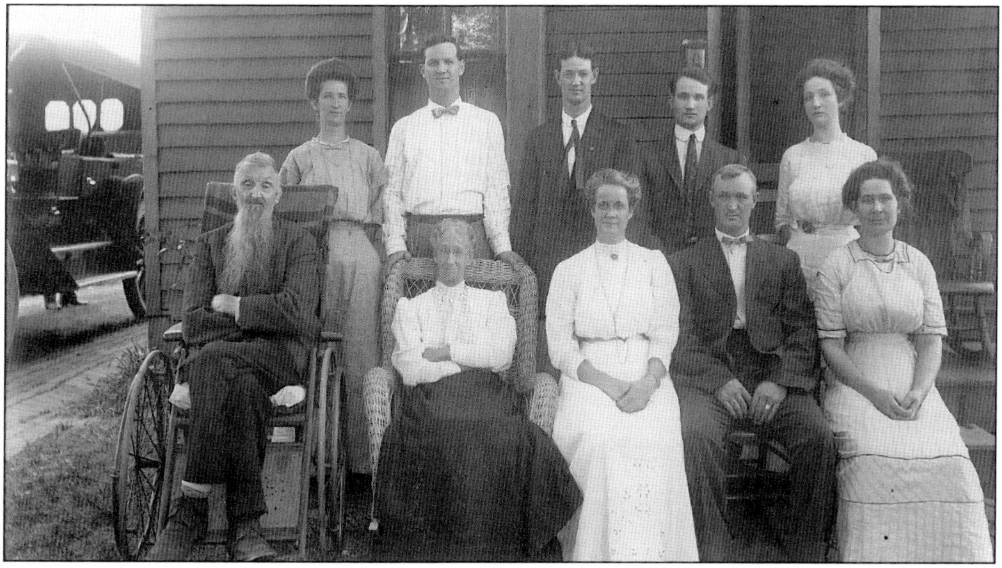

The Frank Gibbons family in 1909 in front of their home on West Third Street. One of this family's ancestors was General John Gibbon, a Union Civil War officer whose troops stood against Pickett's charge of Cemetery Ridge at Gettysburg. He also participated in Lee's surrender at Appomattox. In 1876 Gibbon was involved with Custer's 7th Cavalry in the Battle of Little Bighorn. Gibbon is buried at Arlington Cemetery.

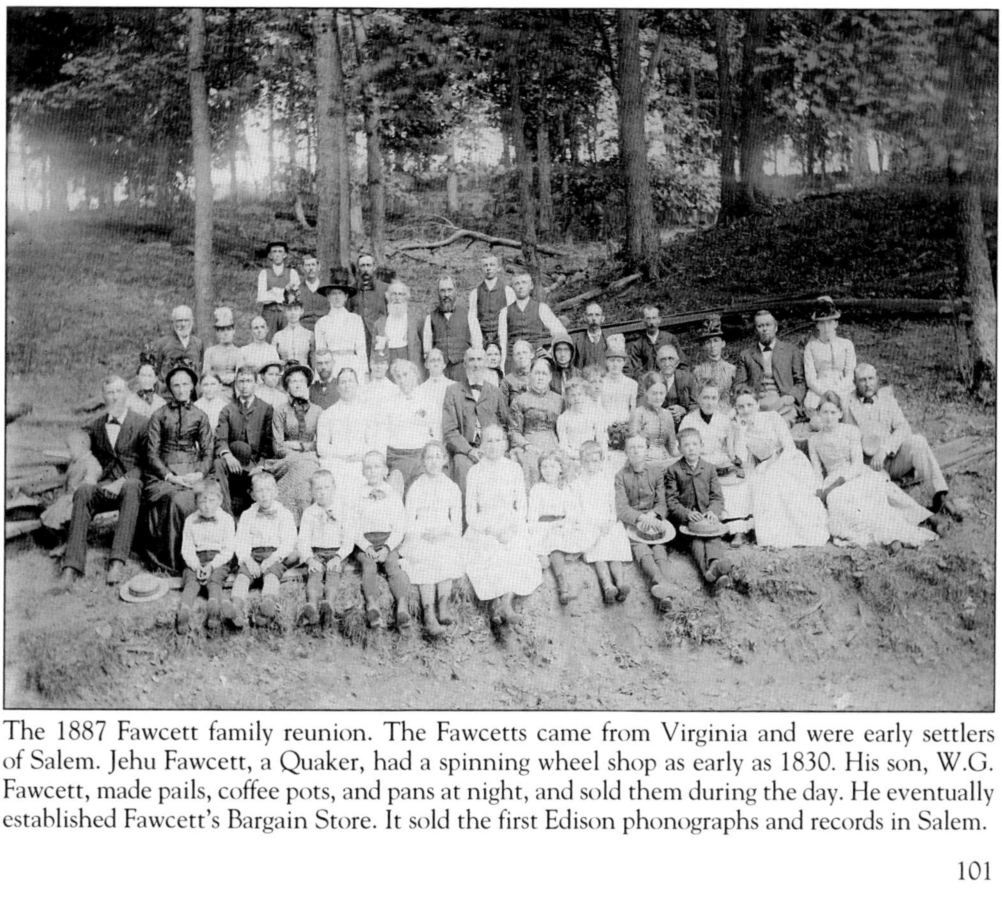

The 1887 Fawcett family reunion. The Fawcetts came from Virginia and were early settlers of Salem. Jehu Fawcett, a Quaker, had a spinning wheel shop as early as 1830. His son, W.G. Fawcett, made pails, coffee pots, and pans at night, and sold them during the day. He eventually established Fawcett's Bargain Store. It sold the first Edison phonographs and records in Salem.

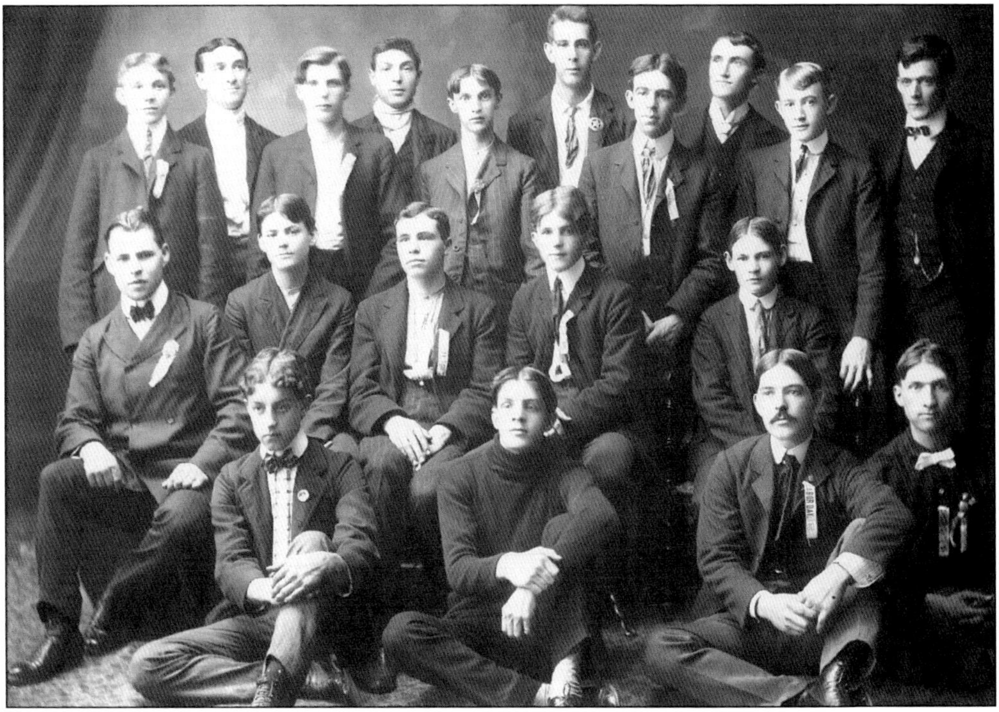

A group of young club members in a photograph taken on Labor Day, 1902.

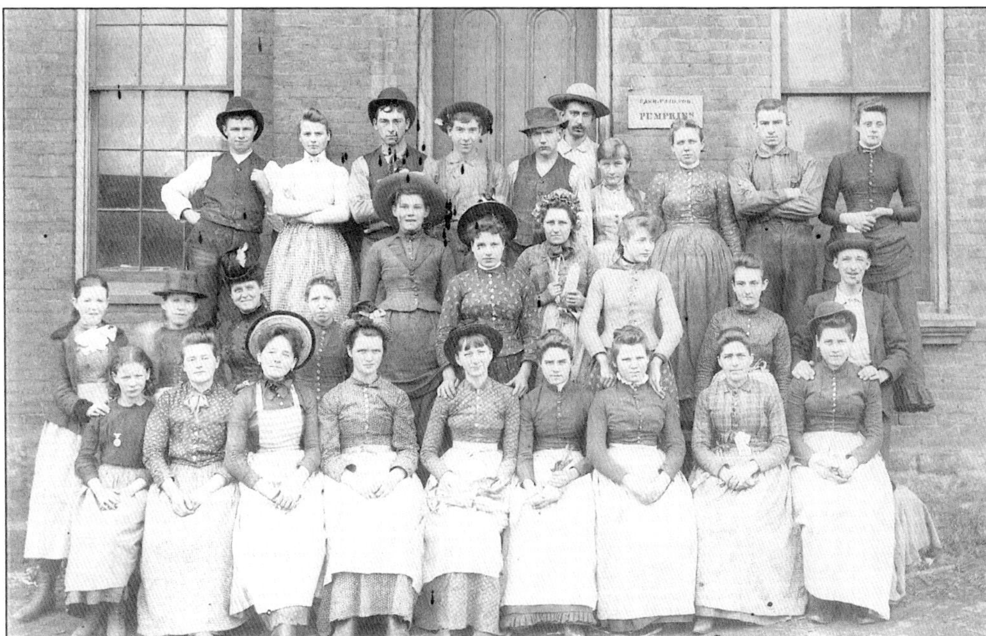

Employees in front of the J.B. McNab Company's canning factory on South Ellsworth Avenue. McNab had the distinction of being the first in the United States to produce canned pumpkin, and for years had a monopoly on the business. The sign reads: "Cash Paid For Pumpkins." His firm canned many kinds of fruits and vegetables, and manufactured cans. This building still stands today.

A 1898 photograph of employees of the Hayes Dry Goods Store, with Albert Hayes at the far right. For 80 years C.I. Hayes and his son Albert operated the Hayes Dry Goods Store on the northeast corner of East State Street and North Lundy Avenue. Their slogan was "Hayes for Linens." The Hayes were Quakers and lived on North Lundy Avenue behind the store.

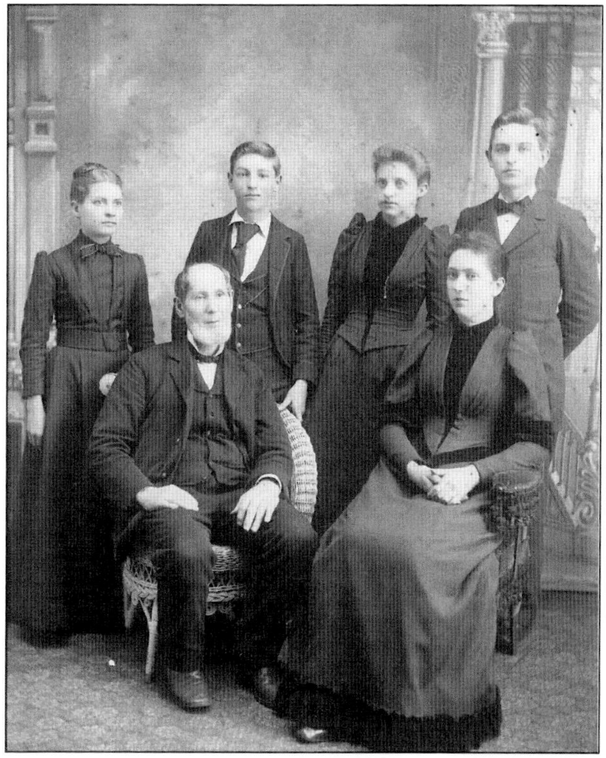

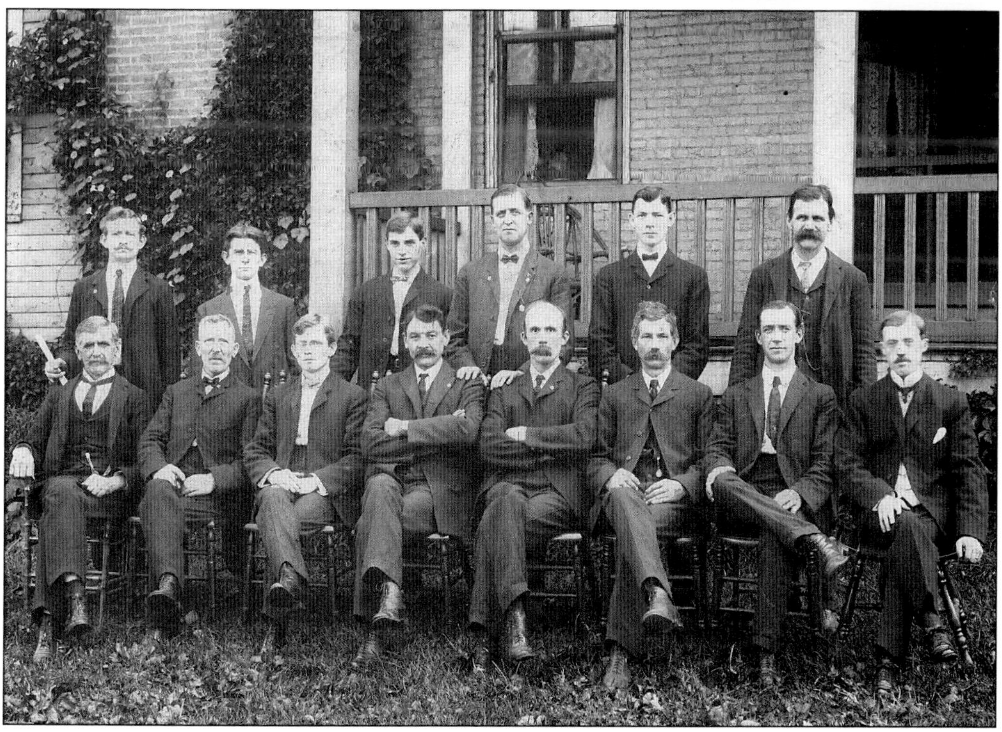

The Trades and Labor Council, 1907. There was considerable manufacturing industry in Salem at this time, with labor-management relations being very good.

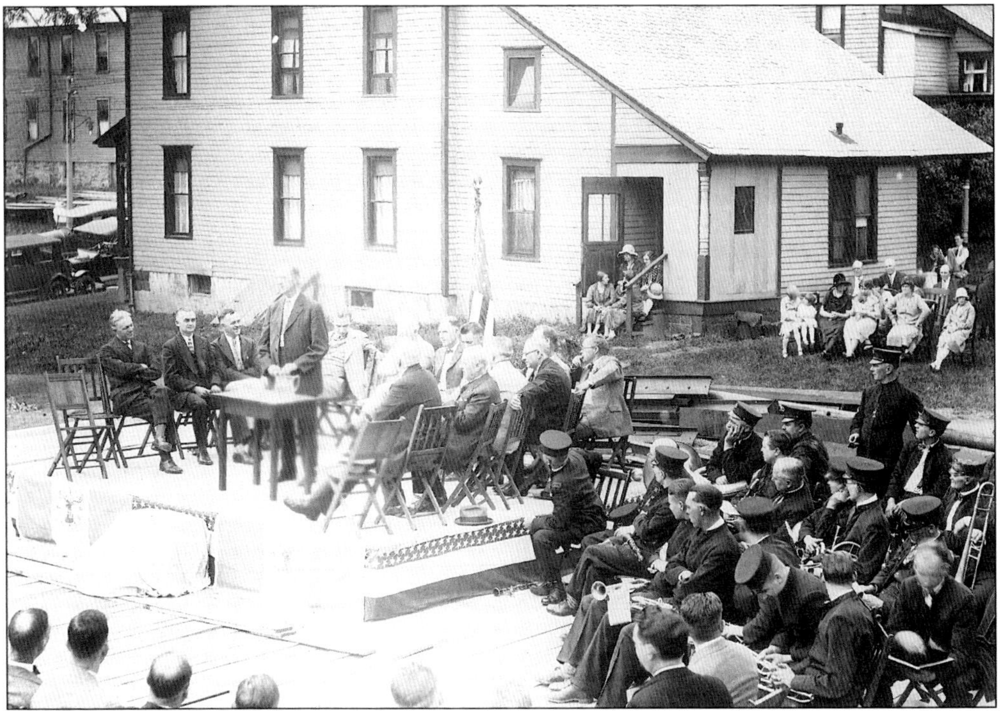

A September 22, 1926 photograph showing members of the Elks Lodge at a ceremony for laying the cornerstone for their new facility on East State Street. The facility was completed April 16, 1927. The Quaker City Band participated in the ceremony. Salem's Elks Lodge was instituted on June 14, 1895.

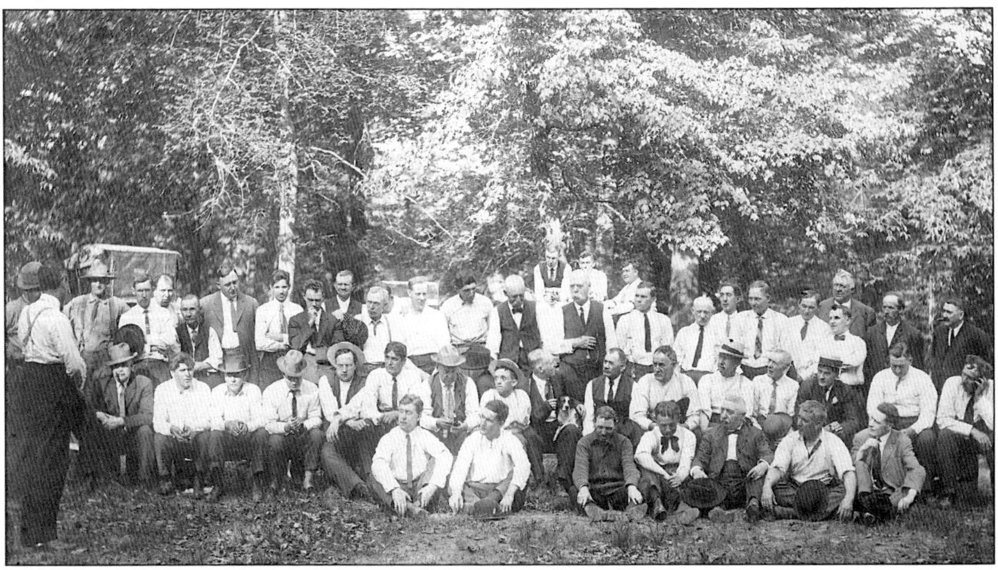

The Daisy Club of Salem, a men's social organization that met two Sundays every month above Redinger's Saloon on South Broadway Avenue. One of their special events was a clambake, held at Fred Redinger's farm on the Albany Road. There were rabbit hunts and rabbit dinners, too. The club also hosted the city's annual Halloween parade, as well as the firemen races along South Broadway Avenue. This photo was taken in the early 1900s.

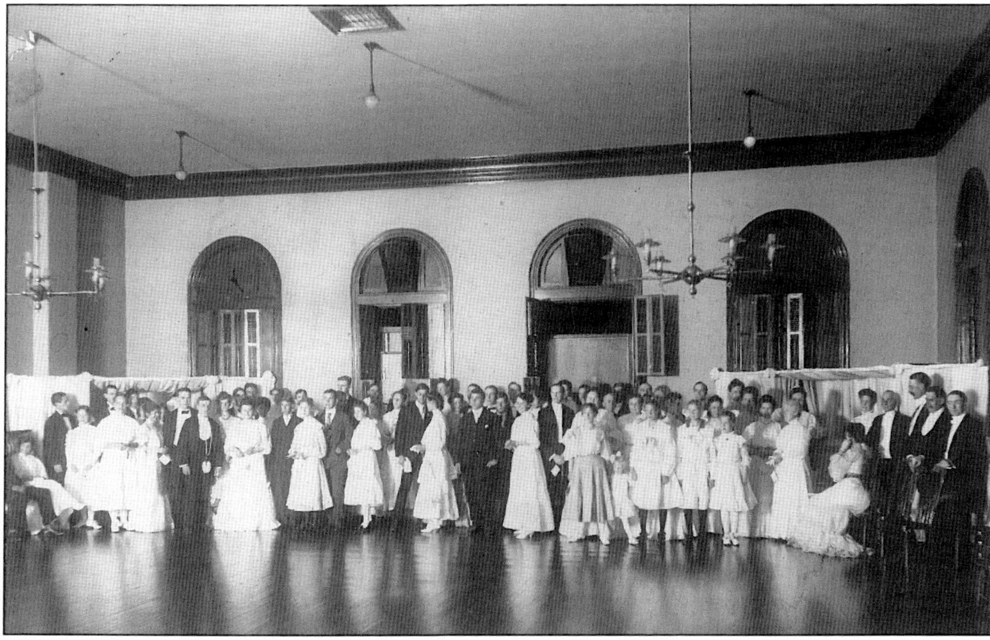

The aristocratic Calumet Club, organized in 1895. The club held its meetings on the second floor of the old Pioneer (Arbaugh) Building, once located on the northeast corner of East State Street and North Lincoln Avenue. Its dance hall was at the front of the third floor. The club's tea dances and Christmas dinner dances were always highlights of the social season. Most of their affairs were formal, conducted with great dignity and decorum.

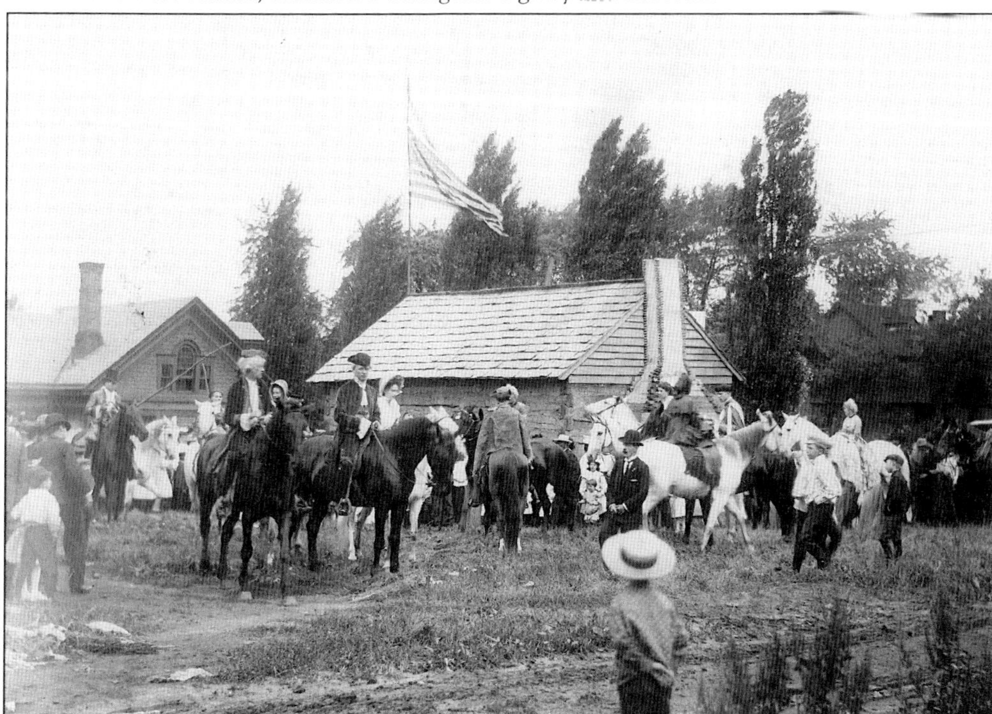

A pageant held on horseback near an old log house during the Salem Centennial celebration.

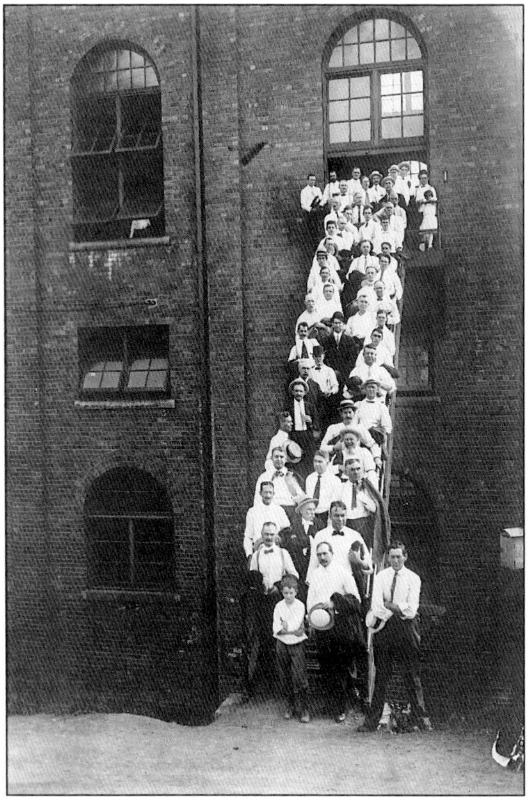

A December 20, 1907 photograph of a group of businessmen and city officials on the steps of the Y&O Railroad power house at West Point, Ohio. The Y&O electric inter-urban operated from 1907 to 1931 between Salem and East Liverpool. It took over the track running between Salem and Washingtonville that originally was used by the Salem Railroad.

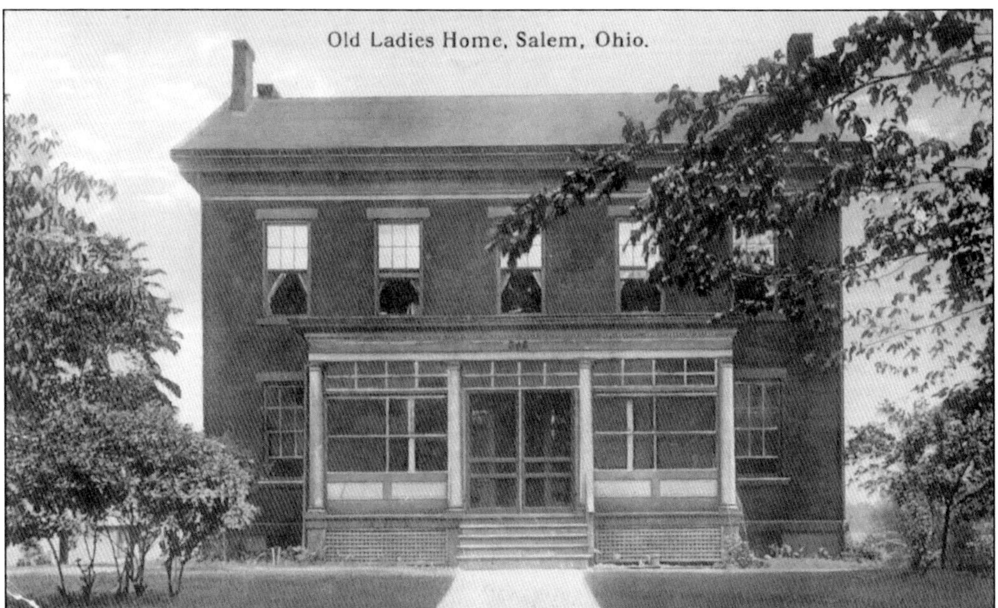

The Home for Aged Women (now known as the Century House) at 1171 East State Street, established October 4, 1888. Originally the property was owned by Phillip Evans. The 1887 group that made this facility possible was headed by Mrs. Joseph Koll.

Six

Homes

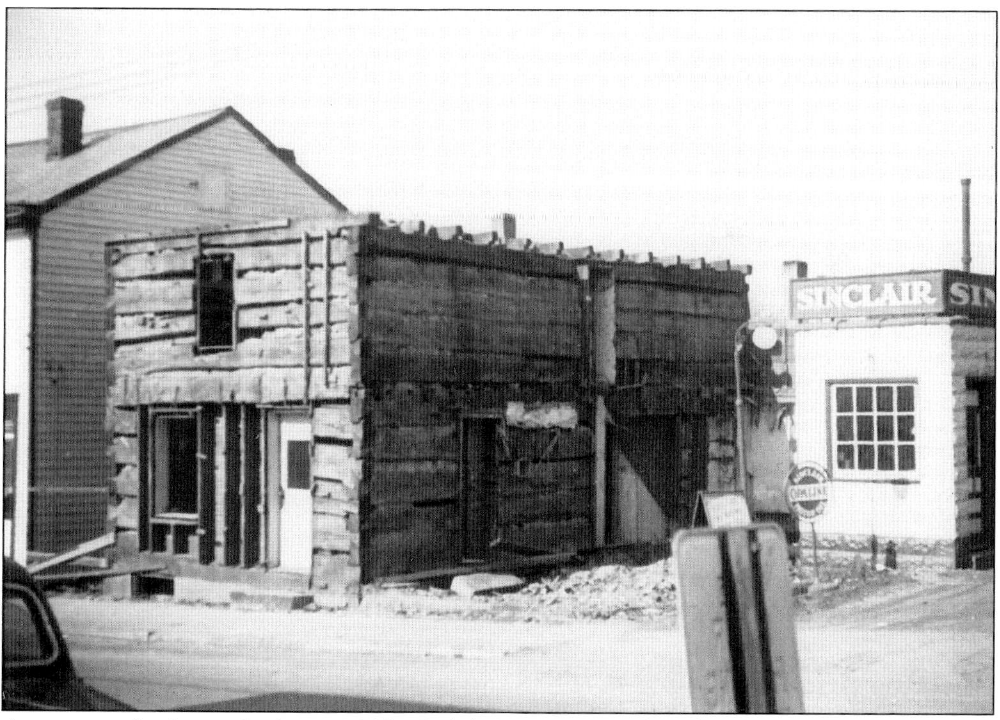

A two-story log house built in 1806 by Zadok Street Sr., co-founder of Salem. This was one of the first houses built in the new settlement. When it was torn down in 1937, some of the logs were saved and used to build a replica of the cabin for the local museum. The photo was taken on West State Street.

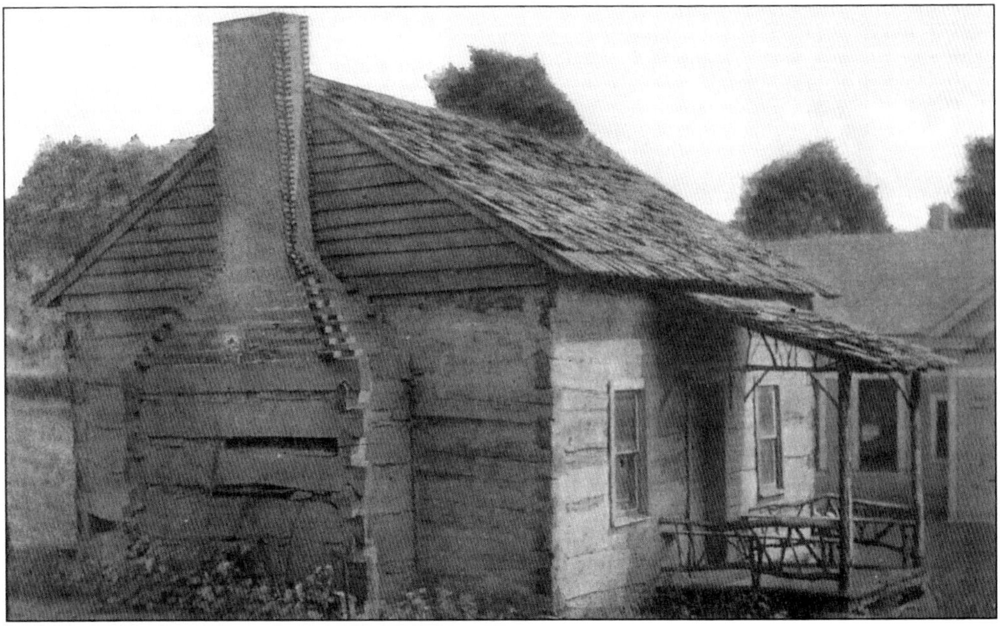

A 1906 photo of the Centennial Log Cabin. The structure was built in the early 1800s. It no longer exists.

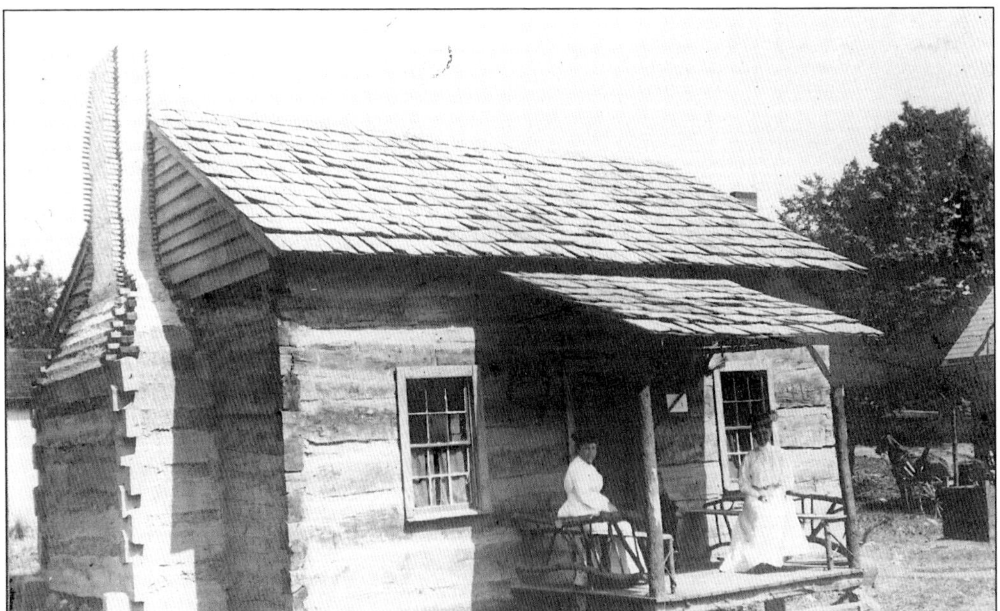

The Centennial Log Cabin, located in 1906 on Garfield (North Lincoln) Avenue near the Salem Junior High School. Frank Cook, an antique dealer, lived here. On September 9, 1914, the cabin was dismantled and reconstructed as a miners' shanty at a coal mine northeast of the city. Note the wood fireplace chimney, clay mortar filling the gap between the logs, and the handmade shingles (shakes) of white cedar.

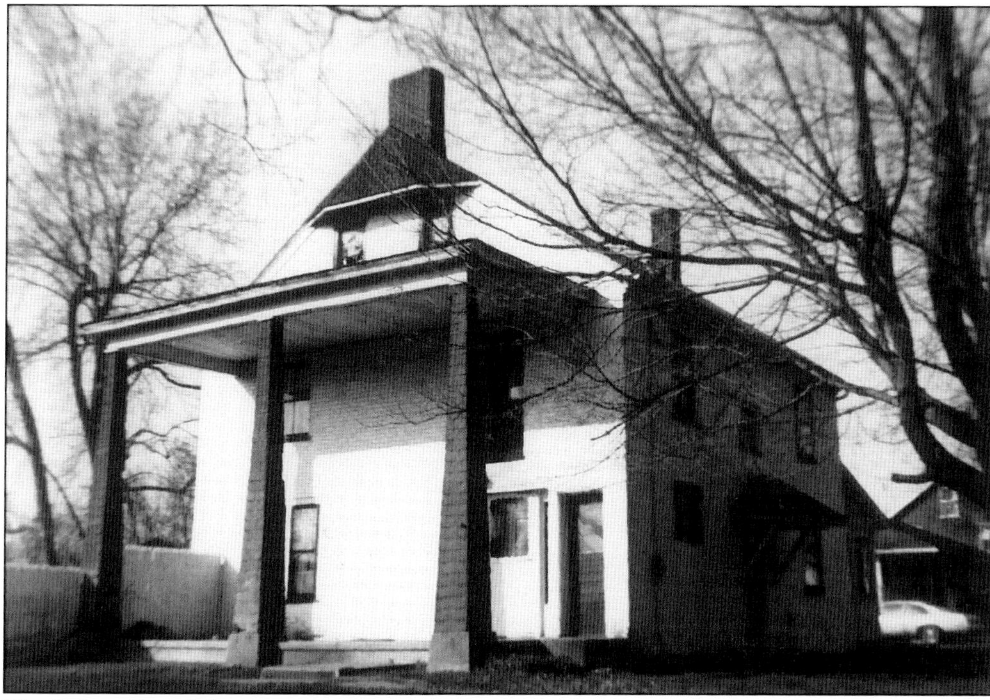

The Robert French house at 291 Jennings Avenue. This is one of Salem's oldest houses. Robert accompanied the Zadok Street Sr. family from Salem, New Jersey, and married Anna Street on February 25, 1807. The couple built this house using 14-inch square, hewn timbers set together by notch and pin, without nails. The cistern is 18 feet deep.

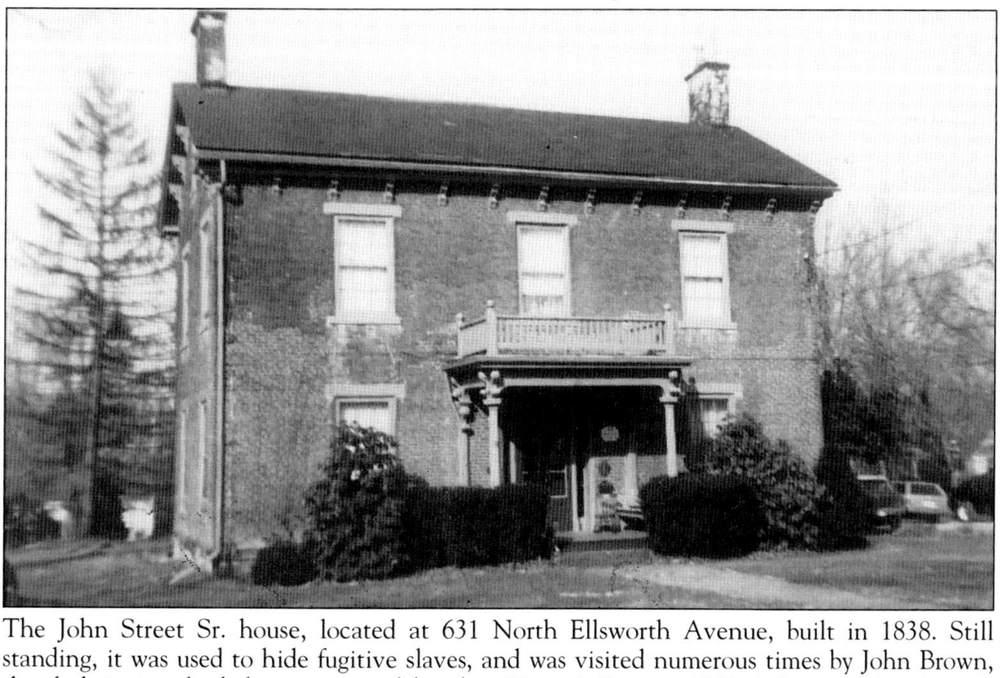

The John Street Sr. house, located at 631 North Ellsworth Avenue, built in 1838. Still standing, it was used to hide fugitive slaves, and was visited numerous times by John Brown, the abolitionist who led an unsuccessful raid on Harper's Ferry in 1859. Salem was the Western Headquarters for the Anti-Slavery Society, and a station on the Underground Railroad.

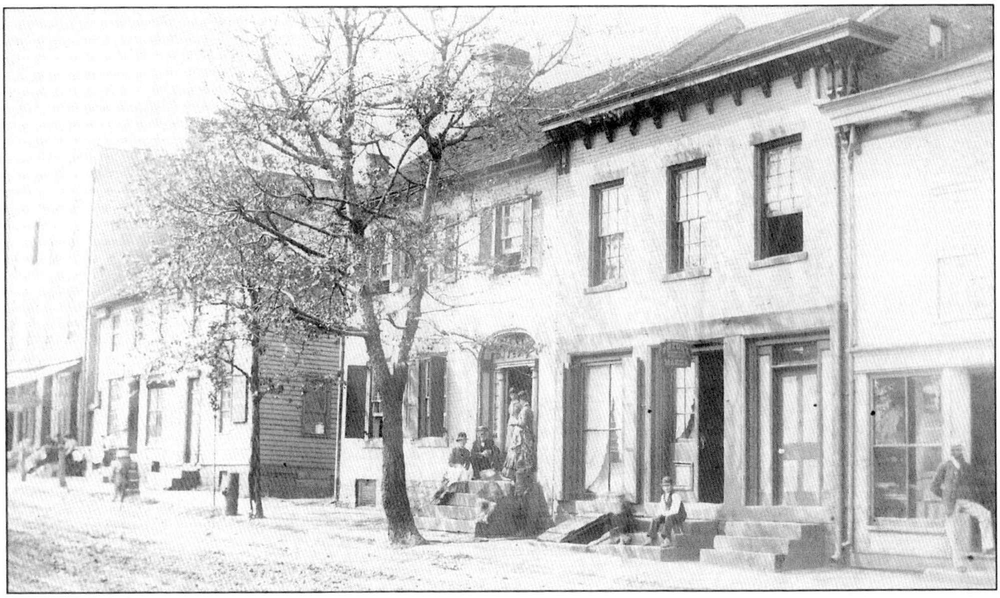

An 1860 photograph of the old Jacob Heaton residence on East State Street. The building still stands today. Heaton was an early pioneer, and is remembered as a businessman and abolitionist. The Heaton home and barn were used to provide shelter and comfort for many fugitive slaves. His "Quaker Tavern" was visited by many well-known figures in the woman's rights movement.

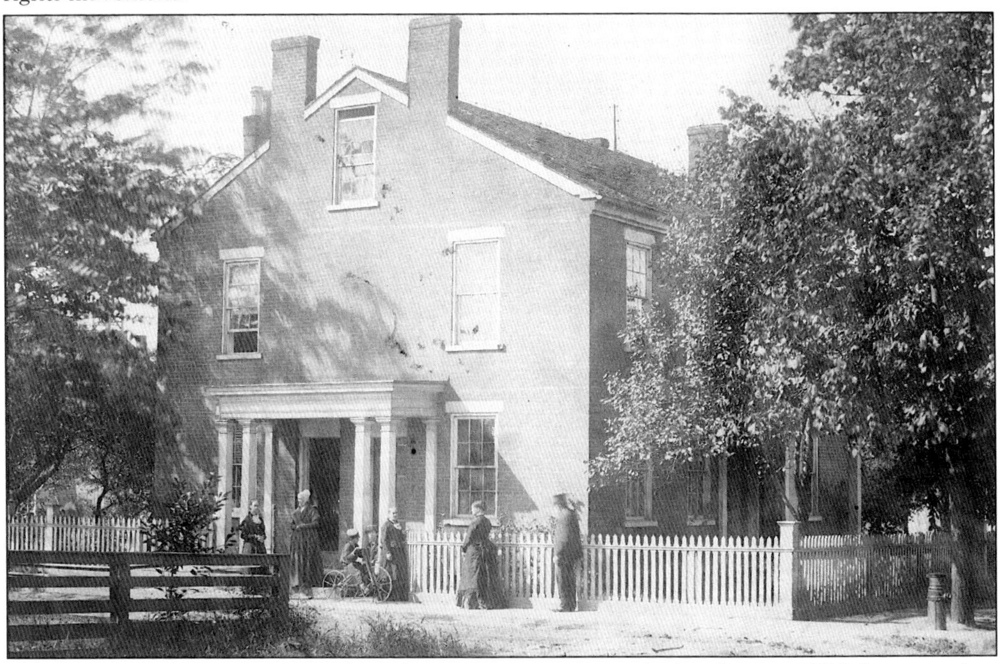

Dr. Benjamin Stanton, Salem's first physician. Born in North Carolina in 1793, he moved to Salem in 1815. His wife, Martha, was one of the town's early teachers. The photo shows family members in front of the Stanton home, once located on the southwest corner of East Second Street and North Broadway Avenue. It was a refuge for many runaway slaves on their way to Canada.

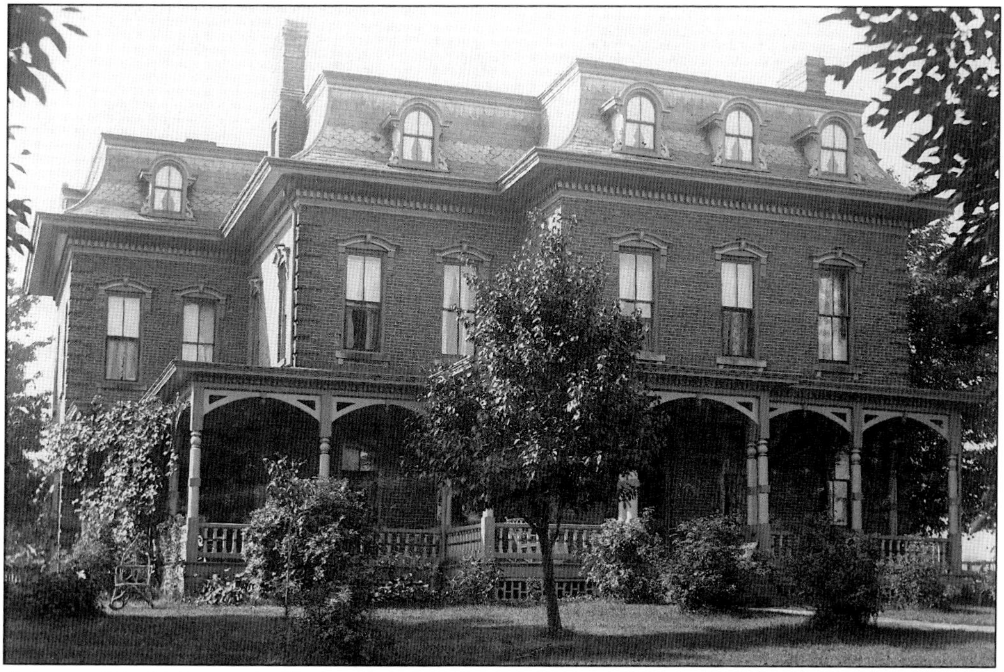

A beautiful old house (still standing) on Painter Road, once owned by John Pow and also known as the Post home. Charles Burchfield, the nationally known artist from Salem, wrote the following comments about the house to a friend: "As a boy I always dreamed of coming back as a rich man, buying the old Post homestead, and spending my reclining days. Funny dreams we have."

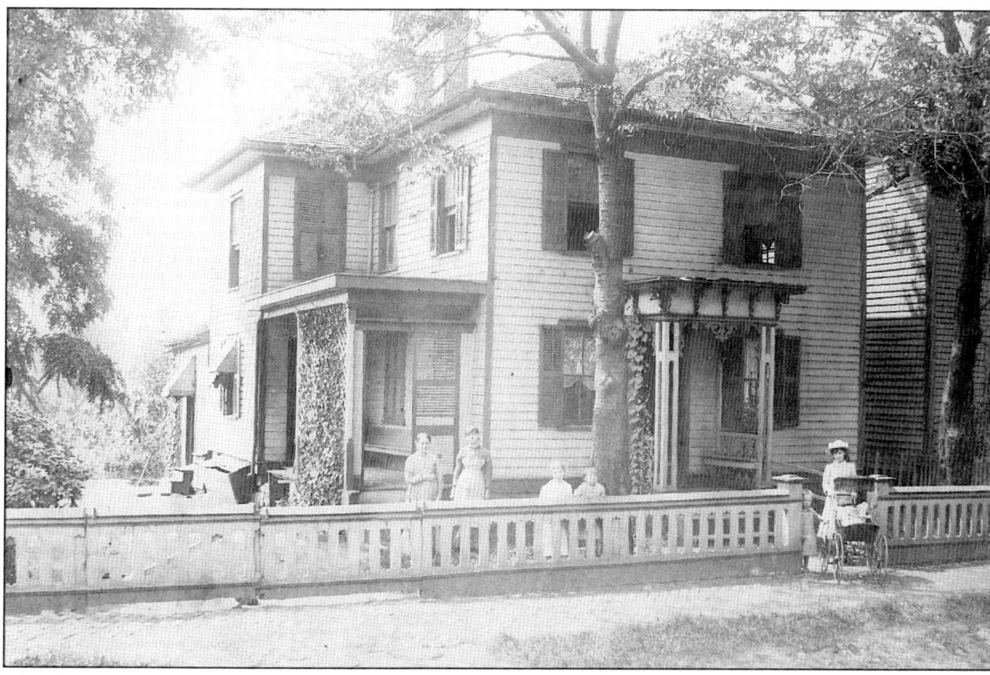

The former residence of W.C. Hutcheson, state representative from 1894 to 1896, located near the corner of East State Street and Rose Avenue. This photograph was taken in 1890.

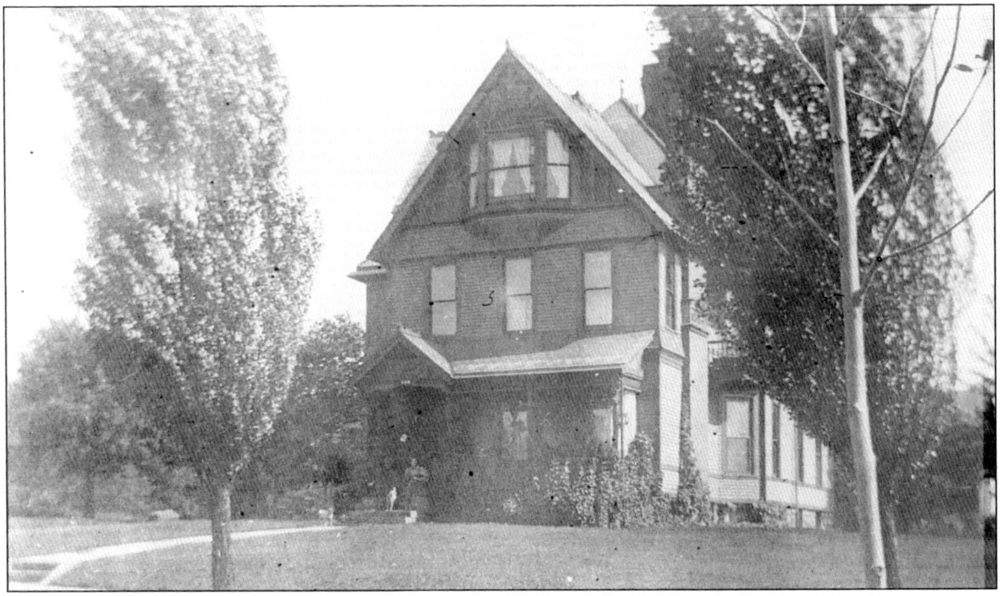

The house (still standing) of Samuel Grove Sr., located at 1383 East State Street. Grove owned the Grove Chewing Gum Company. His firm on South Broadway Avenue flourished from 1882 to 1910. There were about 150 employees, most of them women, producing 12 different flavors. On some days they shipped as much as $50,000 worth of gum. The American Chiclet Company eventually acquired the business.

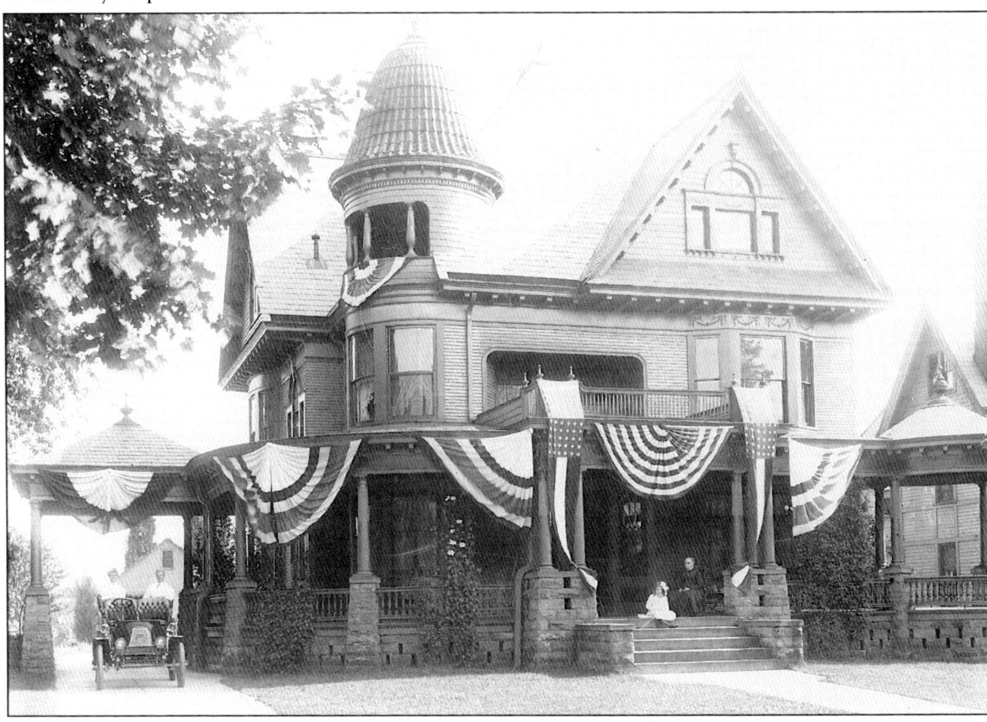

The beautiful mansion at 1241 East State Street, once owned by Samuel Grove Jr., destroyed by fire in 1996. This photograph was taken on June 20, 1906, during Salem's Centennial celebration. Family members are shown in the car at left and on the porch.

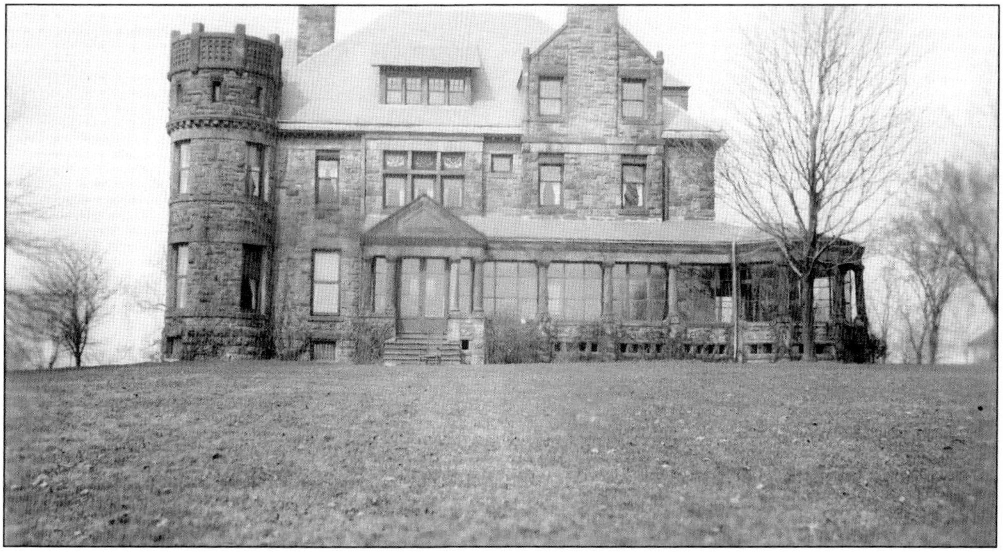

J. Twing Brooks's mansion, once located at 575 Highland Avenue, built in 1891–92. It had 16 rooms, 6 baths, and was constructed of 1,250 tons of sandstone hauled from a quarry near Beaver Falls, Pennsylvania. He named it "Andalusia Place," because of his admiration for a friend's home in Philadelphia. Mr. Brooks, an attorney, owned the Andalusia Dairy, and was a vice-president of the Pennsylvania Railroad.

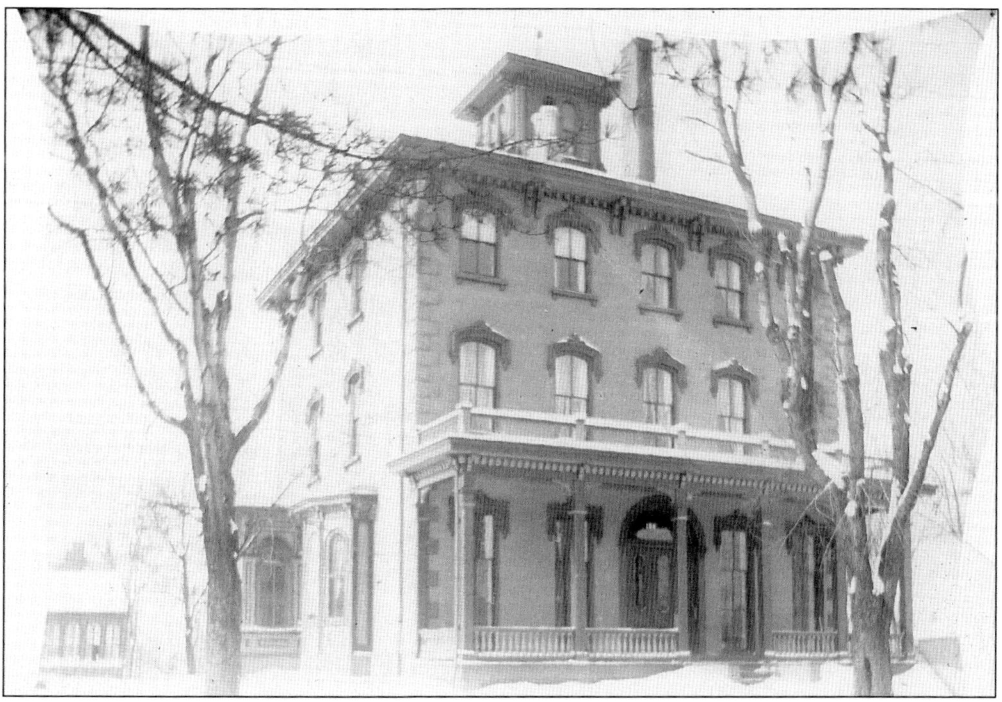

The three-story house with cupola on top, located on the southwest corner of South Lincoln Avenue and Franklin Street, once known as "The Mansion." It dates back to 1882 when the John Wetmore family lived there. In April of 1893 this house was pictured in the local newspaper "as one of the finest homes in Salem." Other families who resided here were the Southworths and Silvers.

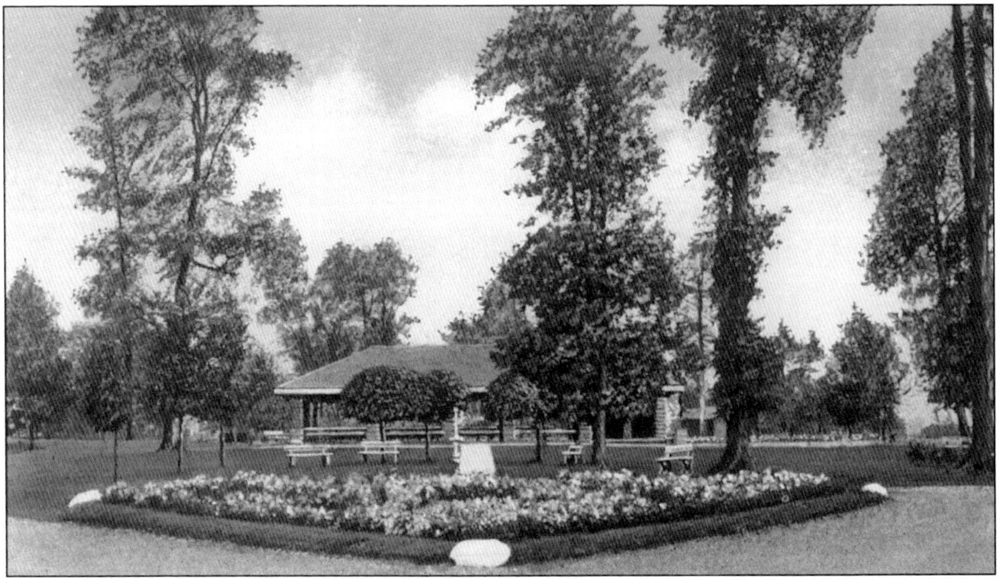

Centennial Park, deeded to the City of Salem on June 25, 1906, the last day of the Centennial celebration. It stands today as a memorial in commemoration of that event. The photo shows the main entrance to the park. In 1906 a campaign was conducted to raise $10,000 from 100 Salemites, each donating $100. The money was used to purchase 15 acres of Jonathan Evans's land for the park.

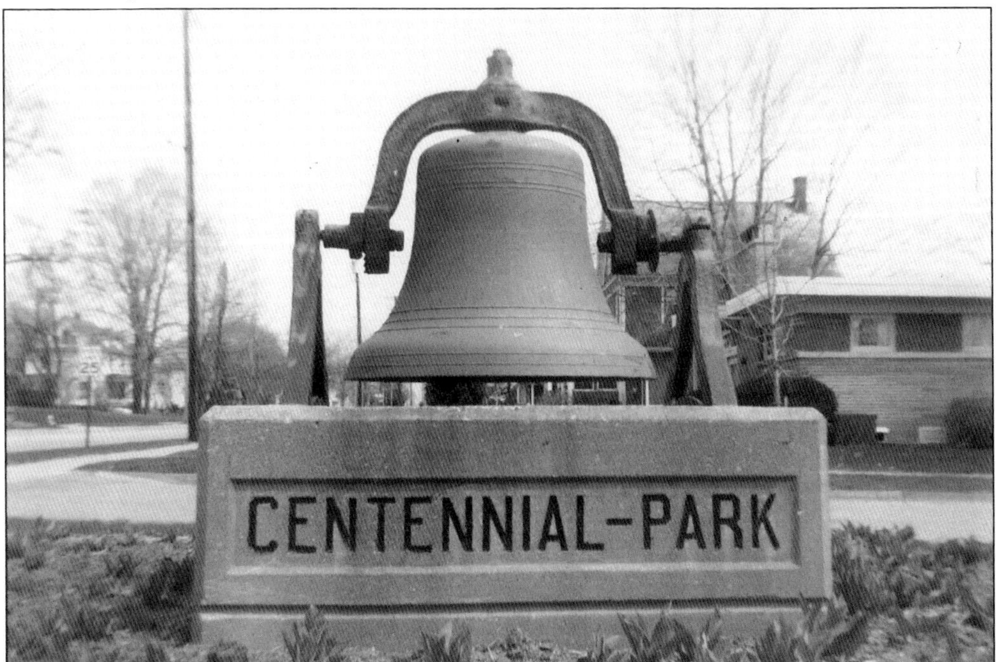

The old town hall bell, which served the city from 1882 to 1933, now mounted at the entrance to Centennial Park. For years this bell was used as a general alarm to call firefighters and patrolmen in periods of emergency. It tolled its last tones on August 9, 1933. In 1956 the bell was dedicated during the sesquicentennial in memory of Miss Alice MacMillan.

Seven

Parks, Recreation, and Bands

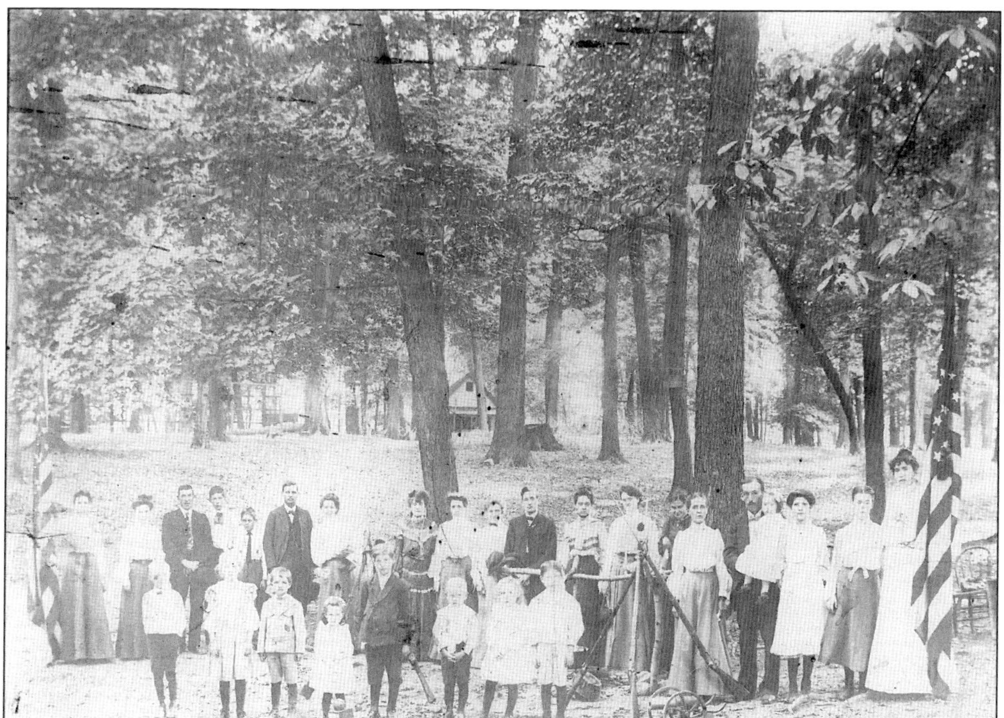

A picnic scene at Salem Centennial Park in the early 1900s. One of the boys is holding a baseball bat, and three rifles are stacked next to a small cannon. Two American flags are part of the scene, so it may be a Fourth of July picnic.

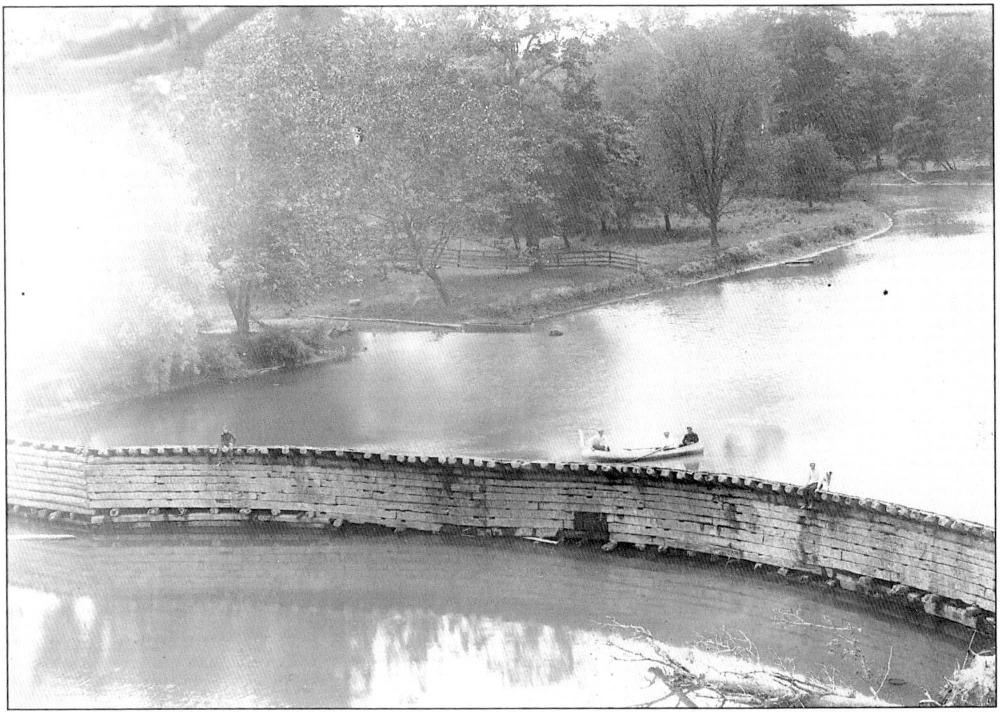

The former Issac Crumrine farm. In 1909 Harold Brian and William H. Dunn purchased the Isaac Crumrine farm and made it into a private picnic ground. They built a dam and diverted a spring to create a large lake for swimming and boating. In 1912 it was incorporated as the Salem Country Club. The 52-acre park is located 1 mile west of Salem. The photo is dated 1910.

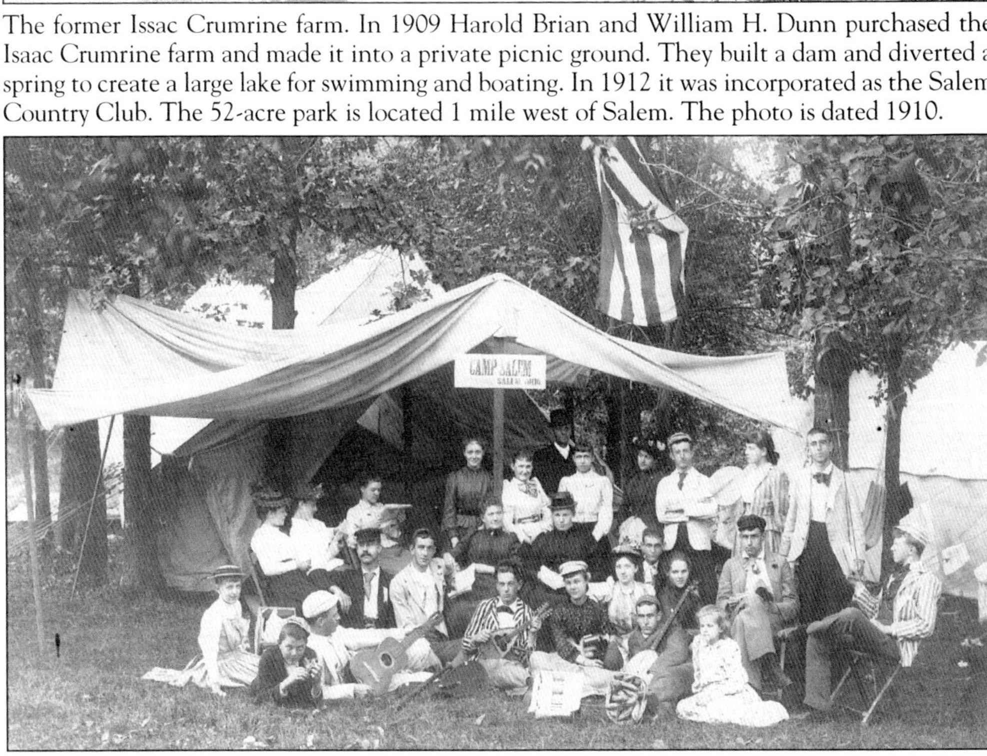

An early 1900s photo of a group of young people at Camp Salem. Considering their fine dress and musical instruments, they must have been there for a special Sunday event. They certainly are not "roughing it," or dressed for sports activities.

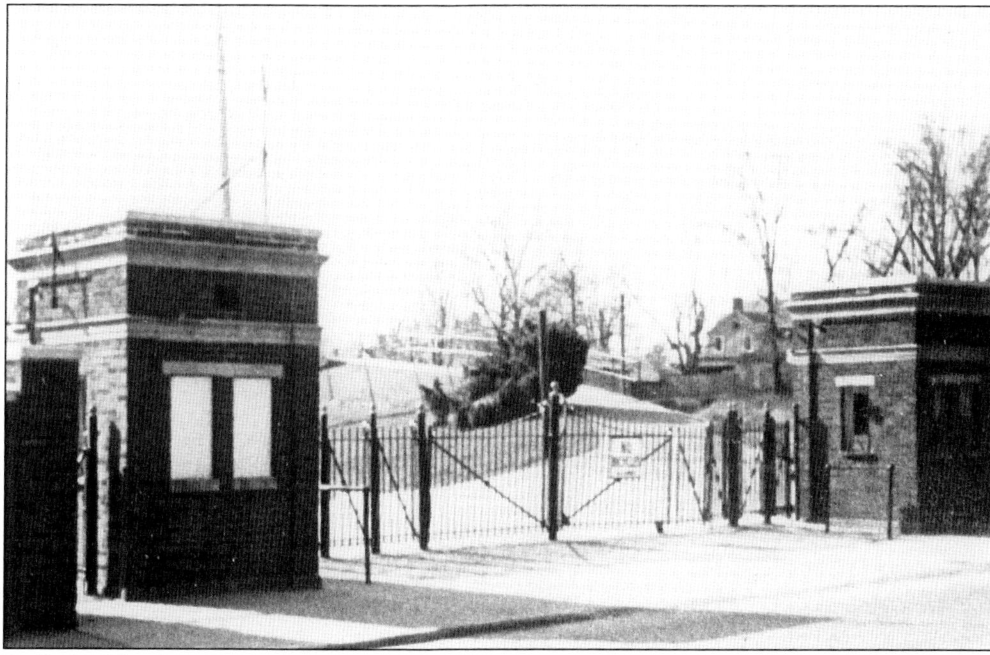

Reilly Field, where the Salem public schools hold their athletic events. The first high school football game in Ohio played under lights was held here on October 11, 1929. General James W. Reilly, a Civil War veteran, died on November 5, 1906, and his estate went to the schools of Columbiana County. On April 15, 1915, Salem used its money to purchase the old Independent Amusement Park.

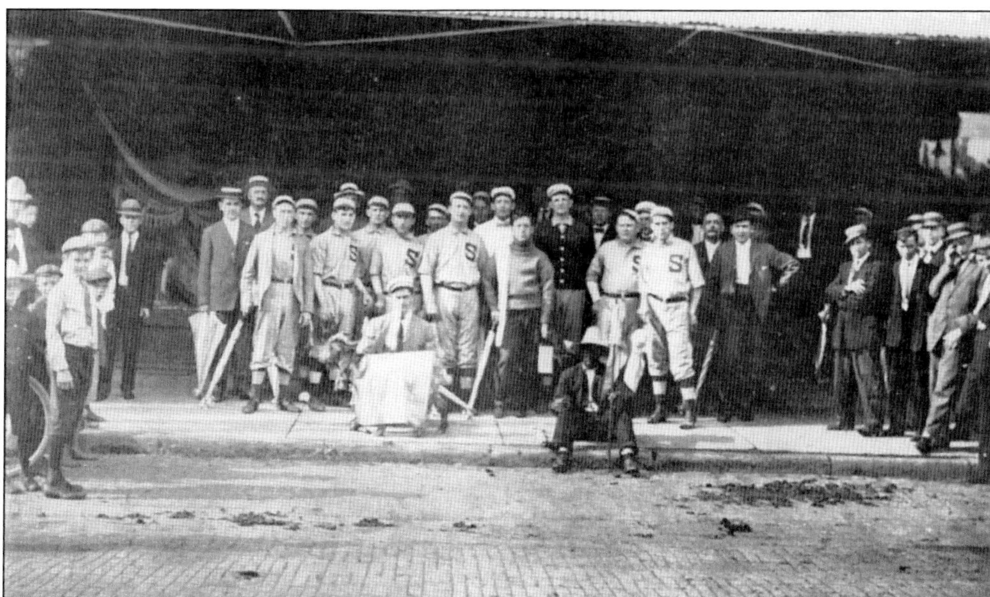

The Salem Elks Lodge baseball team of 1908. This team was unbeaten in 1909. They played at what was called the Independent Amusement Park, now Reilly Field. The Salem lodge was instituted June 14, 1895. They held their meetings in various buildings, until their present home on East State Street was erected in 1927.

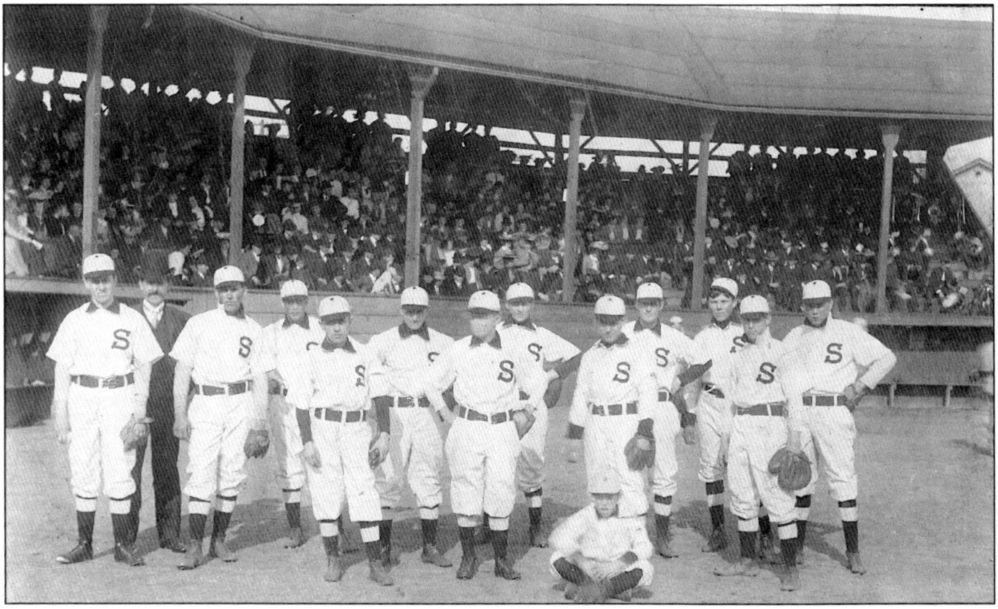

Members of Salem's semi-professional baseball team before a game at Amusement Park (now Reilly Field). Baseball was popular as early as the 1860s. It began with the Independents. Then there were the Stellas, the Starlights, the Meal Ticket team, and the Independent Hose Company team. Some of the players went on to play professional ball.

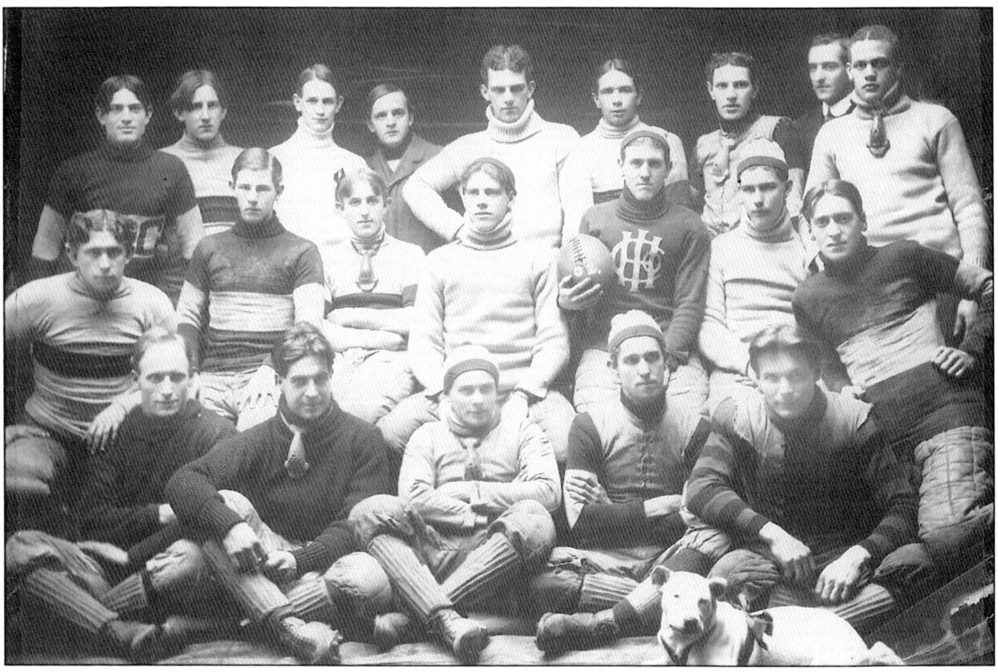

Salem's 1902, semi-professional football team. This team was one of 19 from as many cities—often small towns—that originated the game, particularly in its semi-pro form. They were the prototypes of the professional teams of today. These were the days when the boys played the game simply for whatever fun could be found in the sport. It was roughneck football. They often played at Centennial Park and Reilly Field.

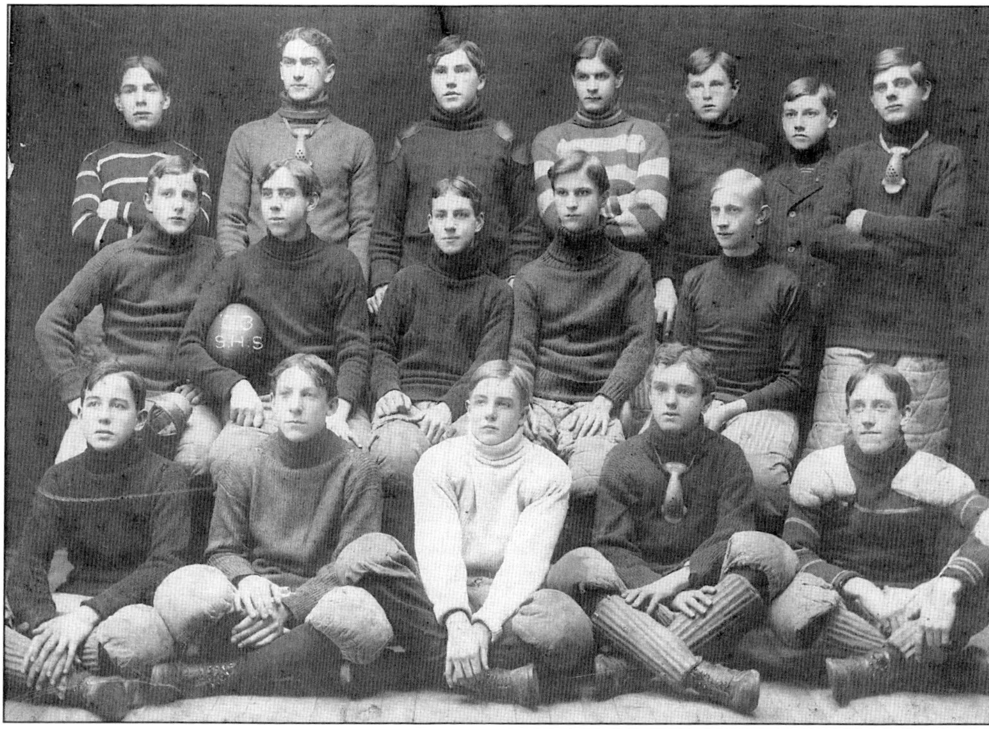

Salem High School's 1903 football team. Note the small amount of padding in the uniforms.

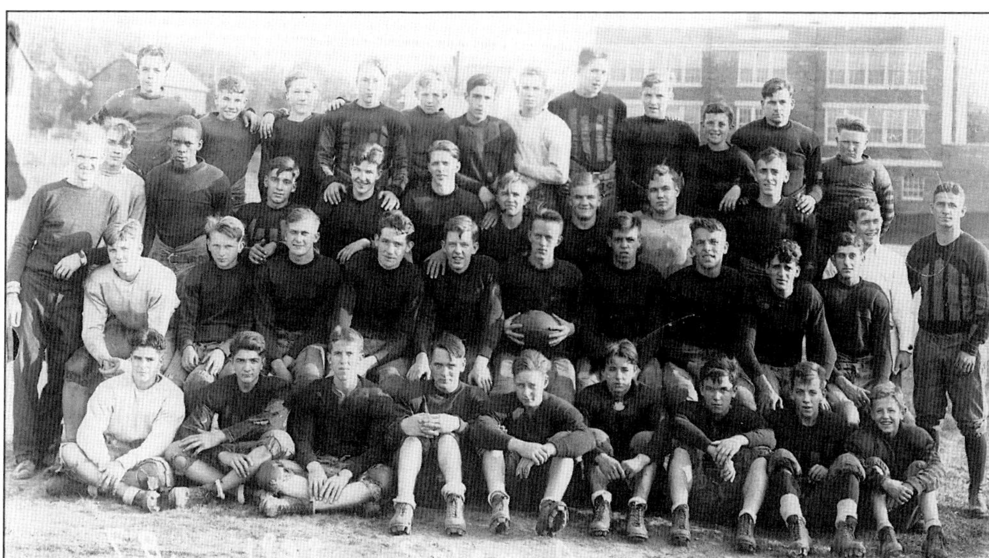

Members of the Salem High School football team of 1928. Although this team lost two games, its players went on the following year to become undefeated. The school's first football game was played on September 1, 1893, at Lisbon.

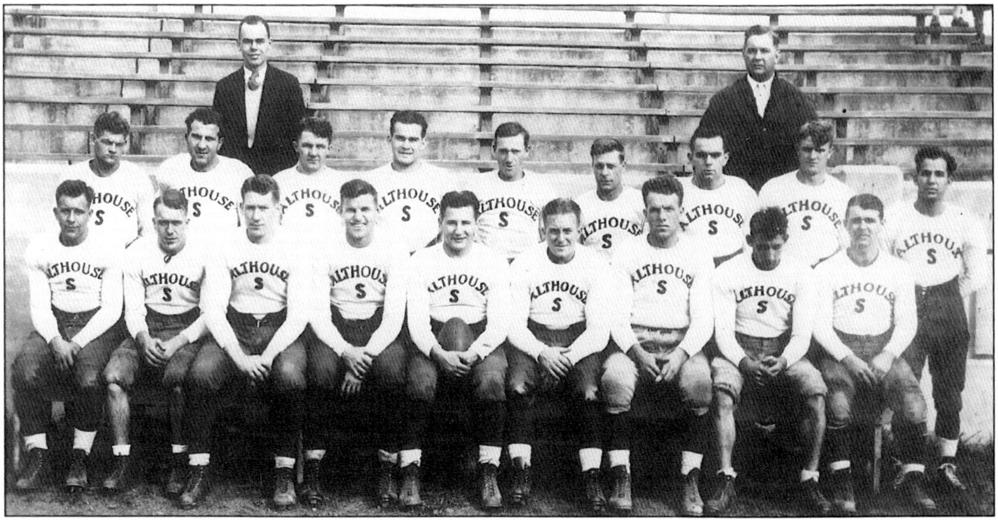

One of Salem's semi-pro football teams in 1934, sponsored by Ernest Althouse (back row, right), an automobile dealer. He entered the auto business in 1916, opening a Ford garage in Winona. His Studebaker agency in Salem was opened in 1922. By 1935 he was also selling Dodge, Plymouth, Packard, and Cadillac cars. He retired in 1951.

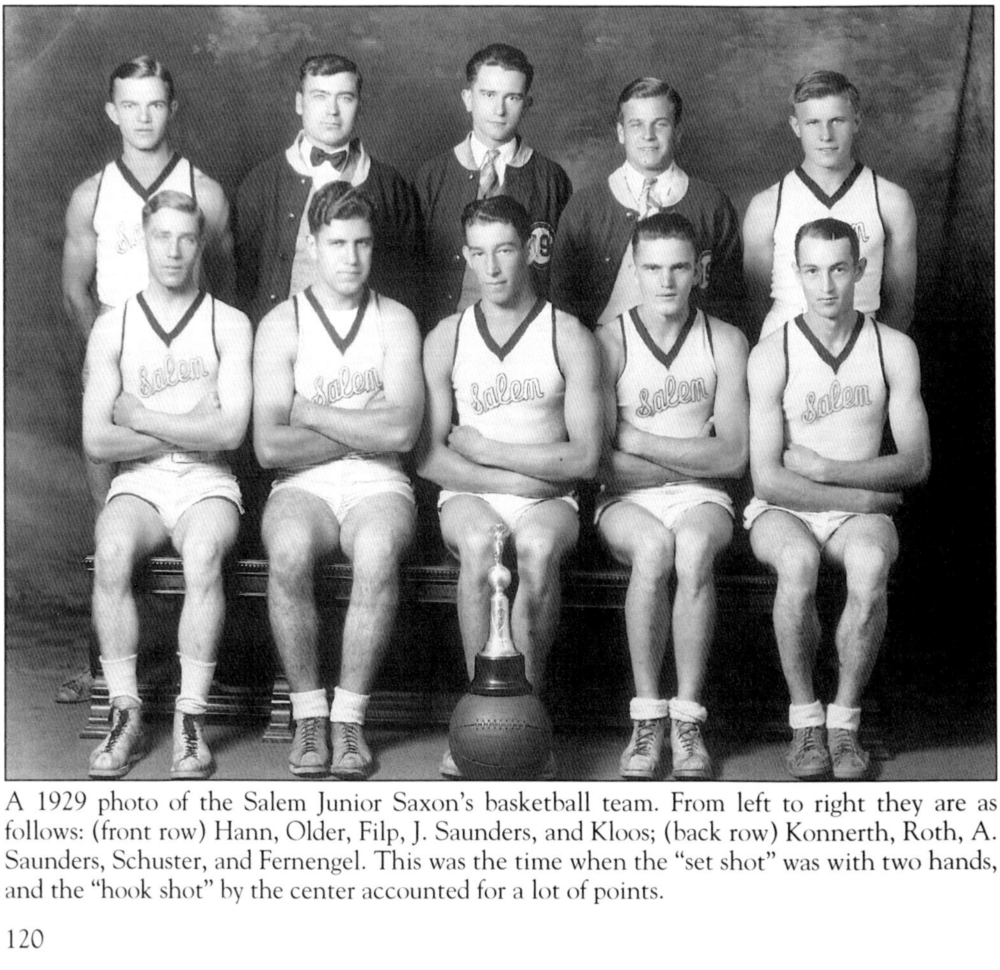

A 1929 photo of the Salem Junior Saxon's basketball team. From left to right they are as follows: (front row) Hann, Older, Filp, J. Saunders, and Kloos; (back row) Konnerth, Roth, A. Saunders, Schuster, and Fernengel. This was the time when the "set shot" was with two hands, and the "hook shot" by the center accounted for a lot of points.

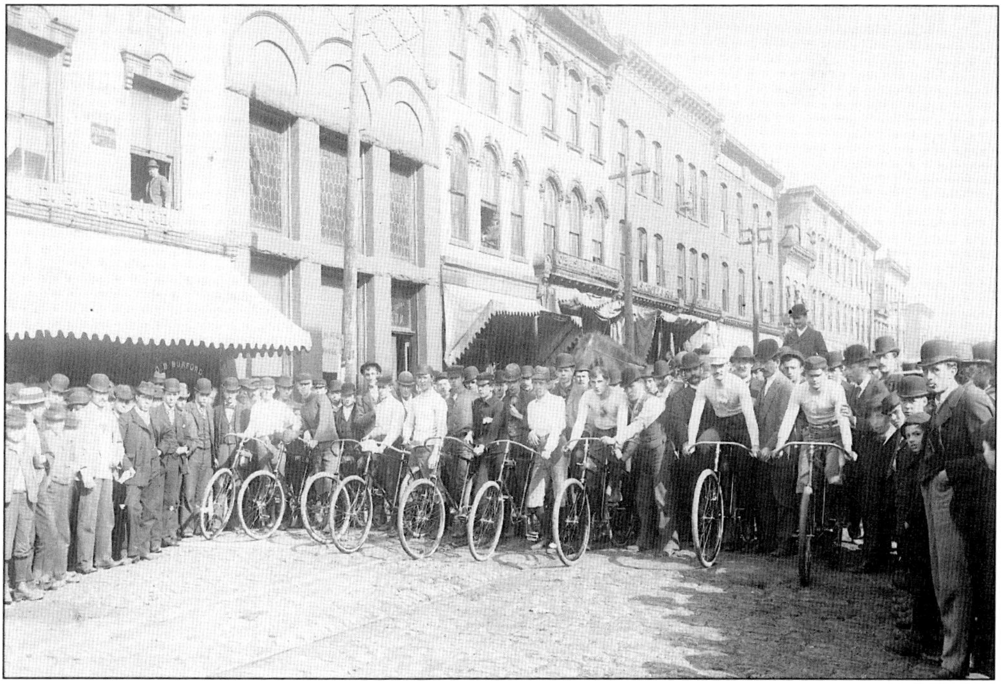

Bicycle racing, a very popular sport in Salem at the turn of the century. The local paper often sponsored races to be run from the corner of East State Street and South Broadway Avenue to the square in Alliance and back. Total distance was 28 miles. Entry fee was 50¢, and riders chose their own routes. The top prize was a $30 gold medal. The winning time was eight hours and nine minutes.

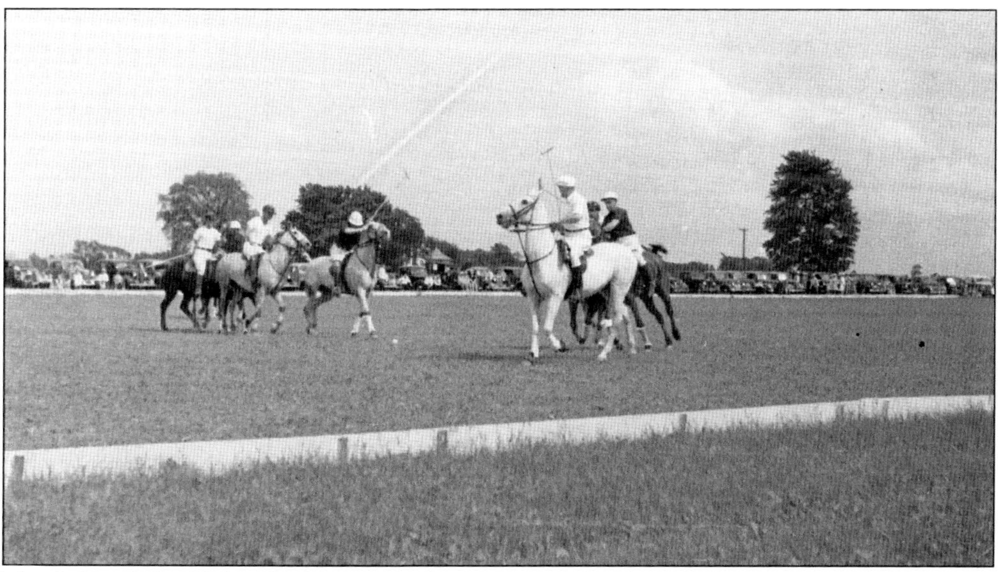

The Salem Polo Club, which originated in 1933. It played at Shelton's Grove, the Canfield Fairgrounds, and the polo grounds on North Ellsworth Avenue. Names associated with this sport in the early days were Votaw, Sheen, Moff, Pidgon, Smith, Fernengel, Hendricks, Duncan, Yates, Loop, Phillips, and Wingard. Families enjoyed watching polo games on Sunday afternoons. Cars lined each side of the playing field, and horns honked when a goal was made.

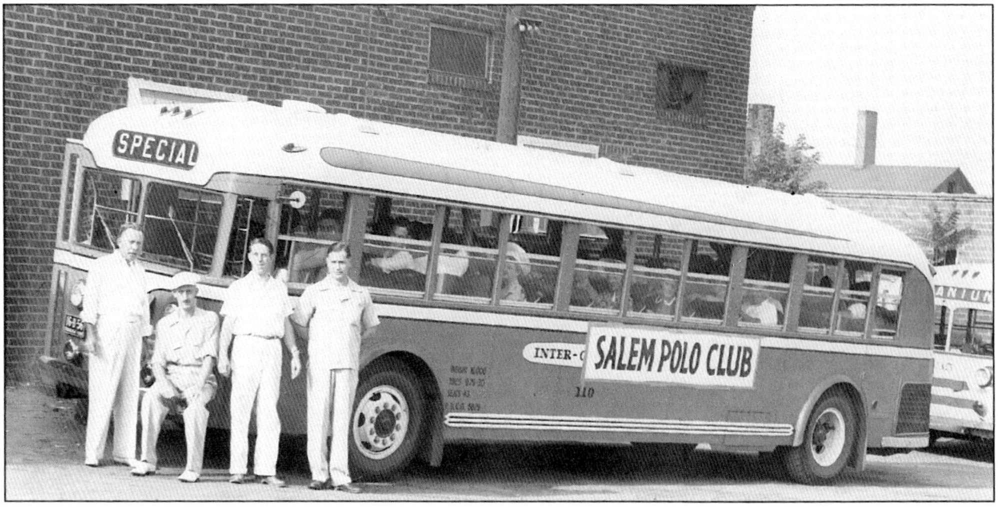

Salem's polo team about to leave for Columbus one summer day in 1940. From left to right are Doyle, Duncan, Loop, and Fernengel. Regular games were held on Saturday or Sunday during the season, which ran from early spring through late summer. In 1953 Salem won the Penn-Ohio Polo League championship. Each player had his own mount and cared for it at his own expense.

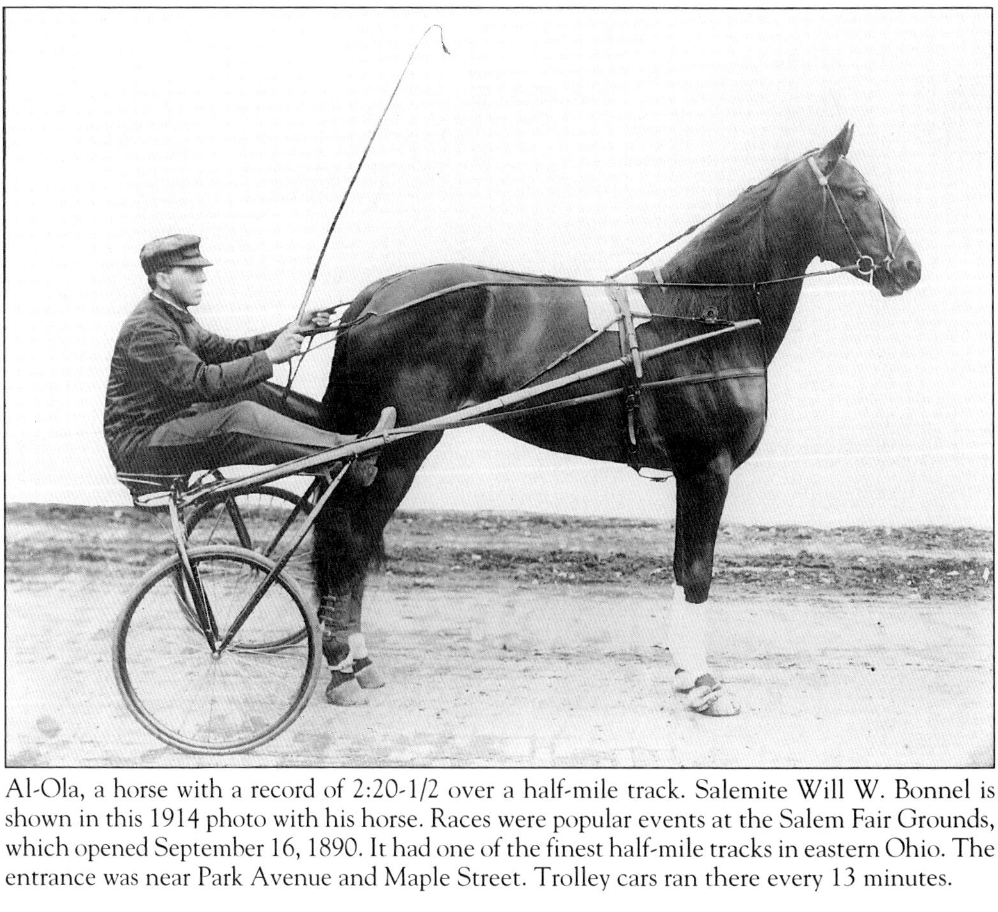

Al-Ola, a horse with a record of 2:20-1/2 over a half-mile track. Salemite Will W. Bonnel is shown in this 1914 photo with his horse. Races were popular events at the Salem Fair Grounds, which opened September 16, 1890. It had one of the finest half-mile tracks in eastern Ohio. The entrance was near Park Avenue and Maple Street. Trolley cars ran there every 13 minutes.

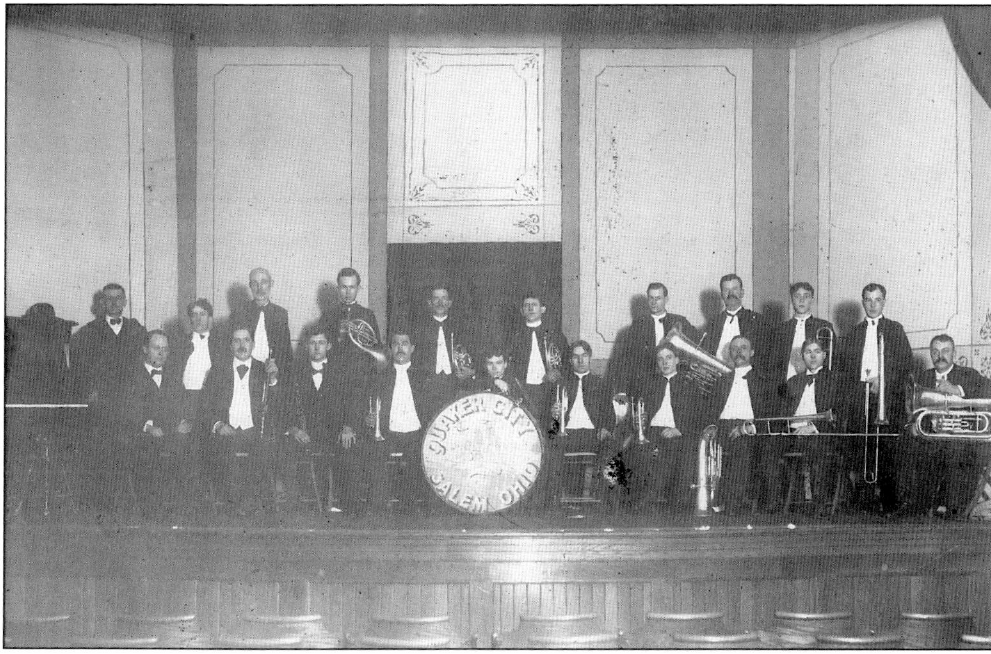

Salem's Quaker City Band, organized in 1896. A small group of men met in Irvin Bard's barbershop. In the fall they rented a room in the Anderson Building (still standing) and practiced by the light of sputtering oil lamps. This photo was taken inside the Grand Opera House before it became the Grand Theater. George Chappell Sr. was the director.

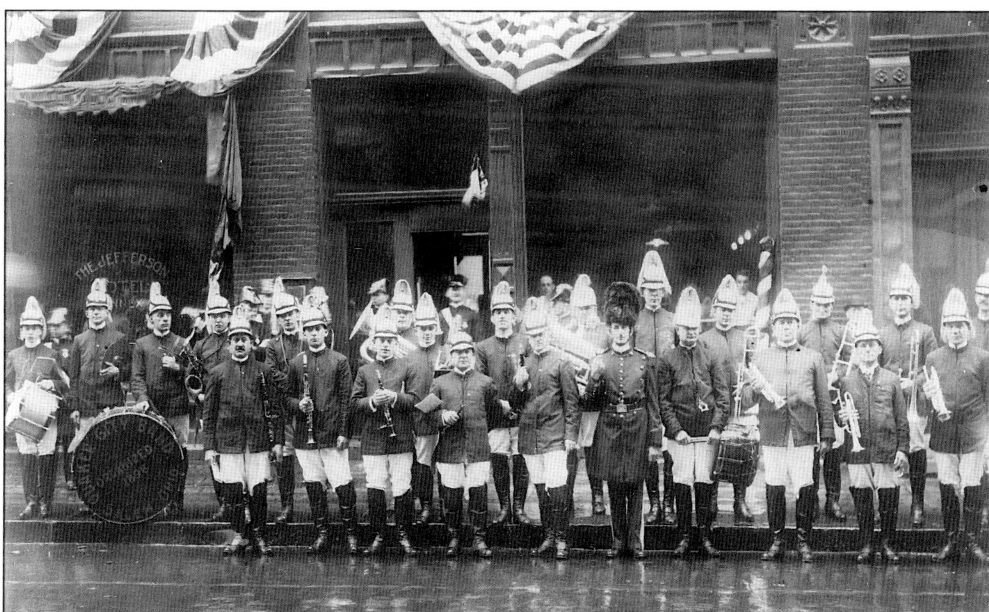

The Quaker City Band at the Knights of Templar Conclave in Toledo, Ohio, on October 13, 1915. John W. Hundertmarck (center) was the director. He took over the band in 1908, directed it for 25 years, and made it into one of the best in the state. When the original 13 members organized the band in 1896 their uniforms were unattractive and the instruments very poor.

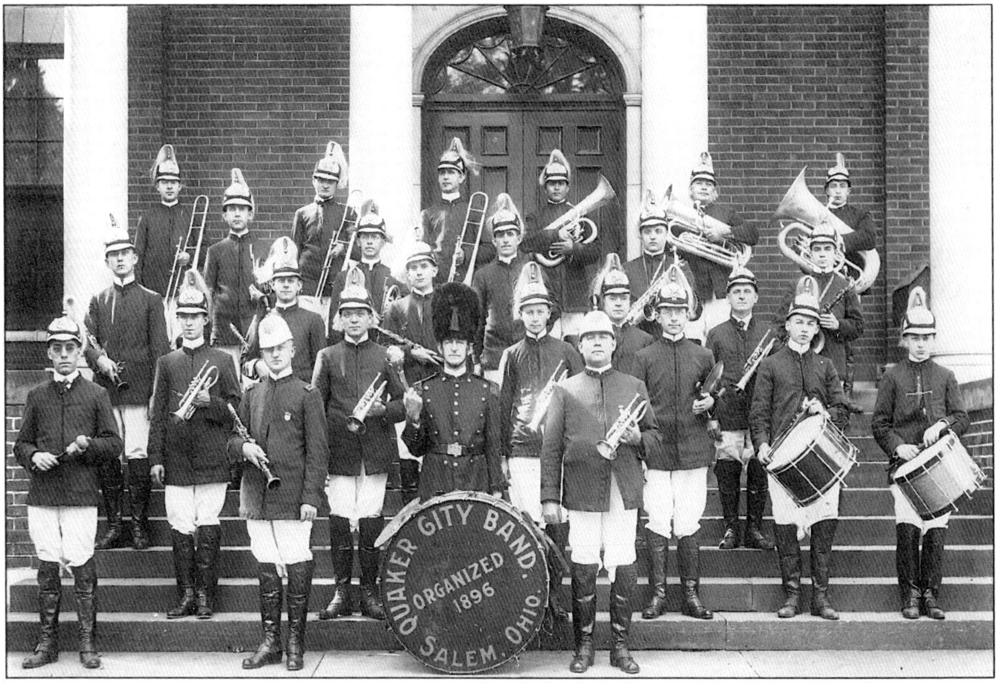

Quaker City Band members in front of the Salem Public Library on Labor Day, September 4, 1916. John W. Hundertmarck, director, and George Chappell, manager, are shown in front. The residents of Salem were very proud of this band. It was quite active with various local organizations, such as the GAR, Eagles, and firemen, accompanying them on trips throughout the country.

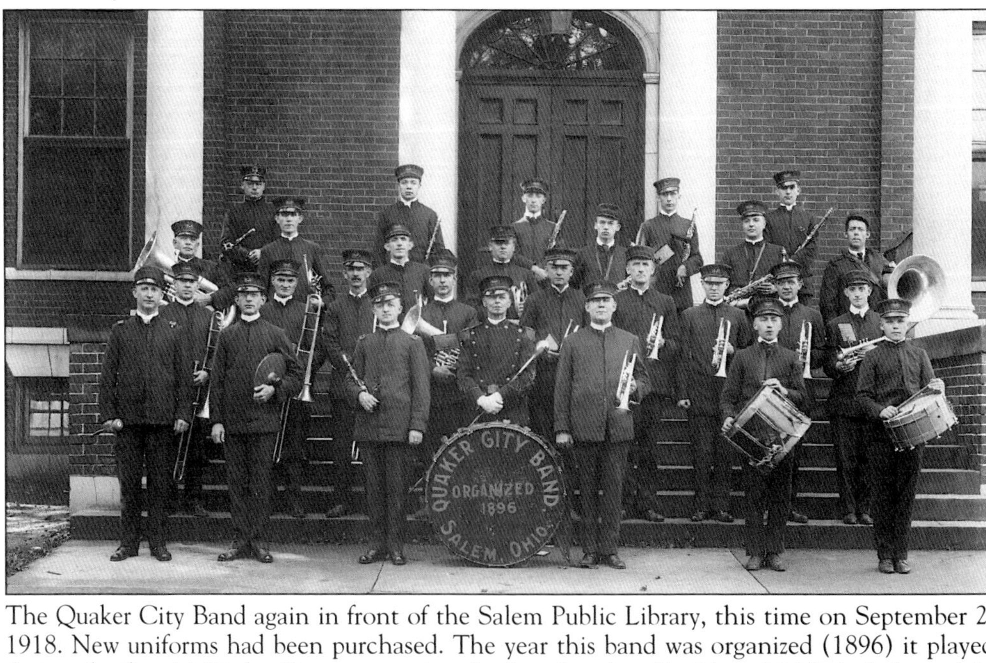

The Quaker City Band again in front of the Salem Public Library, this time on September 2, 1918. New uniforms had been purchased. The year this band was organized (1896) it played during the first McKinley-Bryan campaign. It also played at President McKinley's funeral in Canton in 1901, and again when the McKinley Monument was dedicated in 1903.

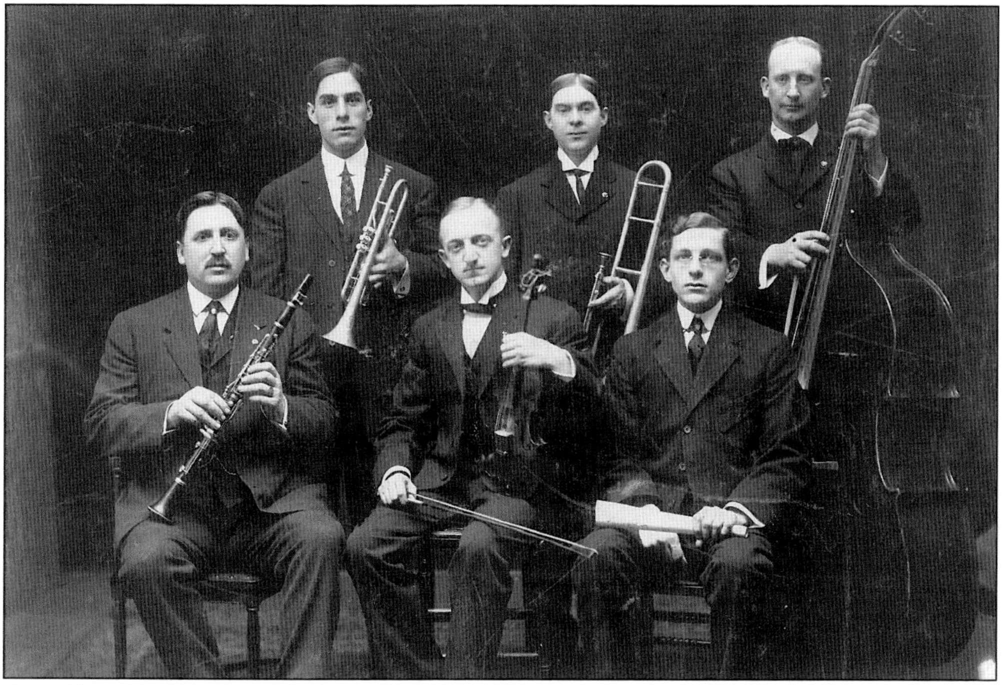

A small orchestra composed of six members of the Quaker City Band. This orchestra played for special events during the early decades of this century. From left to right they are as follows: (front row) Lupton, Hundertmarck, and Coy; (back row) Houghton, Gilson, and Sturgeon. John Hundertmarck (center) was a talented musician and solo violinist. Throughout his lifetime, he played in marching bands, dance orchestras, concerts, vaudeville, and motion pictures. In 1927 he was recognized as "Salem's most versatile musician."

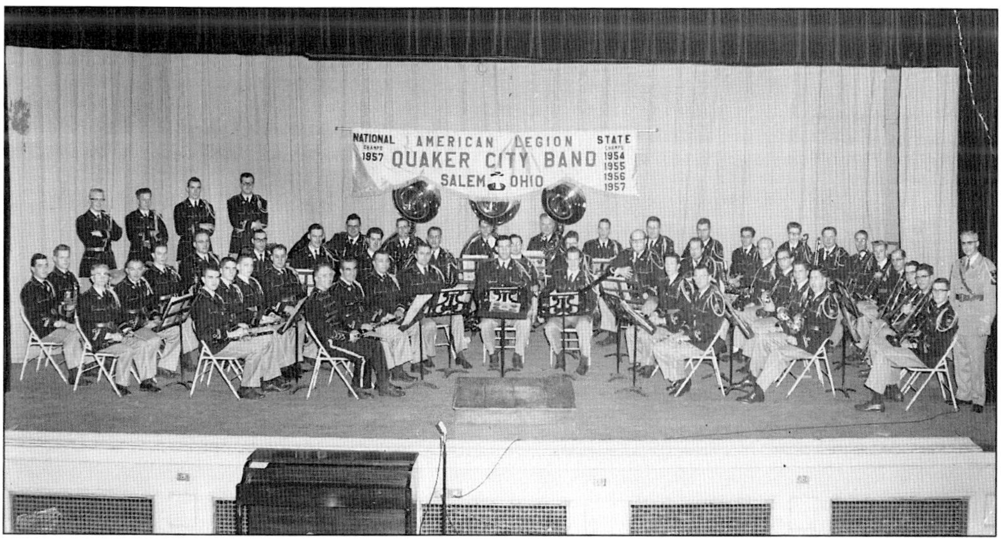

One of Salem's proudest moments in history. On Saturday, September 14, 1957, the American Legion Quaker City Band, under the direction of Chester M. Brautigam (at right), won the coveted 1957 American Legion National Championship at Atlantic City, New Jersey. The band had been runner-up the two previous years, and state champions for four consecutive years. This photograph shows the band performing in concert at Salem High School.

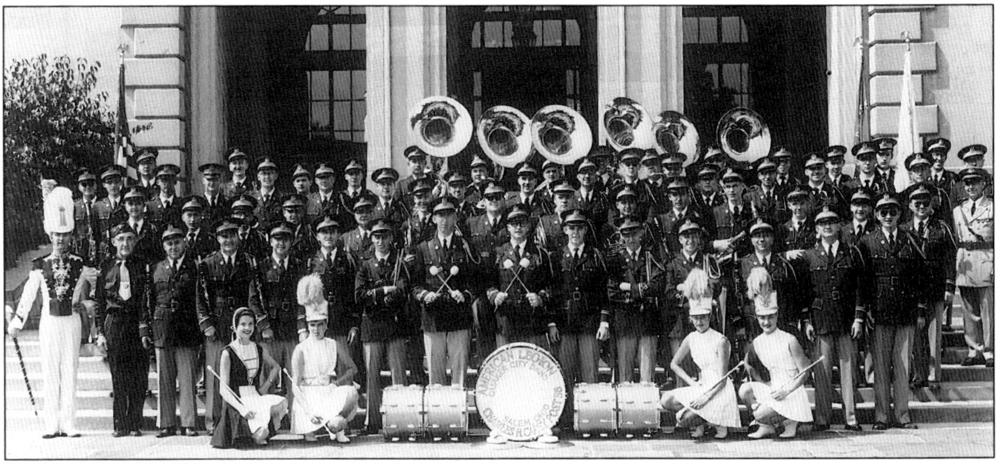

Salem's American Legion Quaker City Band, directed by Chester M. Brautigam (at right), in Columbus, Ohio. The band is shown after winning another state championship in the 1950s. Members brought honors not only to themselves but also to Salem. They were the best ambassadors of goodwill that any city could have. In 1957 the band won national honors, and were welcomed back to town with a huge celebration.

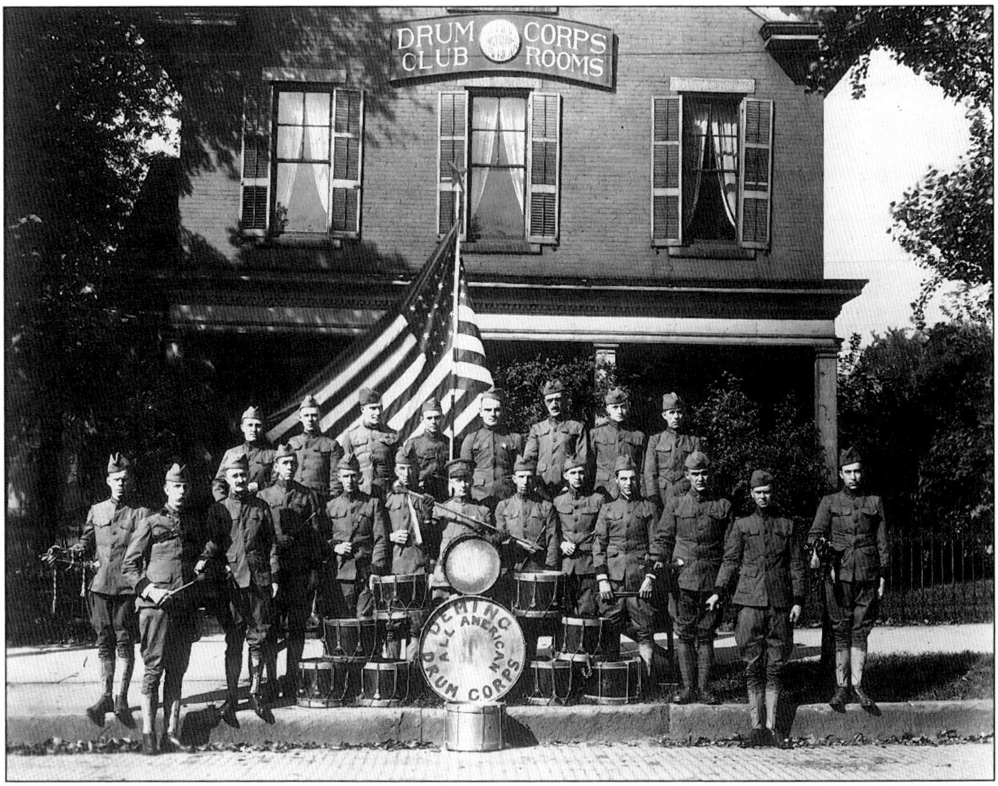

The Deming Drum and Bugle Corps., one of the popular marching units in Salem back in the days of World War I. Organized in 1917 by Joseph Bentley (at right), a machinist at Demings, the group was sponsored by the Deming Company and marched for practically every patriotic occasion during the war period. It disbanded in 1922. This photo was taken on the corner of South Broadway Avenue and Wilson Street.

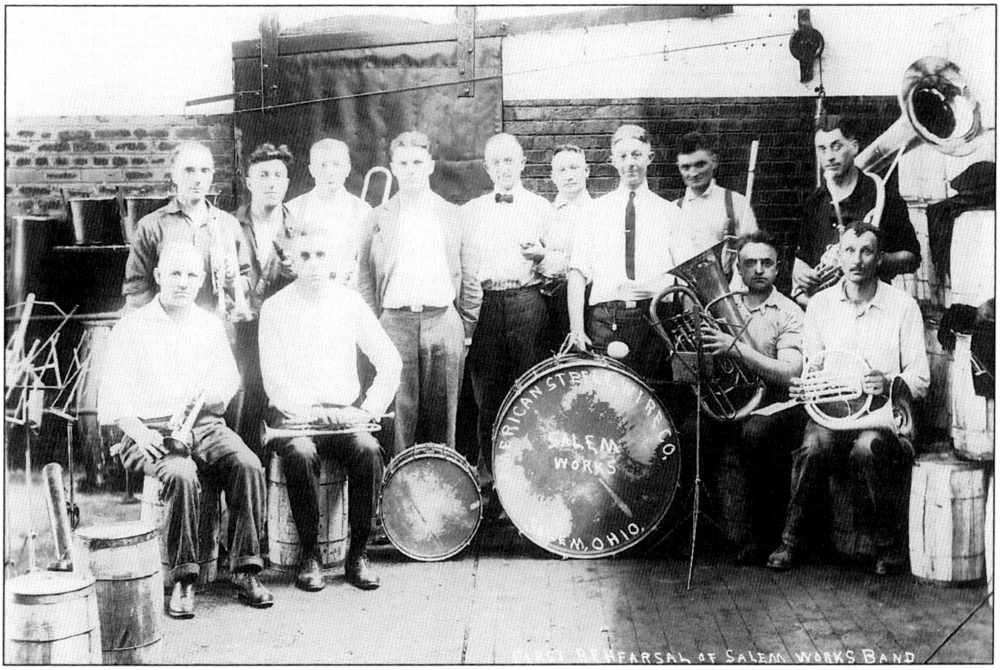

The American Steel and Wire Company band at their first rehearsal on June 13, 1921. Company bands were common in the early 1900s. John W. Hundertmarck, leader of the Quaker City Band, is shown in the center. This company, known as the Nail Mill, was organized in 1884 and produced large quantities of all sizes of wire nails until 1929.

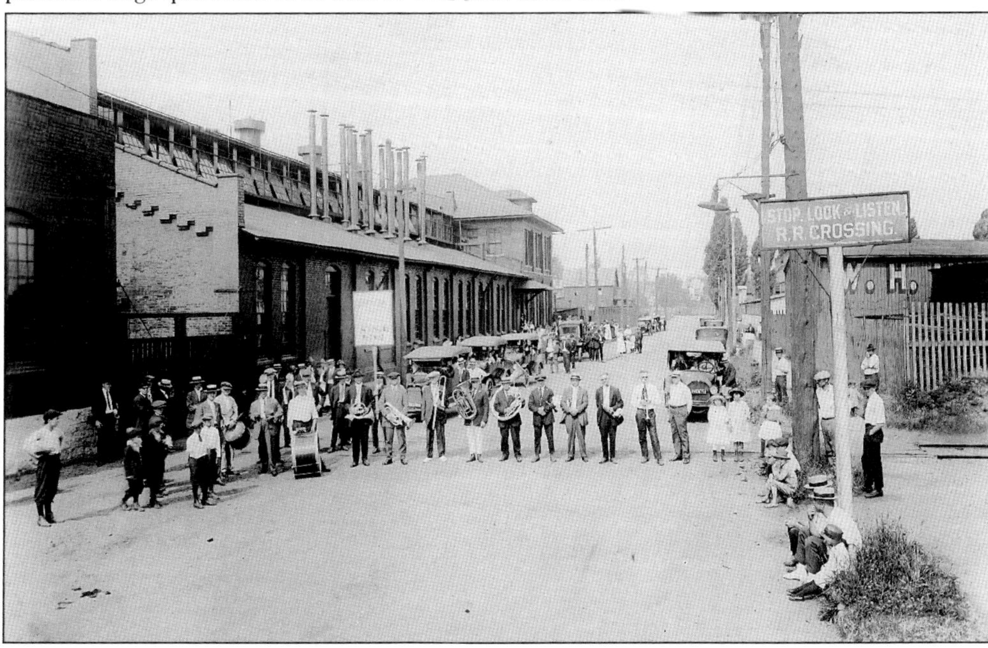

The American Steel and Wire Company band performing for the first time on Mill (Mullins) Street in 1921. On the left is the Nail Mill building (still standing), and on the right is the W.H. Mullins Boat Works. The American Steel and Wire Company closed February 28, 1929, and moved to Cleveland. Eljer purchased the facility in 1940.

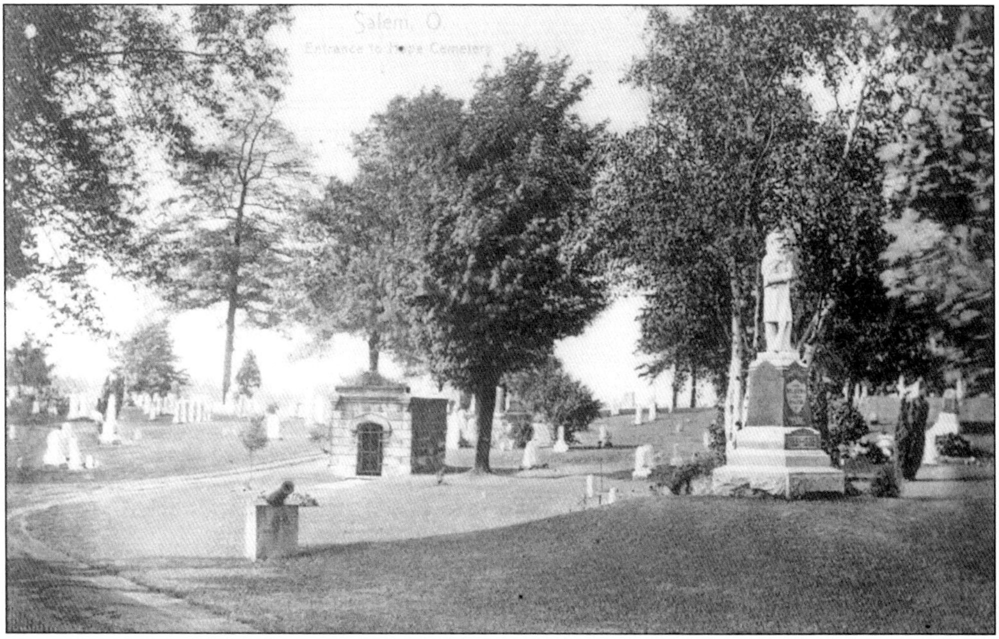

Hope Cemetery, which began in 1833 as a burial ground for Presbyterians. It was formally laid out December 6, 1853, and gradually expanded. Edwin Coppoc, the anti-slavery martyr who participated in John Brown's raid on Harpers Ferry and was executed, is buried here. The cemetery also contains the graves of many of the city's early settlers. Mausoleums contain the names Grove, Sharp, McKee, Wallace, Meyers, and Thomas.

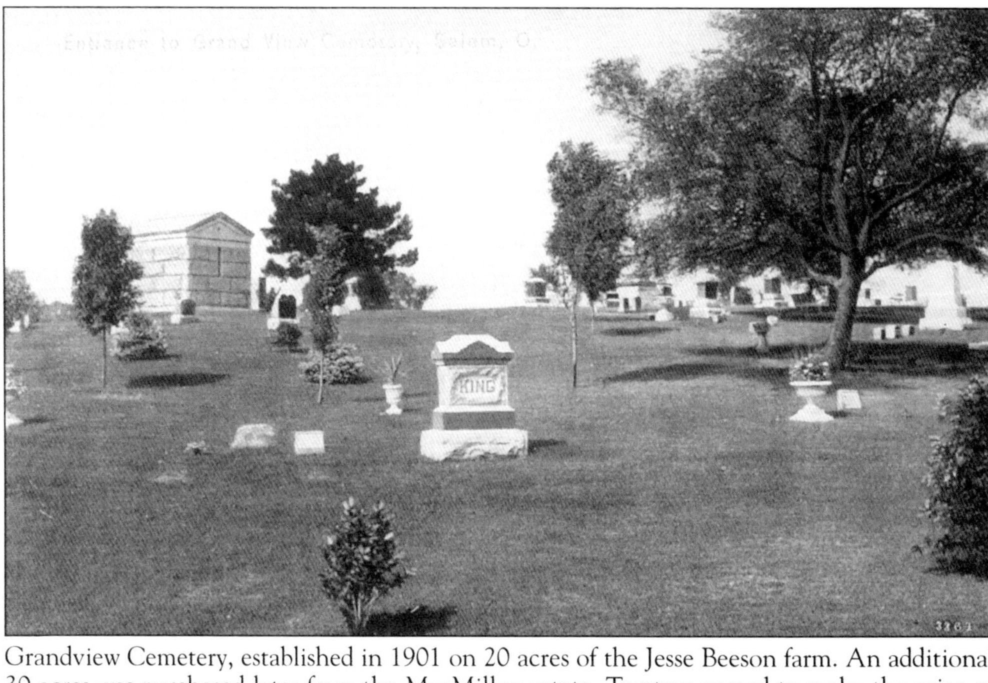

Grandview Cemetery, established in 1901 on 20 acres of the Jesse Beeson farm. An additional 30 acres was purchased later from the MacMillan estate. Trustees agreed to make the price of lots so low that anyone could afford to buy one. Everyone was to pay the same price.